COLUMBIA UNIVERSITY
STUDIES IN THE SOCIAL SCIENCES

(Formerly known as Studies in History, Economics and Public Law)

No. 8

HISTORY

OF

ELECTIONS

IN THE

AMERICAN COLONIES

AMS PRESS

NEW YORK

STUDIES IN HISTORY, ECONOMICS AND PUBLIC LAW

EDITED BY

THE UNIVERSITY FACULTY OF POLITICAL SCIENCE

OF COLUMBIA COLLEGE

Volume III]   [Number 1

HISTORY

OF

ELECTIONS

IN THE

AMERICAN COLONIES

BY

CORTLANDT F. BISHOP, PH.D

COLUMBIA COLLEGE

NEW YORK

1893

COLUMBIA UNIVERSITY
STUDIES IN THE
SOCIAL SCIENCES

The series was formerly known as *Studies in History
Economics and Public Law*

Copyright, 1893, by Cortlandt F. Bishop
Reprinted with the permission of Columbia University Press
From the edition of 1893, New York
First AMS EDITION published 1970
Manufactured in the United States of America

International Standard Book Number:
Complete Set 0-404-51000-0
Number Eight 0-404-51008-6
Library of Congress Catalog Number: 78-137277

AMS PRESS INC.
NEW YORK, N.Y. 10003

TABLE OF CONTENTS.

PART I. GENERAL ELECTIONS.

(iii)

HISTORY OF ELECTIONS

IN THE

AMERICAN   COLONIES.

PART I—GENERAL ELECTIONS.

CHAPTER I.   HISTORY OF GENERAL ELECTIONS.

Throughout the colonial period of American history, beginning at the earliest times and continuing down to the
Declaration of Independence, there existed in the various
colonies some system of popular elections.   Deprived as the
colonists were of a voice in the deliberations of the home
government, the people of every province, whether royal,
proprietary, or chartered, exercised a partial check on the
arbitrary rule of the governor and his council, by means of
a legislative assembly, whose members were chosen on the
basis of a limited popular suffrage.   In several of the more
northern colonies the people possessed the power of electing.
their governor and other general officers, while nearly everywhere the more local officials held their positions by virtue of
popular suffrage.   Nor was this system of election by the
people entirely confined to English colonies; for, as we shall
see in due course, it obtained a partial foothold in the Dutch
province of New Netherland.

§ 1. *Massachusetts and Plymouth.* In Massachusetts the election of a Governor, Deputy-Governor and eighteen assistants on the last Wednesday of Easter term was authorized by the Charter of 1628, under which the colony was founded.[1] Endicott, the first governor, was chosen by the company in London in April, 1629,[2] but in October of the following year it was resolved that the Governor and Deputy-Governor should be chosen by the assistants out of their own number.[3] After 1632, however, the Governor was chosen by the whole body of the freemen from among the assistants[4] at a general court or assembly held in May[5] of each year. The Deputy-Governor was elected at the same time. The charter, as already mentioned, provided also for the annual election of assistants or magistrates, whose number was fixed at eighteen.[6] This number appears not to have been regularly elected, for in October, 1678, in response to the demands of the home government a special election was held in order to bring the assistants up to the required number of eighteen.[7]

Besides the officers mentioned in the charter, an order of 1647 declared that a treasurer, major-general, admiral at sea, commissioners for the United Colonies, secretary of the General Court and "such others as are, or hereafter may be, of like general nature" should be chosen annually "by the freemen of this jurisdiction."[8] The voting took place in

[1] 1 *Massachusetts Colonial Records*, 10, 12.

[2] *Ibid.*, 37 j.   [3] *Ibid.*, 79.

[4] *Ibid.*, 95.   [5] *Ibid.*, 104.

[6] See also letter of Charles II. to the colony in 1662, which states that not more than eighteen, nor less than ten assistants were to be annually chosen. (4 *Massachusetts Colonial Records*, pt. 2, 166.

[7] 5 *Massachusetts Colonial Records*, 195.

[8] *Laws*, chap. 45, § 4, ed. Cambridge 1660, 28; ed. 1814, 107; 2 *Massachusetts Colonial Records*, 220; Commissioners for United Colonies first chosen in 1644, 2 *Massachusetts Colonial Records*, 69.

Boston in May, at a "court of election" held annually, and freemen could vote at first only in person, but eventually by proxy also, if they desired to do so.[1] The last election of general officers under the Charter of 1628 was held on May 12th, 1686,[2] and soon afterward the government passed into the hands of a President and Council appointed by the English crown.[3]

In Plymouth, as in Massachusetts, general officers were elected every year by the freemen of the colony. The first governor was chosen on January 1st, 1620–1,[4] though the existing records do not mention an election before 1632–3.[5] The other general officers were the assistants.[6] At first but one was chosen.[7] From 1624 till 1633 four were elected and it was not until the latter year that the full number of seven was chosen.[8] The last annual election of governor before the merging of New Plymouth into the province of Massachusetts Bay took place in June, 1691.[9] Besides the governor and assistants, two commissioners for the United Colonies and a treasurer were annually elected.[10] Just before Plymouth was incorporated into the royal province of Massachusetts Bay, a law was passed providing that county magistrates or associates should be elected by the freemen of each county.[11]

[1] See chap. iii, § 6, page 127, *post.*

[2] 5 *Massachusetts Colonial Records*, 513.

[3] 3 *Connecticut Colonial Records*, 207.

[4] 1 Palfrey, *History of New England*, Appendix.

[5] 1 *Plymouth Colony Records*, 5.

[6] *Laws*, 1636; Brigham ed., 1836, 37; 11 *Plymouth Colony Records*, 7. The laws in the edition of 1836 are also reprinted in the eleventh volume of the *Plymouth Colony Records.*

[7] 1 Palfrey, *History of New England*, Appendix.

[8] *Ibid.*

[9] 6 *Plymouth Colony Records*, 264.

[10] *Book of General Laws*, 1671, chap. 5, § 2, Brigham, 257.

[11] *Laws*, 1691, Brigham, 237.

In both Massachusetts and New Plymouth all freemen had originally a personal voice in the transaction of public business at the general courts or assemblies which were held at stated intervals. One of these was known as the Court of Election, and at this were chosen the officers of the colony for the ensuing year. As the number of settlements increased, it became inconvenient for freemen to attend the general courts in person and they were allowed to be represented by deputies. Massachusetts provided for this contingency by an act of 1634,[1] and required all towns containing more than thirty freemen to send not more than two deputies. Towns with less than thirty freemen had the option of sending two deputies, although, if they had less than twenty, they could send but one. In case there were not as many as ten freemen in a town, they could unite with their nearest neighbor in sending a deputy to the general courts. These deputies were to serve for a year and were granted the "full power of all the freemen deputed to them for the making and establishing of laws, granting lands, *etc.*, the matter of election of officers only excepted."[2] In the course of time the number of deputies became so large that several attempts were made to restrict each town to one representative, but they were unwilling to surrender their privilege of sending two if they so preferred.[3] The inconvenience of compelling all freemen to attend the courts of election finally gave rise to the proxy system, by means of which, as will be explained in a later chapter, the deputies carried the votes of their townsmen to Boston.[4]

In Plymouth the system of sending deputies originated in 1639, when Plymouth was represented in the general court

---

[1] 1 *Massachusetts Colonial Records*, 118.

[2] *Laws*, chap. 35, §§ 1, 2; ed. 1660, 25; ed. 1814, 97.

[3] 2 *Massachusetts Colonial Records*, 3, 88, 209, 217, 231.

[4] 1 *Massachusetts Colonial Records*, 166 (1636–7), 188.

by four deputies and each of the other towns by two.[1]   The function of these deputies was, as in Massachusetts, to assist the magistrates in making laws, but these enactments were for a time subject to the approval of the freemen, who were required to attend the June court for that purpose.[2]   It was not till 1652 that the deputies were permitted to carry the proxies of their fellow townsmen to the court of election,[3] though Rehoboth had been granted this privilege five years before.[4]   In 1638 a law was passed which gave the general court power to reject deputies who had been sent by the towns for the purpose of assisting the magistrates in making laws, if they judged them unfit; in such cases the towns were required to elect other representatives.[5]

During the rule of Dudley and of Andros, the whole legislative power of Massachusetts was lodged in a council,[6] appointed by the crown through its governor, and popular election in the New England colonies was limited to the choice of selectmen at a single meeting held annually in each town, on the third Monday in May.[7]

The ultimate result of the revolution of 1688 in England, was to unite Massachusetts and New Plymouth under the Charter of 1691.   By virtue of this instrument, " the Great and General Court of Assembly" was to consist of "the Governor and Council or Assistants for the time being, and such Freeholders of our said Province or Territory as shall be from

[1] See 1 *Plymouth Colony Records*, 126.

[2] *Laws*, 1638, Brigham, 63; *Laws*, 1646, Brigham, 88.   These deputies were called committees.

[3] *Laws*, 1652, Brigham, 94; *Book of General Laws*, 1671, chap. 5, § 1; Brigham, 256.

[4] *Laws*, 1647, Brigham, 89.

[5] Brigham, 112; *Book of General Laws*, 1671, chap. 5, § 8, Brigham, 259.

[6] 2 *New Hampshire Provincial Papers*, 3.

[7] 3 *Connecticut Colonial Records*, 427.

time to time elected or deputed by the Major parte of the Freeholders and other Inhabitants of the respective Townes and Places." The governor, deputy governor, and secretary and the first assistants were appointed. After the first year, the assistants were to be annually elected by the general assembly.[1] The number of deputies to be returned by towns having more than a hundred and twenty freeholders, was fixed at two by a statute passed in 1692–3. If it had less than this number of freeholders, it could elect but one. Boston alone could return four.[2] Under this charter, with the exception of these deputies, the only elective officers whose functions were at all general in their nature were the county treasurers, and they were chosen upon the basis of the town rather than upon the basis of the provincial suffrage.[3]

§ 2. *New Hampshire.* In the detached settlements which sprang up in the southern portion of what is now New Hampshire, all officers were originally elected. Thus in Dover, after 1633, a governor was annually chosen,[4] while Exeter[5] and Hampton[6] seem to have had a similar custom. In Portsmouth before 1640, a governor and two assistants appear to have been elected.[7] In 1641 these towns were taken into the colony of Massachusetts, and as such sent deputies to the general court at Boston.[8]

The crown, in 1679 constituted a separate government for New Hampshire, claiming that the towns had been unlawfully taken possession of by Massachusetts. The commission of John Cutts as first President of the new province

---

[1] See charter, 3 Will. and Mary; Poore, *Constitutions*, 949; 1 Ames and Goodell, ed., 1869, *Acts and Resolves*, 10, 11, 12.

[2] *Laws*, 1692–3, chap. 38; 1 Ames and Goodell, 88.

[3] *Laws*, 1692–3, chap. 27, § 1; 1 Ames and Goodell, 63.

[4] 1 *New Hampshire Provincial Papers*, 119.   [5] *Ibid.*, 144, *et seq.*

[6] *Ibid.*, 147.   [7] *Ibid.*, 111.

[8] *Ibid.*, 154, 369, *etc.*

ordered him to call a general assembly by summons under the great seal, in such a manner as he and his council saw fit.[1] By virtue of the authority thus granted, the first assembly elected by the province met at Portsmouth, on March 16th, 1679–80, and was opened with prayer and a sermon.[2] After this, assemblies were to be called annually at Portsmouth, and this appears to have been done except during the years from 1686 to 1692, during a part of which period the power of Andros obtained in New Hampshire.[3] Governor Allen's commission of 1692 again provided for an assembly of the freeholders,[4] and the last assembly elected under the royal government, met in May, 1775.[5] A statute requiring assemblies to be re-elected every three years seems to have been proposed in 1723.[6]

§ 3. *Rhode Island.* Before the charter of 19 Charles I., the several towns that finally formed the colony of Rhode Island appear to have been independent of one another and to have elected their own officers. The early records are incomplete, but in 1638 we find that Portsmouth established a government "according to the Word of God."[7] Providence in 1636 also did something similar.[8] In Portsmouth during the year 1638, a chief magistrate with the title of judge and also several elders, a constable, and a sergeant appear to have been chosen.[9] Providence had some part in this election.[10]

The earliest evidence on the subject of elections in the

[1] 1 *New Hampshire Provincial Papers*, 379.

[2] 1 Belknap, *History of New Hampshire*, 177; 1 *New Hampshire Provincial Papers*, 395.

[3] 2 *New Hampshire Provincial Papers.*   [4] *Ibid.*, 58.

[5] 7 *New Hampshire Provincial Papers*, 371.

[6] 4 *New Hampshire Provincial Papers*, 114.

[7] 1 *Rhode Island Colonial Records*, 53, 85.   [8] *Ibid.*, 14.

[9] *Ibid.*, 52, 64, 65.   [10] *Ibid.*, 64.

Newport records speaks of the presence of the judge and elders from Portsmouth. A joint government was set up for the three towns and it was determined to have the judge, elders and all other officers of the "Bodie Incorporate" annually chosen at a general court or assembly "by the greater body of freemen present."[1] At the first election which took place in the month of March, 1639–40, the chief magistrate was given the title of governor, and the next that of deputy-governor, the remainder being assistants. Two of the assistants and either the deputy-governor or the governor were to be chosen from each of the towns. Two treasurers and a constable for Newport, as well as one for Portsmouth and a "sarjeant" were also chosen.[2] At the election of the following year the government was declared a democracy and the power of the freemen to make laws and depute officers to execute them was established.[3]

The charter of Providence Plantations granted not by the crown but, on account of the civil war which was then raging in England, by Commissioners under authority of Parliament, allowed the inhabitants of the colony power to rule themselves.[4] In addition to the three towns already mentioned, Warwick was taken into the colony.[5] It seems that this town had established no government of its own, not because it was opposed to such a thing, but because it considered legal authority from England necessary.[6] The officers of the colony, chosen at the first election in 1647, were a President, four assistants (one from each town), a recorder, a treasurer and a "general sargant," who seems to have been a sort of high sheriff.[8] One of the assistants often

[1] 1 *Rhode Island Colonial Records*, 90, 98.

[2] *Ibid.*, 100, 101, 112, 120, 126, 127.

[3] *Ibid.*, 112.

[4] *Ibid.*, 145.

[5] *Ibid.*, 129, 148.

[6] *Ibid.*, 129.

[7] *Ibid.*, 191.

[8] *Ibid.*, 197.

held the office of treasurer as well.[1] It was not long before a schism took place in the colony. Portsmouth and Newport, which were situated on Rhode Island, séparated themselves from Providence and Warwick. Each half of the confederacy had a separate legislative assembly and elected its own governor and two assistants.[2] After various negotiations between the opposing factions, the breach was closed in the summer of 1654 and the old form of government resumed.[3] About this time an "attorney" and a solicitor were annually elected.[4]

After the accession of Charles the Second, in order to avoid any question of the validity of the first, a second charter was obtained. In the new instrument, under date of 1663,[5] the officers of the colony were named, and it was provided that in future a governor, a deputy-governor and ten assistants were to be elected annually by the company, which was composed of all the freemen.[6] By a resolution of the legislature in the following year, it was provided that annual elections should be held for minor officers as under the old charter.[7] A plurality of votes was declared sufficient to elect, but in case the person chosen refused to serve—and this happened quite frequently—the general assembly was empowered to fill vacancies.[8] Except during the Andros régime,[9] elections were held regularly until the Revolution.[10]

The bond of union between the Rhode Island towns was at first very loose, and there seems to have been no occasion for a general legislative assembly. It was not until after the charter of 1644 that steps were taken toward

---

[1] 1 *Rhode Island Colonial Records*, 209.   [2] *Ibid.*, 233, 244, 262, 265.
[3] *Ibid.*, 268, 278, 282.   [4] *Ibid.*, 278, 282.
[5] 15 Car. II.   [6] 2 *Rhode Island Colonial Records*, 7.
[7] *Ibid.*, 38.   [8] *Ibid.*, 83.
[9] 1686–1690; 3 *Rhode Island Colonial Records*, 187, 267.
[10] 7 *Rhode Island Colonial Records*, 510.

a meeting of deputies from the towns. Thus we find that in 1647 Providence sent a "committee" to Portsmouth to join with committees from other towns in order to form a government.[1] The fifth " act and order " established by this convention provided that each town should send a committee to every general court, and these, like the deputies in Massachusetts and Plymouth, could exercise the powers of the freemen in all matters excepting the election of officers.[2] The committee from each town should consist of six members.[3]

The power of making laws, possessed by these committees, was subject to popular approval expressed by means of a process somewhat resembling the French *plebiscite* or the *referendum* as it exists in Switzerland at the present day.[4] Matters of general import were required to be proposed in some town meeting, and notice must be given of this to each of the other towns. Towns which approved of the proposition were ordered to declare their opinion at the next general court through their committees. If the court decided in favor of the proposition a law was passed which had authority only until ratified by the next general assembly of all the people. The general court was also allowed to debate matters on its own motion, but its decisions must be reported to each town by the committee representing that town. A meeting of the town was held to debate on the questions so reported, and then the votes of the inhabitants were collected by the town clerk, and forwarded with all speed to the recorder of the colony. The latter was to open in the presence of the governor all votes so received, and if a majority

[1] 1 *Rhode Island Colonial Records*, 42.

[2] *Ibid.*, 147.

[3] *Ibid.*, 229, 236.

[4] 1 Bryce, *American Commonwealth*, 448.

voted affirmatively the resolution of the court was to stand as law until the next general assembly.[1]

This complex method of *referendum* was repealed in 1650, and instead, it was ordered that all laws enacted by the assembly should be communicated to the towns within six days after adjournment. Within three days after the laws were received, the chief officer of each town was to call a meeting and read them to the freemen. If any freeman disliked a particular law he could, within ten days, send his vote in writing, with his name affixed, to the general recorder. If within ten days the recorder received a majority of votes against any law, he was to notify the president of that fact, and the latter in turn was to give notice to each town that such law was null and void. Silence as to the remaining enactments was assumed to mean assent.[2]

After 1658 the recorder was allowed ten days instead of six, as the period within which the laws must be sent to the towns. The towns were given another ten days for consideration, and then if the majority of the free inhabitants of any one of them in a lawful assembly voted against a given enactment, they could send their votes sealed up in a package to the recorder. If a majority from every town voted against the law it would be thereby nullified; but unless this was done within twenty days after the adjournment of the court the law would continue binding. The recorder must always canvass the votes of the towns in the presence of the president of the colony, but if the latter were absent, the presence of the assistant in the town where the recorder lived was needed.[3] A further modification of the *referendum* was made in 1660. By the act of that year, three months ("fowre score and six daies") were allowed for

[1] 1 *Rhode Island Colonial Records*, 149.

[2] *Ibid.*, 229. [3] *Ibid.*, 401.

the return of the votes to the recorder. Instead of a majority of each town, a majority of all the free inhabitants of the
colony was sufficient to nullify a law, although indeed, any
one town should be wholly silent on the subject.[1] No mention of the *referendum* under the second charter has been
found. Under that charter four deputies from each of the
four original towns, except Newport, which was still allowed
six, and two deputies from each of the other towns, were
constituted a general assembly which was to sit in May and
October of each year in cönjunction with the assistants.[2]
With the exception of the years from 1686 to 1690 the
assembly sat regularly under this charter until the revolution.

§ 4. *Connecticut and New Haven.* The colony of Connecticut was fully organized in 1665, under authority of the
charter of 14 Charles II.[3] Before that time there had been
two separate governments, the one at New Haven, the other
at Hartford. In order, therefore, to get a clear idea of their
development, it will be necessary to trace the history of each
part with special reference to the subject of popular election.

The first meeting of all the "free planters" of New Haven
took place on the fourth day of the fourth month (June)
1639, for the purpose of "settling ciuill Gouernm^t according to God, and about the nominatiō oſ persons thatt
might be founde by consent of all fittest, in all respects for
the foundacō work of a church w(hich) was intended to be
gathered in Quinipieck." The meeting was opened by "a
solemn invocatiō of the name of God in prayer (for) the
presence and help of his speritt, and grace in those weighty
businesses." There was considerable discussion as to

[1] 1 *Rhode Island Colonial Records,* 429.
[2] 2 *Rhode Island Colonial Records,* 8.
[3] 2 *Connecticut Colonial Records,* 5.

whether the planters should give to free burgesses the power of making ordinances, but it was ultimately decided to do so. The minutes of the meeting show that this decision was arrived at on the authority of several passages from the Bible—such as " Take you wise men and understanding, and known among your tribes and I will make them rulers over you,"[1] and "Thou shalt in any wise set him king over thee whom the Lord thy God shall choose; one from among thy brethren shalt thou set king over thee; thou mayest not set a stranger over thee, which is not thy brother."[2] The model followed in the governmental organization was the liveries of the city of London which chose the magistrates and were themselves elected by the companies. Accordingly, the planters of New Haven elected a committee of eleven men, and gave them power to choose the seven pillars of the theocracy they had decided to establish.[3] The seven pillars met as a court of election in October of the same year and admitted upon oath several members of " approved churches." After reading a number of passages from the Bible bearing on the subject of an ideal ruler, they proceeded to the election of a chief magistrate and four deputy magistrates, with a marshal and a " publique notary," to hold office for the ensuing year.[4] At this meeting, all members of the church were admitted to membership in the general court. In 1643 Stamford was admitted to a share in the government, and New Haven chose for that town a magistrate and four assistants.[5] Other towns were admitted later, the franchise in them being likewise restricted to church members.[6]

In 1643 the towns in General Court assembled adopted a set

[1] *Deuteronomy* i. 13.

[2] *Deuteronomy* xvii. 15; also *Exodus* xviii. 21, and 1 *Corinthians* vi. 1 to 7.

[3] 1 *New Haven Colonial Records*, 11–14.   [4] *Ibid.*, 20.

[5] *Ibid.*, 85.   [6] *Ibid.*, 110.

of " Fundamental Orders," or written constitution, which
provided among other matters, for the election of a governor,
deputy-governor, and other magistrates, with a secretary and
a marshal.[1] Commissioners for the United Colonies were
chosen this year[2] by the general court, and after October,
1644 by the freemen.[3] As has already been noticed, the principle of representation by deputies in the making of laws
seems to have been recognized at the meeting of 1639.
Deputies appear to have been chosen semi-annually after
May, 1641,[4] and at first were little more than a jury to assist
the magistrates. In 1643 Stamford sent two deputies to the
general court at New Haven.[5] The fundamental orders
passed in the same year called for a " general court for the
jurisdiction," and to this two deputies were sent from each
plantation in the colony. The court was to meet in April
and in October, or oftener if called, and the governor, deputy-
governor and magistrates sat with the deputies from the
towns.[6] There was, therefore, at New Haven, the general
court "for the jurisdiction" as well as a general court for the
town of New Haven at which deputies were chosen for the
jurisdiction court.[7]

In the Hartford colony, which was Connecticut proper,
the earliest mention of elections is found in the Fundamental Orders of 1638, which have become famous as the
first written constitution framed on the American continent.
It was enacted that a governor and six magistrates should
be chosen annually by the freemen of the jurisdiction.[8] A
deputy-governor was also chosen.[9] The charter of 14

---

[1] 1 *New Haven Colonial Records*, 112, 191.

[2] *Ibid.*, 87, 117.   [3] *Ibid.*, 147.

[4] *Ibid.*, 51, 58, 69, 78, 85.   [5] *Ibid.*, 85.

[6] *Ibid.*, 114.   [7] *Ibid.*, 125, 129.

[8] 1 *Connecticut Colonial Records*, 21.   [9] *Ibid.*, 27.

Charles II, which placed the New Haven and the Hartford colonies under one government, provided for the same general officers, together with twelve assistants.[1] In 1689 it was ordered that a secretary and a treasurer should also be elected.[2] Although, as is well known, Andros did not succeed in taking away the charter of Connecticut, he, nevertheless, took the government into his hands in the autumn of 1687.[3] Upon his imprisonment in Boston in 1689 the old officers took up their duties again,[4] and a new election was held in the spring of the following year.[5] The Fundamental Orders of 1638 also provided that deputies should perform all the business, legislative or judicial, of the freemen, except the election of colonial officers.[6] If, however, a change in the constitution was proposed, notice to that effect must be inserted in the warrants calling for an election of deputies, and those towns which sent proxies to the general elections were requested to send in their votes in a similar manner on the question of the projected change.[7] There were two general courts each year, namely, in October and in May[8] so that there was, accordingly, a semi-annual election of deputies in each town. Under the charter the custom of sending deputies to the general courts was continued, and they ultimately formed the lower house of the legislature. The only occasions on which officers of the colony were elected by the assembly were when vacancies were caused by the death of

[1] 2 *Connecticut Colonial Records,* 5; also *Session Laws,* 1715, 30.

[2] 4 *Connecticut Colonial Records,* 11.

[3] 3 *Connecticut Colonial Records,* 248.

[4] *Ibid.,* 250. For a contemporaneous account of the proceedings at this time see *ibid.,* 455, *et seq.*

[5] 4 *Connecticut Colonial Records,* 22.

[6] 1 *Connecticut Colonial Records,* 25.   [7] *Ibid,* 346, 7.

[8] *Ibid.,* 21.

persons in office.   Thus, in 1707,[1] 1724,[2] and again in 1741,[3] a governor was chosen by both houses of the legislature. In the early part of the eighteenth century it was enacted that all officers must have a majority of votes in order to be elected.   If this number was not secured, the assembly had the power to choose the officers.[4]

In all colonies south of New England, as we shall see in due course, the governor was appointed either by the English crown or by the proprietors, who held by charter or grant from the crown.   There was, however, everywhere, at some time or other, a legislative assembly chosen by the colonists.

§ 5. *New York*.   While New Netherland remained under Dutch rule the people had no voice in the choice of those officers whose duties were more than local in character. The governor was an appointee of the West India Company, and responsible solely to it; though the latter was subject to a certain amount of control from the States General.   That the people desired the privilege of electing their general officers, is shown by a petition sent in 1649 to the States General from the Nine Men.   A request was made in this document for a suitable system of government, and it was accompanied by a sketch of the methods of written proxies used by the New England colonies in selecting their governors.[5]   On the other hand, a letter sent two years later by the magistrates of Gravesend to the directors at Amsterdam, stated that it would involve "ruin and destruction" to frequently change the government by allowing the people to elect the governor, partly on account of the numerous factions, and partly because there were no persons

[1] 5 *Connecticut Colonial Records*, 38.   [2] 6 *Connecticut Colonial Records*, 484.

[3] 8 *Connecticut Colonial Records*, 416.   [4] *Ibid.*, 453.

[5] 1 *New York Colonial Documents*, 266

in the province capable of filling the office.[1] Nor did the Dutch colonists possess any voice in the making of laws. There was no regular representative assembly, although we find that there were several emergencies when the advice of the people was asked by the governors. Thus in 1641 Governor Kieft requested the commonalty to elect a board of twelve men to advise him. But he dissolved the board as soon as they failed to comply with his wishes.[2]

Two years later Kieft again asked the commonalty to elect a board. But they preferred not to do so and requested the Governor and his council to make the selec tion, reserving to themselves, however, the right to reject any person they disliked. As a result of this action, the "Eight" were chosen, and for a time they sat at intervals and sent complaints to the Amsterdam chamber of the West India Company.[3] The Eight finally met with the fate of the Twelve. A third board, this time consisting of nine men, was formed in 1647 under Governor Stuyvesant. The people of New Amsterdam elected eighteen persons and from these the director and his council selected the members of the board. As this body was self-renewing, popular election ceased after the first eighteen names were submitted to the governor. A charter was granted to the Nine, but their existence was shortlived.[4] In 1653 there was more than the usual amount of dissatisfaction in the colony at the arbitrary rule of the governor, chiefly, perhaps, on account of Indian troubles. Delegates from several of the villages met at Flushing, and a meeting was held in the city hall of New Amsterdam. Finally, Governor Stuyvesant sent out writs for

[1] 2 *New York Colonial Documents*, 155.
[2] 1 O'Callaghan, *History of New Netherland*, 242, *et seq.*
[3] *Ibid.*, 283 *et seq ;* 1 *New York Colonial Documents*, 191, 213.
[4] 2 O'Callaghan, *History of New Netherland*, 38, *et seq.*

the election of delegates to an assembly at New Amsterdam. When the delegates met on December 10th, eight towns were represented, and on the following day a lengthy remonstrance was drawn up for transmission to the States General.[1] This assembly like the others, had a short existence.

In 1664, however, when the English were threatening immediate invasion and the affairs of New Netherland were in a precarious condition, Governor Stuyvesant, in the extremity of the danger, determined to call a representative assembly—(*eene Laenddagh*). He therefore, at the request of the Burgomasters and Schepens of New Amsterdam, sent out writs to all the towns under his rule, calling on them to elect deputies by a plurality of votes. Two representatives from each town were chosen and composed the assembly which met in the city hall of New Amsterdam on the tenth day of April.[2] This was the last assembly convoked by a Dutch Director, for in August of the same year New Amsterdam fell into the hands of the English.

The patent of Charles II., under date of March, 1664, by virtue of which the Duke of York acquired his title to New York, granted the fullest powers of government.[3] Soon after the conquest of the territory, Col. Nicolls, who had been appointed to his position as governor by the Duke of York, addressed a letter to the people of Long Island, calling on them to elect " Deputyes chosen by the major part of the

[1] 2 O'Callaghan, *History of New Netherland*, 239, *et seq.*

[2] 1 Brodhead, *History of the State of New York*, 728; 2 O'Callaghan, *History of New Netherland*, 505. The latter gives a copy of the certificate of election for the deputies from Wiltwyck. This is signed by a number of inhabitants, and states, among other matters, that the election was held on March 31st by the sheriff and commissaries at the summons of the Director General and Council of New Netherland.

[3] 2 Brodhead, *History of the State of New York*, 652; Leaming and Spicer, *Grants and Concessions*, 3.

freemen only, which is to bee understood, of all Persons rated according to their estates, whether English or Dutch." Four days notice of the election was to be given and each town was to send two deputies to meet the governor at Hampstead in the latter part of February 1664–5.[1] This assembly was not as representative as the Lantag of Stuyvesant, for only Long Island towns were summoned or sent delegates. When the convention came together it adopted the code known as the Duke's Laws. The delegates thought at first that they were to organize a government even more liberal than that existing in the Puritan colonies, with provision that general officers should be elected by the votes of the freemen; but when Governor Nicolls showed that he was authorized to appoint all officers they submitted and were dissolved.[2]

The government constituted by the Duke's Laws lasted practically till 1691. Only local officers were elected under this code. There sat during this period a limited legislature, known as the court of assizes, whose members were appointed by the governor, but they merely registered the decrees of the governor's council and had no more power than a French *lit de justice*.[3] During the second Dutch occupation in 1673 and 1674 there was a provisional government, and only local officers were elected by the people.[4]

When New York was again surrendered to the English crown in 1674, the Duke of York obtained a fresh charter, similar to his first. A desire for a popular assembly soon sprang up, and in 1680 a petition was sent to the Duke

---

[1] *Introduction to Journal of New York Legislative Council,* Albany, 1861, iv.

[2] 2 Brodhead, *History of the State of New York,* 69; *Introduction to Journal of New York Legislative Council,* v, vi.

[3] 2 Brodhead, *History of the State of New York,* 71; *Introduction to Journal of New York Legislative Council,* vi.

[4] 2 *New York Colonial Documents,* 574, 579, 680, *etc.*

[5] Leaming and Spicer, 41.

by the court of assizes, asking that the freeholders should be allowed to elect a legislature.[1] In March, 1681–2 James wrote that he would grant the request, and the instructions of Governor Dongan authorized him to call such an assembly,[2] by sending out not more than eighteen writs thirty days before the date chosen for the meeting of the legislature. Dongan reached New York in August, 1683, and soon issued writs calling an assembly to meet on October 17th. The most important act passed by this body was the Charter of Liberties and Privileges. It declared that the

"Supreme legislative authority under his Majesty and Royall Highnesse, James, Duke of York, Albany, etc., shall forever bee and reside in a Governor, Councell and the People met a general assembly. . . That every freeholder within this province, and every freeman in any corporation shall have his free choice and vote in the Electing of representatives, without any manner of constraint or imposition, and that in all elections the Majority of voices shall carry itt, and by ffreeholders is understood every one who is so understood according to the Laws of England."

The charter then proceeded to apportion the seats in the assembly among the various counties.[3] The representatives together with the governor and council were declared to be " forever the supreme and only legislative power, under his Royall Highnesse, of the said province."

The charter was presented to the duke for his approval, and seems to have been amended and affirmed, and then ordered sent to New York, as ratified.[4] This order does not appear to have been carried into effect, for at a meeting of the

[1] 2 Brodhead, *History of the State of New York*, Appendix, 658.

[2] 1682–3, 3 *New York Colonial Documents*, 317, 330.

[3] 2 Brodhead, *History of the State of New York*, 659, where the charter is given in full.

[4] 1684, 3 *New York Colonial Documents*, 348; 2 Brodhead, *History of the State of New York*, 416, note.

Privy Council in March, 1684–5, very soon after James became King and New York a royal province, it was noted that
his majesty did not "think fit to confirm it."[1]   In a report on
the charter presented at this meeting of the Privy Council
objections were made to the phrase "the People," because
such words "are not used in any other constitution in
America; But only the words General Assembly."[2]   Dongan's first assembly was dissolved in August, 1685, and
he had called another, when orders arrived from the crown
vesting all legislative authority in the governor and his
council.[3]   Andros took New York, as well as all New England, under his rule; and in accordance with his instructions, as already explained,[4] no assemblies were called.
After Andros' imprisonment Lieutenant-Governor Leisler
usurped the government of New York and called an assembly in June, 1689.[5]   He was superseded and executed by
authority of Governor Sloughter, who reached America in
March, 1691, with a commission from William and Mary
authorizing him to call an assembly.[6]   Within a month after
his arrival an assembly met and passed a modified form of
the Charter of Liberties and Privileges which had been
vetoed by King James in 1684–5.[7]   From this time assemblies were called at intervals until the royal government
ceased.   Representatives were elected by the residents of
the manors, cities and counties, and the privilege of voting
is described as the subject's "chiefest Birth Right."[8]

---

[1] 3 *New York Colonial Documents*, 357.   [2] *Ibid.*, 357.

[3] *Ibid.*, 370.   [4] *Ibid.*, 544. See *ante*, p. 5.   [5] *Ibid.*, 655.

[6] 3 *New York Colonial Documents*, 624; *Introduction to Journal of the New
York Legislative Council*, xxiv, xxv.

[7] Bradford, *Laws*, ed. 1710, 1; 2 Brodhead, *History of the State of New York*, 642.

[8] 11 Will. III., chap. 74, Van Schaack's *Laws*, 28. During the later colonial
period members were returned by the borough of Westchester and by the town
of Schenectady. 1 Jones, *History of New York*, ed. 1879, 506.

§ 6. *New Jersey.* The territory included in the present state of New Jersey was originally under the rule of the Director General and Council of New Netherland, and it also formed a portion of the country granted to James, Duke of York, by the patent of 1664.[1] By indentures of lease and release dated respectively June 23rd and June 24th, 1664, the proprietor conveyed all his rights in the territory now known as New Jersey to John, Lord Berkeley, and Sir George Carteret.[2] The country was to be settled under the name of Nova Caesarea. The lords proprietors, in order to encourage settlement in their newly acquired province, issued, on February 10th, 1664–5, a " Concession and Agreement." By virtue of this constitution, all persons who became subjects of the King of England, and who swore fidelity to the Lords Proprietors should be admitted as freemen of the colony. Those inhabitants who were either freemen or chief agents to others were authorized to choose twelve representatives for a general assembly, to be summoned by writs issued as soon as Philip Carteret, who had been appointed governor, reached the province.[3] Carteret came to America in the latter part of 1665,[4] but did not issue a proclamation calling an assembly till April, 1668.[5] This body was elected by the freeholders and met in Elizabeth in May of that year, and after transacting some business adjourned till the following November.[6] No further assemblies were called by the governor, although in 1672 there was great discontent in the province, and some of the settlers elected delegates to an illegal assembly held at Elizabeth. This pretended to act for the whole province, and chose as governor an illegitimate son of

---

[1] 1 *New Jersey Archives*, 3.   [2] *Ibid.*, 8, 10.

[3] *Ibid.*, 30; Leaming and Spicer, *Grants and Concessions*, 12.

[4] 1 *New Jersey Archives*, 48.   [5] *Ibid.*, 56.

[6] *Ibid.*, 56; Leaming and Spicer, 81, 85.

Sir George Carteret.[1] In 1673, New Jersey was recon-
quered by the Dutch and placed, with New York, under a
provisional government.[2]

When peace was restored, the Duke of York received
from the crown, under date of June 29th, 1674, a new
grant.[3] This included New Jersey and all the other territory which had been bestowed on him ten years before.
Two days later, July 1st, Major Andros was commissioned
governor of all the Duke's territories in America. In spite of
this, on the 28th and 29th of the same month (July), indentures of lease and release were executed by the Duke
conveying East Jersey to Sir George Carteret.[4] The interest
of Lord Berkeley in the western half of New Jersey had been
conveyed by deed of bargain and sale to a certain John
Fenwick, in trust for Edward Byllinge. Byllinge failed and
assigned his interest to William Penn and two associates
as trustees. On July 1st, 1676, Sir George Carteret, Byllinge
and the trustees executed the famous Quintipartite Deed,[5] by
which their several claims were satisfied and New Jersey
separated into two parts, known thereafter as East Jersey
and West Jersey. The government of East Jersey had already been for some time in the hands of Carteret's representatives. He had issued a charter confirming the concession and agreement promulgated before the Dutch conquest,[6] and an assembly, elected by the freeholders, had met
under his authority in the month of November, 1674,[7] and
thereafter. In 1680, however, Governor Andros under claim

---

[1] Whitehead, *East Jersey under the Proprietors*, 66, 67. Reference is made to
the second edition of this work.

[2] 1 *New Jersey Archives*, 121, 125, *et seq.*   [3] Leaming and Spicer, 41.

[4] 1 *New Jersey Archives*, 160, 161; Leaming and Spicer, 46.

[5] 1 *New Jersey Archives*, 205; Leaming and Spicer, 61.

[6] 1 *New Jersey Archives*, 167, *et seq.*; Leaming and Spicer, 50, 58.

[7] Leaming and Spicer, 93, *et seq.*

of royal authority exercised governmental powers in East Jersey;[1] but the death of Carteret and the subsequent release from the Duke of York to his heirs, again restored the province to the Carteret family.[2] In 1682 a number of conveyances were executed, which resulted in transferring East Jersey from the trustees under Carteret's will to twelve proprietors. These in turn divided their shares with twelve others, and the Duke of York confirmed the whole twenty-four in their ownership.[3]

The twenty-four proprietors issued in 1683 an elaborate instrument, known as the "Fundamental Constitutions of East Jersey."[4] Sixteen of the proprietors were to elect the governor from nominations made by each of the twenty-four. The power of making laws was placed in a great council, consisting of the proprietors or their proxies and a hundred and forty-four persons elected by the freemen. On account of the small number of towns in the province, however, there were to be but ninety-six delegates at first, twenty-four of whom came from each of the eight towns and forty-eight from the country at large. A third of this number was to go out of office and be renewed by popular election each year. A common council was to be formed by adding twelve freemen, chosen by ballot from the members of the great council, to the proprietors or their proxies. All officers except magistrates were to be chosen by the council and the governor. It is doubtful whether this constitution was ever put into operation.

The proprietors had appointed a governor for life[5] and had given him the privilege of remaining at home and ruling his province by a deputy. The latter convoked the first as-

---

[1] Whitehead, *East Jersey under the Proprietors*, 92.

[2] 1 *New Jersey Archives*, 337.   [3] Leaming and Spicer. 73, 141.

[4] *Ibid.*, 153; 1 *New Jersey Archives*, 395.   [5] Leaming and Spicer, 166.

sembly under the proprietors at Elizabeth in March 1682–3.[1] When Andros was carrying out the wishes of James II. by reducing the American colonies to submission, he siezed East Jersey.[2] Being threatened with a writ of *quo warranto*, the proprietors had caused a surrender to be drawn up, but never executed it;[3] they, however, abandoned their property till 1692.[4] After that year assemblies were elected annually until 1698.[5]

The proprietors of West Jersey, who as a matter of fact were mostly Quakers, drew up, with the assistance of the freeholders and inhabitants of their dominions, a long series of Concessions and Agreements.[6] These were supposed to form a complete constitution; but in default of a sufficient number of settlers the country was to be governed for the time being by a number of commissioners appointed by the proprietors. The constitution was to go into effect in March, 1680, at which time the proprietors, freeholders and inhabitants resident in the province were to meet and elect "Ten honest and able Men fit for Gouernment, to officiate and execute the Place of Commissioners for the Year Ensuing."[7] The thirty-second chapter of the concessions provided that where "divisions or tribes or other such like distinctions are made" an election should be held annually in each of the one hundred proprieties or parts for a freeholder or proprietor from each, to be deputy, trustee or representative for the "Benefit, Service and Behoof" of the people of the province in a "General and Supream Assembly." This body was to choose ten commissioners to adminster the

[1] Leaming and Spicer, 227.

[2] Whitehead, *East Jersey under the Proprietors*, 147, 159.

[3] 2 *New Jersey Archives*, 26.

[4] Leaming and Spicer, 605.   [5] *Ibid.*, 312, 380.

[6] *Ibid.*, 382–409; *New Jersey Archives*, 241–270.

[7] Leaming and Spicer, 385.

affairs of the province while the General Assembly was not in session.[1]

In August, 1680, the Duke of York made another grant of the soil to the proprietors of West Jersey,[2] and in the fall of the following year the deputy-governor who had been appointed in England convoked the first legislature. Ten fundamental laws were passed, providing among other things for a general assembly to be elected yearly by the free people of the province. This elected body was to choose all officers of state.[3] The members of the next assembly, which met at Burlington in May, 1682, had been returned by the sheriff from the province as a whole.[4] To do away with this, a statute was passed, requiring each of the ten proprieties to choose " their representatives where they are peopled." As new proprieties were settled in the future, each tenth was to choose ten representatives. The members of the next assembly were returned by tenths, ten sitting for each tenth.[5] The next year (1683) the assembly debated the question, and decided that it had power to elect a governor. This was done by construing liberally the clause of the constitution permitting changes to be made by six-sevenths of the people. They accordingly chose a governor " *nemine contradicente,* saue only one member was dubious therein."[6] Freemen were allowed by an act of this year to attend the first meeting of each assembly.[7] From 1685 to 1692, no assemblies were elected, for though no *quo warranto* was sought against New Jersey, the proprietors of both provinces joined in the proposd surrender.[8]

[1] Chap. 38, Leaming and Spicer, 385.

[2] Leaming and Spicer, 412.   [3] *Ibid.*, 423.

[4] *Ibid.*, 442.   [5] *Ibid.*, 455.

[6] *Ibid.*, 471.   [7] *Ibid.*, 482.

[8] Whitehead, *East Jersey under the Proprietors*, 159; 2 *New Jersey Archives*, 26. The elaborate system of proprieties and tenths seems to have been abro-

During the later years of the seventeenth century there was more or less disorder in both of the provinces, and the proprietors of East and West Jersey being for the most part the same, a memorial was addressed to the Lords of Trade and also to the Lords Justices of England, asking that East Jersey be annexed to New York.[1] The Lords of Trade approved of the suggestion, but would not give New Jersey as many representatives as were desired: one sixth of the whole New York assembly was suggested as the proper proportion for each of the Jersey provinces.[2] At last, in 1701, both sets of proprietors addressed a memorial to the crown, requesting that an assembly be elected annually and that it sit alternately in Perth Amboy and Burlington, two members being elected from each of these towns by the inhabitants, who were householders, and sixteen being chosen by the freeholders of each province.[3] The Board of Trade reported in favor of a form of government consisting of a governor, council and assembly.[4] A deed of surrender was executed in April, 1702, and accepted by the Queen.[5] Lord Cornbury was appointed the first royal governor, and his commission[6] and instructions[7] required him to call an assembly on the lines suggested by the proprietors, except that there were to be but ten members from each half and only twenty-four in all. In the autumn of 1703 the first royal legislature under this authority was elected.[8] By a

gated by the establishment of counties, (*Laws*, 1694, chap. 11, Leaming and Spicer, 533,) Burlington being given twenty members, Gloucester twenty, Salem ten, and Cape May five. Each of the first two counties contained two tenths, and the third only one. In 1699 (chap. 3, Leaming and Spicer, 567), the representation of each county was reduced by one-half; but the old number was restored two years later (Leaming and Spicer, 581).

[1] Leaming and Spicer, 588, 591. [2] *Ibid.*, 594.
[3] *Ibid.*, 599. [4] *Ibid.*, 603.
[5] *Ibid.*, 609. [6] *Ibid.*, 647.
[7] Art. 14, *Ibid.*, 623.
[8] 1 Smith, *History of New Jersey*, 275; Allinson's *Laws*, 1.

statute of 1767 new assemblies were to be elected at least once in seven years.[1]

§ 7. *Pennsylvania and Delaware.* The country from which the provinces of Pennsylvania and Delaware were formed was conquered by the Dutch from the Swedes, and a portion of it came under the rule of the Duke of York, and the code known as the Duke's Laws probably had effect after 1676. Charles II. by charter of 1681 granted to William Penn a large tract of land between Maryland and the Duke of York's territory. The fourth section of the royal charter gave the proprietor power to make laws "with the advice, assent and approbation of the freemen of the said country or the greater part of them or their delegates or deputies, whom, for the enacting of the said laws," Penn was authorized to assemble.[2] By a deed from the Duke of York in August, 1682, Penn was enfeoffed with the country lying within a radius of twelve miles from New Castle, while another instrument gave him additional land to the south of that town.[3]

In April of the last mentioned year Penn drew up and promulgated a "Frame of Government." This provided that laws should be made by the governor and freemen. The latter were to meet in the month of February, 1682–3, and elect seventy-two persons of most note for their "wisdom, virtue and ability," to form the provincial council. One third of this number was to go out of office every year, and their seats were to be filled by vote of the freemen. The first assembly was to consist of all the freemen, but thereafter it was to be representative. The freemen were at first to return two hundred members, though, as

[1] 8 Geo. III, Allinson's *Laws*, 306, 307.

[2] 1 *Pennsylvania Colonial Records*, 19.

[3] *Laws*, Adams ed., New Castle, 1797, 1.

the country increased in population, the number of assemblymen might be increased to five hundred.[1] The "Laws agreed upon in England" at this time fixed the qualifications to be possessed by freemen,[2] and Chalmers in his *Political Annals*,[3] says that Penn derived suggestions in reference to this matter from Harrington's *Oceana*. The proprietor reached America in the latter part of October, 1682, and convoked at Chester an assembly of as many freemen as saw fit to appear. It met on the fourth day of December.[4] Freemen attended not only from Pennsylvania but from the "territories" recently granted to the proprietor by the Duke of York, and which were now annexed to the province by legislative action. An act of settlement was passed at this meeting, and from this statute we find that the freemen had been summoned by writs issued by the Proprietary to the sheriffs of each of the six counties (three in the "province" and three in the "territories" as the Delaware country was called), and requested to elect twelve persons from each county to form the first provincial council. The freemen had been requested to attend the assembly in person; but, the act goes on to declare, "the Fewness of the People, their inability in Estate and Unskilfulness in Matters of Government" would render impracticable so large an assembly as had been provided for. Therefore, the statute enacts, that, of the twelve persons returned by each county, three should serve in the provincial council, and nine in the assembly, while the frame of government was declared to be modified in this particular.[5]

---

[1] Articles 1, 2, 14, 16; 1 *Pennsylvania Colonial Records*, 133, *et seq.*

[2] *Pennsylvania Colonial Records*, 37; *Laws*, ed. Harrisburg, 1879, 99.

[3] *Political Annals*, 642.

[4] Chalmers, *Political Annals*, 645; 1 Proud, *History of Pennsylvania*, 206.

[5] Colden, *History of the Five Nations*, pt. ii., 245; 1 *Votes, Assembly*, 1752, 1.

This meeting having been preliminary, Penn called a regular assembly to meet in Philadelphia the following March.[1] A new charter or frame of government was passed by this body, and approved by Penn. It incorporated the provisions of the act of settlement already given, except that each county was allowed but six assemblymen instead of nine.[2] One-third of the council, that is, one member from each county, was to go out of office each year.

Except in 1684[3] and in 1690,[4] when the assembly sat in Newcastle, legislatures met every year in Philadelphia, until 1693 when Penn's government was taken away by the crown and given to Governor Fletcher of New York. The commission of the latter empowered him to call an assembly elected by freeholders in the same way as the New York body.[5] He did so in 1693,[6] but in the following year Penn's government was restored to him by letters patent from William and Mary.[7] Penn appointed William Markham governor, and the latter caused legislatures to be elected in September 1695 and again in 1696.[8] The body last mentioned enacted a new frame of government which reduced the membership of the council from three to two for each county, making in all but twelve. The total number of assemblymen was likewise reduced from thirty-six to twenty-four.[9] This frame continued to be the constitution of the province till 1701, when Penn, just before his final departure for England, granted the Charter of Privileges, which remained in force down to the revolution. This charter provided for an assembly to be annually elected by the freemen, and to

---

[1] 1 *Votes, Assembly,* 7.
[2] 1 *Pennsylvania Colonial Records,* 42.
[3] 1 *Votes,* 24.
[4] *Ibid.,* 56.
[5] 1 Proud, *History of Pennsylvania,* 378.
[6] *Ibid.,* 382.
[7] *Ibid.,* 403.
[8] *Ibid.,* 405, *et seq.*
[9] 1 *Pennsylvania Colonial Records,* 49.

meet on the 14th of October of each year.[1] By another charter
a council of state was instituted, and the governor was given
power to fill vacancies, so that the assembly was now the
only legislative body whose members were chosen by the
votes of the people.[2]

Except on the two occasions already mentioned, the inhabitants of the "territories" had never favored the sending
of representatives to the legislature which sat at Philadelphia. In 1699 New Castle defied the writ sent out
by the governor, and refused to elect assemblymen. In
consequence of this action a law was passed imposing a
fine of £100 on counties which were delinquent in sending representatives, and providing that the members from those
counties holding elections should act for all.[3] The Charter
of Privileges allowed two-thirds of the counties to act for all,
in such a contingency.[4] Penn, fearing that there might at
some time be trouble on this point, inserted a clause in the
Charter of Privileges giving the province and the territories
power to hold separate legislatures, if they saw fit. In that
case, each county in Pennsylvania was to be allowed eight
members and the city of Philadelphia two. The Delaware
counties could have as many delegates to their assembly as
they saw fit, and both legislatures, if separated, were to have
the same power as if they had remained together.[5]

The proprietor had scarcely left America when a dispute
broke out, and the territories refused to send delegates to the
Philadelphia assembly, and instead held one of their own in
October, 1700.[6] In 1703 the separation permitted by the
charter was made, and from that time there were two distinct
legislatures, one sitting at New Castle for the government of

---

[1] 1 Proud, *History of Pennsylvania*, 444.   [2] *Ibid.*, 451, note.
[3] 1 *Votes, Assembly*, xiii.
[4] 1 Proud, *History of Pennsylvania*, 444.   [5] *Ibid.*, 444.
[6] Franklin and Hall ed., *Delaware Laws*, 1752, 1.

New Castle, Kent and Sussex upon Delaware, and the other at Philadelphia for the province of Pennsylvania. Both remained under the proprietorship of Penn and the same governor acted for both. The Charter of Privileges was the constitution in both governments, and we shall see that the legislation of the two in regard to the management of elections was almost precisely identical.[1] Penn expressed a willingness to surrender the provinces to the crown in 1712, but on account of a fit of apoplexy he was unable to execute the necessary instruments.[2] He died in 1718, leaving his province to three English noblemen to be by them held in trust and disposed of for the benefit of his heirs.[3] After nine years of litigation on the subject of this bequest it was decided that the grant was void, and the government, therefore, descended to his heirs, who administered it either in person or by deputy, until independence was declared.[4]

Besides the members of the legislature as already explained, the frame of government drawn up in the early part of 1683 provided for the election by the freemen of a double number of sheriffs, justices and coroners. The persons chosen were in each case to be presented to the governor and he could grant a commission to the one he preferred. If within three days he took no action, the person first named on the return received the office.[5] The third paragraph of the Charter of Privileges of 1701 provided in like manner, for the election of a double number of sheriffs and coroners.[6] The idea of giving the governor a partial check on the election of certain officers, by compelling the electors to chose one or more alternates was undoubtedly borrowed

---

[1] 1 Proud, *History of Pennsylvania*, 454.
[2] 2 Proud, *History of Pennsylvania*, 57. [3] *Ibid.*, 105.
[4] Gordon, *History of Pennsylvania*, 178.
[5] 1 *Pennsylvania Colonial Records*, 42; Section 16 of Frame.
[6] 1 Proud, *History of Pennsylvania*, 444.

from Holland, where it had been for many years practiced in the choice of Burgomasters and Schepens,[1] and, as we shall see, it was introduced in New Netherland.[2]

§ 8. *Maryland.* Maryland was settled under a charter granted by Charles I. to Lord Baltimore in 1632. The proprietor was given the power of making laws with consent of the freeholders[3] or freemen.[4] The first legislative assembly under this grant was held at St. Mary's on February 16th, 1634-5, but all records of its proceedings have been lost.[5] Probably all the freemen attended. The second assembly was called for the early part of 1637-8.[6] Certain gentlemen were summoned to this meeting by writs specially addressed to them, and all freemen were ordered to attend in person or by proxy. For the latter purpose the freemen were permitted to assemble in their hundreds and elect "one, two or more able and sufficient men" to be "the deputies or burgesses for the said freemen, in their name and steed to advise and consult in the same manner as burgesses from an English borough."[7] All freemen not participating in the election of a burgess were required to send a proxy or attend in person. We find

---

[1] See 1 O'Callaghan, *History of New Netherland*, 392.

[2] For details of the methods used in electing these officers, see *Pennsylvania Statutes*, 4 Anne, chap. 153, Franklin ed. *Laws*, 1742, 105; *Delaware Statutes*, 12 Will. III, chap. 21a; Franklin and Hall, ed. 1752, 29; Adams ed. 1797, 63.

[3] § 8, "Liberi tenentes."

[4] § 37, "Liberi homines." For a copy of charter in the original Latin, and also a translation, see Bacon's *Laws* (1765).

[5] See 2 Bozman, *History of Maryland*, 33, 34.

[6] See *Maryland Archives*, 1 *Proceedings and Acts of Assembly*, 1; 2 Bozman, *History of Maryland*, 47; also Appendix A, to this work, for a copy of one of the writs; Bacon's *Laws*, ed. 1765, 7 Cæcilius Lord Baltimore, chap. 1, chap. 26. The pages in Bacon are not numbered.

[7] *Maryland Archives*, 1 *Proceedings and Acts of Assembly*, 74, 81, 82.

even as late as 1642 that freemen not represented were fined twenty pounds of tobacco.[1]

The reason why the freemen of Maryland were permitted to be represented by proxy and thus apparently act in contravention to the well known rule of the common law which forbade the exercise of a public franchise by proxy, was that they were supposed to sit in their own right as did the Peers in the English House of Lords. Like the peers, therefore, they could be represented by proxy.[2] It followed from this, and it was so held in an actual case, that freemen represented by proxy were exempt from arrest until a reasonable time after the dissolution of the assembly, just as if they had actually occupied their seats.[3] Of course this state of affairs did not continue after the population of the colony became relatively larger. The custom disappeared about 1658.

In 1689, because the Baltimore family adhered to the Roman faith, the British crown took the government into its own hands and did not restore it until 1715. Then it was given to a member of the family who professed the Protestant religion.[4] Assemblies were called, however, at intervals throughout Maryland's colonial history, and the following quotation from a letter of Governor Sharpe to Lord Baltimore, under date of June 6th, 1754, shows that elections were held at intervals of three years:

"I will beg leave to submit to your Lordship's Consideration whether it be impracticable or improper to fall on any method to put a Stop to such Perverseness as might generally be perceived in the proceedings of our Lower Houses of Assembly which is in great measure owing to the short Duration of our Sessions which termin-

[1] *Maryland Archives,* 1 *Proceedings and Acts of Assembly,* 169; also 2, 3, *et seq.*
[2] Bozman, *History of Maryland,* 48, 49.
[3] *Maryland Archives,* 1 *Proceedings and Acts of Assembly,* 8.
[4] See Bacon's *Laws.*

ate at the end of 3 years: few Gent[n] will submit so frequently to the inconveniences that such as canvass for Seats in that House must necessarily subject themselves to; by which means there are too many Instances of the lowest Persons at least men of small fortunes no Soul & very mean Capacities appearing as Representatives of their respective Counties; As there would be no want I apprehend of Gent[n] to appear as Candidates if the Drudgery of Electioneering was to return less frequently. I submit to your Lordships Wisdom whether there may be any impropriety (if a more agreeable Choice of Members should be made) in continuing the next assembly for more years than has been lately usual or customary."[1]

§ 9. *Virginia.* The first Virginia Charter (1606) placed the legislative power in the hands of a council whose members were appointed by the crown.[2] The second (1609) made the council a corporation[3] to meet in England. The third and last charter (1611–12) provided for four great courts to be held annually in England for managing the affairs of the company.[4] By virtue of this charter, the treasurer, council and company in England issued on July 21st, 1621, an Ordinance and Constitution which placed the legislative power in Virginia in the hands of a council of state and an assembly. The assembly was to consist of two burgesses to be elected by the inhabitants of each hundred, town or other particular plantation, and to be called " once a year and no oftener."[5]

But this ordinance had been anticipated, for the first legislative assembly of Virginia met " in the church quire" at James City on July 30th, 1619. It was called by the governor, Sir George Yeardley, who " sente his summons all

---

[1] *Maryland Archives;* 1 *Correspondence Gov. Sharpe*, 68.

[2] 1 Hening, *Statutes at Large*, 61, 68. [3] *Ibid.*, 90.

[4] *Ibid.*, 103.

[5] *Ibid.*, 110, *et seq.* See also Sir Francis Wyatt's commission as governor, 1 Hening, 113; 3 Hening, 236.

over the country," ordering two burgesses " out of each In-
corporation and Plantation freely to be elected by the inhabitants." This was without doubt the first election held on
the American continent by men of Anglo-Saxon lineage
under an organized government, and, on that account, is of
especial importance.[1] A second assembly was called in
November, 1621,[2] but the first legislature whose records are
preserved in Hening's *Statutes at Large* was that of 1623–4.[3]
The House of Burgesses (as the Virginia assembly was
called) met with greater or less regularity until 1773.[4] During Bacon's rebellion in 1676, a house of burgesses, elected
by the insurgents, met and passed laws.[5] Throughout the
eighteenth century members were returned by the counties,
cities and towns, and by the College of William and Mary.[6]
According to a statute enacted in 1763,[7] elections were to
be triennial.

§ 10. *The Carolinas.* Both North and South Carolina
were included in the two charters under which the Carolina
proprietors derived their rights. The first charter, that of
1663, gave to the proprietors the fullest power of making
laws " with the advice, assent, and approbation of the
freemen of the said province or of the greater part of them
or of their deputies." Laws could be made by the proprietors themselves until they exercised their power of
calling the freemen together.[8] The second charter (1665)

---

[1] *New York Historical Society Collections*, 2d Series, vol. iii., 331 *et seq.*, 1857,
Stith, *History of Virginia*, 160.

[2] 1 Hening, 119.   [3] 1 Hening.

[4] 8 Hening, 647.   [5] 2 Hening, 356.

[6] 4 Anne, chap. 2, § 7, 3 Hening, 236. In England it has long been a custom for the two universities to return members to the House of Commons. See
Statute, 9 Anne, chap. 5, 3dly.

[7] 3 Geo. III., chap. 1, § 3, 7 Hening, 519.

[8] 1 *North Carolina Colonial Records*, 23.

gave similar authority, as well as a limited ordinance power, whenever assemblies could not be called.[1] But the first charter speaks of the whole territory as one province,[2] while the second grants power to divide the country into " counties, baronies and colonies with separate and distinct jurisdictions, liberties and privileges."[3] The latter provision is of importance from our point of view, because from it resulted the final division into two provinces, each with a separate, elective legislature.

Before the Lords Proprietors received their charter, some settlers from New England had established themselves in the Carolina territory, and it may not be presumptuous to suppose that they chose their own officers.[4] In a " declaration and proposals to all that will plant in Carolina," issued by the proprietors in 1663, it was provided that the undertakers, before leaving for America, should select thirteen persons from among their number, and out of these a governor and six members of the council should be commissioned. The successors of the governor were to be chosen from the council, while the number of the latter was to be completed from the six persons remaining. On the 25th of March, preceding the expiration of the official terms of these magistrates, a new set of thirteen names was to be presented by the freeholders of the colony, or " by such persons as they shall constitute." By the tenth of the following month, the new governor and council were to be commissioned from this list. The freeholders, in person or represented by two deputies from each parish, tribe or division, were to make laws which should be binding, unless

[1] 1 *North Carolina Colonial Records*, 104.
[2] 5th Paragraph, *ibid.*, 23.
[3] 4th Paragraph, *ibid.*, 104.
[4] 2 Hawks, *History of North Carolina*, 70, *et seq.*

abrogated by the proprietors within a year.[1]   Dr. Hawks[2]
states that these proposals were put into force at Cape Fear
but not in the settlement at Albemarle, which ultimately
developed into North Carolina.   If this is true, it is the
only instance within the knowledge of the writer, in which
the inhabitants of any of the colonies south of New England had any share in the choice of their governor, or
of his council, except, perhaps during the twenty years
when the Pennsylvania council was elected by the people,
and the occasions on which, as we shall see, the same
was done in South Carolina.[3]   The proprietors received at
about the same time a letter from certain "gentlemen from
Barbadoes," who proposed settling in Carolina, and asked
for permission to elect their own officers.[4]   They were told
that proposals which we have just described would be followed.[5]

In this same year, the proprietors issued a commission
to Sir William Berkeley, governor of Virginia, empowering him to establish a government in Albemarle.   He was
to have a council which in the making of laws should act
with the advice and consent of the freeholders or freemen,
of the major part of their delegates or deputies.[6]   In the
"concessions" of 1665,[7] and in the instructions issued ten
years later to the governor of Albemarle,[8] it was provided
that the inhabitants who were freemen or chief agents to
others, should choose deputies to coöperate with a governor
and council in making laws.   As soon as the country was

[1] 1 *North Carolina Colonial Records*, 43; Rivers, *South Carolina*, 335; 2
Hawks, *History of North Carolina*, 27.

[2] 2 *History of North Carolina*, 144.

[3] See also as to West Jersey, *ante*, p. 26.

[4] 1 *North Carolina Colonial Records*, 40.   [5] *Ibid.*, 58.

[6] *Ibid.*, 50.   [7] *Ibid.*, 80, 81.

[8] *Ibid.*, 166.

sufficiently settled, each district was to have a representative. In a book published in London in 1665, and describing the advantages of Carolina, it was stated that the inhabitants would have a governor and council, chosen from among themselves, as well as an annually elected assembly.[1] The instructions of Governor Stephens in 1667, however, gave his council power to fill its own vacancies.[2]

We shall at present confine ourselves to the history of the Albemarle settlement, and treat it with particular reference to the subject of elections. The time of the election of the first assembly is not positively known; it has been placed as early as 1663.[3] The legislature of 1670 is the first of which the records remain.[4] The assembly was elected under instructions to the Governor that writs should be sent to four precincts in Albemarle county, commanding each of them to elect four representatives. The assembly so formed was to choose four members of the council.[5] As soon as the government just described had been established, the first edition of the celebrated constitution which the philosopher Locke had drawn up at the request of the proprietors was received. Four subsequent editions were sent over, and attempts were made to enforce it until after 1698. But these were futile, and it had little influence, either in the northern or in the southern part of the Carolinas. The constitution provided for a parliament to be composed of the proprietors or their deputies, the various ranks of the nobility, and representatives elected biennially by the freeholders of each precinct. As all the members were to sit in one room and each had a single vote, and as one of the chief reasons why

[1] 1 *North Carolina Colonial Records*, 157.

[2] *Ibid.*, 164; Chalmers, *Political Annals*, 524.

[3] See 1 Moore, *History of North Carolina*, 17; 2 Hawks, *History of North Carolina*, 144, where the various authorities are collected and discussed.

[4] 1 *North Carolina Colonial Records*, 183.   [5] *Ibid.*, 181, 235, 333.

the constitution proved impracticable was the lack of a sufficient number of persons to form the nobility, it will readily
be seen that the freeholders would have a large share in the
business of the parliament.[1] Constables and other minor officers were to be annually elected.[2]

The governor of Albemarle was known as such until 1690,
when the name North Carolina seems to have come into use.[3]
In 1691 Governor Ludwell " of Carolina " was empowered to
order the election of five delegates from Albemarle county
who should join with fifteen from the counties in the more
southern settlements, to form one assembly for all Carolina.[4]
However, this order was almost immediately rescinded, on
account of the impracticability of having North Carolina send
delegates to Charleston.[5] Until 1712, there was but one
governor for the entire province, though each part elected
its own assembly.[6] The last legislature under the rule of the
proprietors was elected in 1728.[7]

The first assembly in North Carolina under royal authority
met in April, 1731,[8] and the last in November, 1774.[9] The
authority for electing these assemblies is found in the commission of Burrington, the first royal governor.[10] He was told
to follow the laws and usages of North Carolina on this subject. It is thus presumed that the members of the assembly
were to be elected biennially.[11] The separation between the

---

[1] Arts. 71, 72, 73, 75, *etc.;* 1 *North Carolina Colonial Records,* 199, *et seq.*

[2] Art. 91.

[3] " That part of our province that lies north and east of Cape Feare." 1 *North
Carolina Colonial Records,* xxiv., 360.

[4] *Ibid.,* 377.   [5] *Ibid.,* 380.

[6] 2 Hawks, *History of North Carolina,* 493.   [7] *Ibid.,* 569.

[8] 1 Moore, *History of North Carolina,* 54.

[9] 2 Martin, *History of North Carolina,* 328.   [10] Jan'y 15th, 1729-30.

[11] 3 *North Carolina Colonial Records,* 68. For the law as to biennial assemblies, see 2 *North Carolina Colonial Reeords,* 213.

two Carolinas was not legally recognized until after they became royal provinces, though each of them had always elected its own assembly.

The "gentlemen from Barbadoes" already mentioned, settled near Cape Fear under Governor Yeamans,[1] in 1665, at a spot where a New England settlement had once stood.[2] It is said that an attempt was made to introduce the Locke constitutions here, but however that may be, the colony gradually dwindled away, so that in 1690 there was not a settler left.[3]

In 1669 the proprietors issued a commission to Governor Sayle for the country south and west of Cape Fear.[4] He was instructed to call together the freemen as soon as he reached Port Royal and cause them to elect four persons to join with him and his council in making laws. He was also to require the freeholders to choose twenty persons to form a parliament; the other requirements of the first issue of Locke's constitution being dispensed with for the time being. These instructions appear to have been carried into effect, not at Port Royal, but at a new settlement on the Ashley river, near the present site of Charleston.[5] The instructions of Governor Yeamans, two years later, contained similar provisions[6] and required a biennial parliament.[7]

In 1682 the proprietors ordered ten members of the biennial parliament to be chosen at "Charlestowne in Berkly county," and ten at London in Colleton county.[8] The latter had so few inhabitants that this apportionment was considered

---

[1] Chalmers, *Political Annals*, 523.

[2] 1 *North Carolina Colonial Records*, 36; see *ibid.*, 95, for Yeamans' commission.

[3] 2 Hawks, *History of North Carolina*, 455, 6; Rivers, *South Carolina*, 71.

[4] Rivers, *South Carolina*, 340.

[5] *Ibid.*, 95, 97.　　　　　　　　　　[6] *Ibid.*, 366.

[7] *Ibid.*, 379. Election of twenty members took place in April, 1672, *ibid.*, 109.

[8] *Ibid.*, 406.

unfair, and at the election of 1683 no attention was paid to the order.[1] About this time a vacancy in the office of governor was filled by vote of the council, and as some of the members of this body were elected by the parliament, the people had an indirect voice in the matter.[2] Governor Ludwell's instructions of 1691, as already mentioned, gave five of the twenty seats in the parliament to delegates from North Carolina, each of the three southern counties being allowed the same number.[3] When this order was rescinded, Berkeley county was given seven members, Colleton the same number and the remaining one, six.[4] The admission of Craven county to a share in the election of delegates to the parliament is of importance, because this portion of the country was inhabited almost exclusively by Huguenots, who had previously had no share in the making of laws.[5]

In 1695 the freemen were called together in general assembly to decide about the number of representatives. Twenty was the number fixed upon for Berkeley county and ten for Colleton, while Craven was omitted altogether.[6] Elections after this time do not seem to have been carried on in a very orderly manner.[7] The apportionment of delegates to the commons house of assembly, as the popular branch of the legislature was called, appears to have furnished a subject of contention, and the people were well pleased when an act of 1716 provided that the parish instead of the county should be the election district.[8] The privilege of

---

[1] Rivers, *South Carolina*, 136.   [2] *Ibid.*, 141.

[3] 1 *North Carolina Colonial Records*, 371.   [4] *Ibid.*, 380; Rivers, 160.

[5] The journals of the Parliament show that Huguenot members were returned and that they swore allegiance to William III. Rivers, 176.

[6] Rivers, 181, 453, *et seq.* About this time the first mention of the name South Carolina is to be found. Act 1696, 2 Cooper, 124.

[7] Rivers, 453, 462, 196, 206.

[8] Act no. 365, 2 Cooper, 683, see in particular the preamble; Rivers, 287.

elections was always jealously guarded by the settlers of South Carolina; and when, in 1719, the proprietors repealed the last mentioned statute; the people rose in revolt, elected a governor and appealed to the king.[1] The crown sent over a governor in 1721, and his commission authorized him to call an assembly.[2] This royal government was only provisional, pending a settlement with the Lords Proprietors. The latter, with the exception of Lord Carteret, sold out their interest in both North and South Carolina, and the purchase was confirmed by act of Parliament.[3] The undivided one-eighth interest of Carteret, Earl of Granville, was set apart by royal charter in 1744, but as the right of calling assemblies to be elected by the freemen was expressly reserved, this does not concern us.[4] Except for a period of two years, from 1745 to 1747,[5] when annual assemblies were required, it seems to have been the law that elections must be held every two years,[6] although from 1721 to 1745 the duration of an assembly was fixed at three years.[7] The dissolution of the last royal legislature took place on September 15th, 1775.[8]

§ 11. *Georgia.* The government of Georgia was vested by royal charter of 1732, in the hands of a council whose legal title was the "Trustees for establishing the colony of Georgia in America." The trustees filled vacancies among their own number, but their power was

---

[1] Rivers, 292 to 310.   [2] 1 Ramsay, *History of South Carolina*, 95.

[3] *Statute,* 2 Geo. II., chap. 34, 1 Cooper, 60.

[4] 4 *North Carolina Colonial Records,* 655.

[5] Act 1745, no. 730, 3 Cooper, 656.

[6] Act 1747, no. 746, 3 Cooper, 692; Locke's *Constitution,* Art. 75; Act 1694, Trotts' *Laws,* 36; Act no. 108, 2 Cooper, 80.

[7] Act 1745, no. 556, 3 Cooper, 135.

[8] 1 Ramsay, *History of South Carolina*, 249.

limited to twenty-one years.[1] These trustees appointed all
the officers of the colony, whether judicial or otherwise.[2]
In 1750, the affairs of the colony were in a bad way and
the trustees, hoping to provide a remedy, proposed that each
town, village or district should depute one delegate if it had
ten families or more, and two if it had thirty, to attend an
assembly held annually at Savannah. As the whole power
of making laws was in the hands of the trustees, this assembly
could have power only to "propose, debate and represent"
their grievances.[3] By virtue of this resolution, the assembly
met on January 15th, 1751, elected a speaker, and on the
following Sunday listened to a sermon "suitable for the
occasion." They transacted no business beyond drawing
up bills of grievances,[4] and as the trustees surrendered their
charter in June, 1752, no more assemblies were elected, under
the authority of the trust.[5] The crown appointed a governor
and council, and, as was generally the case, gave the governor

[1] Hotchkiss, *Digest of Laws of Georgia*, 20, *et seq.;* 1 Stevens, *History of Georgia*, 476, *et seq.*

[2] 1 Stevens, *History of Georgia*, chap. vii.

[3] 3 *Minutes of Common Council*, 235; 1 Stevens, *History of Georgia*, 245, *et seq.* The qualifications to be possessed by these delegates were so remarkable and therefore furnish so good an example of the absurd theories which the home governments were fond of attempting to put into practice in America, that they are inserted in this connection. From June, 1751, to June, 1753, no person could be a deputy unless he had "a hundred mulberry trees planted and properly fenced upon every fifty acres he possessed." After 1753, a deputy must be a person who had strictly conformed to the limitation of the number of negro slaves in proportion to his white servants, who had at least one female in his family instructed in the art of reeling silk, and who yearly produced fifteen pounds of silk upon fifty acres of land, and the like quantity upon every fifty acres he possessed. "But as the Trustees are desirous of seeing some immediate good effects from this assembly, and are sensible that at present there are not many in the province who may have the necessary qualifications," the members of the first assembly were wisely exempted from the operation of these rules.—3 *Minutes of Common Council*, 235; 1 Stevens, *History of Georgia*, 245, *et seq.*

[4] 1 Stevens, *History of Georgia*, 248, *et seq.*   [5] *Ibid.*, 258.

authority to call an assembly. Writs were sent out and the first election held in the latter part of 1754.[1] The members of the Commons house of assembly continued to be chosen at intervals until 1780. In that year writs were sent to all the provost marshals, but those whose territory was in the hands of the rebels were permitted to prove that fact by affidavits, instead of returning a member.[2]

[1] 1 Stevens, *History of Georgia*, 381–393.
[2] 2 Stevens, *History of Georgia*, 318.

CHAPTER II. THE SUFFRAGE.

QUALIFICATIONS REQUIRED OF ELECTORS.

In the early part of the history of each colony the qualifications required of electors were neither numerous nor well
defined.   On account of the small number of inhabitants, it
was at first hardly necessary, and perhaps not advisable, to
limit the elective franchise to any particular class of individ-
uals.   Consequently, in the summons that was sent out by
the first royal governor or proprietor, the " freeholders " or
the " freemen," of a certain district were ordered to elect a
certain number of deputies or representatives, as the case
might be.[1]   In Virginia, on the contrary, the " inhabitants "
were to elect the first house of burgesses.[2]   In the colonies
under royal rule the qualifications of voters were very frequently fixed by the commissions of the governors.   But in
the instructions, as well as in the commissions of the early
governors, the definition of a voter rarely went beyond the
single word " freeholder," and the fixing of a more precise
meaning to this general term seems to have been left for legislative action.   In the preceding chapter care has been taken to
mention in many instances the authority from the crown

---

[1] See for example in Maryland " freemen" (Act of 1637–8, *Maryland Archives*,
I *Assembly*, I, 27, 28, 87, 88, 114, 121, *etc.*, *etc.*); in Pennsylvania " free-
holders," writ of 1682 (I Proud, *History of Pennsylvania*, 234); also in New
York, (*Introduction to Journal Legislative Council*, xiv.) and in New Jersey (I
New Jersey Archives, 56).   These writs are published in appendix A of this work.

[2] I Hening, 110, 113.

through which the qualification of an elector was originally derived.[1]

Thus far we have been treating of the elective franchise in the colonies at a time when they were most closely under royal rule. But in New England, while she retained her independence, the case was different, and the right of voting for officers was inherent in all freemen and incidental to membership in the corporation. Thus in the four colonies of Plymouth, Massachusetts, Rhode Island and Connecticut the word *freemen* had a special significance, which was taken away when the two former became a royal province by the charter of 1691, and which remained in the two latter until the revolution. A *freeman* did not become such, unless he possessed certain prescribed qualifications, and until he had been approved, admitted and sworn, in a manner which will be described in a subsequent section of the present chapter. When a man had been admitted to the freedom of one of these colonies, his position was analogous to that of a freeman in a city or borough, and as such he became entitled to the exercise of the elective franchise. That the privilege of voting in the elections of the province was regarded as a right, vesting inherently in the freemen of a corporation, is shown by the New York Charter of Liberties and Privileges, and by the election laws of the same province, which contained a clause exempting freemen of the cities of Albany and New York from their operation.[2]

---

[1] See references to governors' commissions and instructions mentioned in the previous chapter. New Hampshire (1 *Provincial Papers*, 379) is an example of a province where the governor and his council were originally given full authority to fix the qualifications of an elector, while New Jersey under her first royal governor in 1702, had the qualifications definitely prescribed (Leaming and Spicer, 623). Massachusetts as a royal province had the definition of an elector fixed by the charter of 1691 (Poore, *Constitutions*, 949).

[2] See for instance, Charter of Liberties and Privileges (2 Brodhead, *History of the State of New York*, 642) as passed in 1683, and again in 1691 (Bradford's *Laws*

The fact that qualifications could be imposed on candidates for the freedom of a colony enabl&d Rhode Island[1] and Connecticut[2] to ultimately require the possession of a freehold as a prerequisite to the exercise of the suffrage. In all of these colonies[3] freemen could, under certain conditions, be deprived of their freedom, and incidentally of their rights as voters. In Rhode Island a law passed in 1724 provided that the privilege of electing deputies should not be limited to freemen of the colony, to the exclusion of freemen of the·town.[4] This seems to indicate a distinction, in Rhode Island at least, between the freedom of the colony and that of a particular town.

The term *freeman* occurs also in the early history of some
ed. 1710, 1); 11 Will. III, chap. 74, § 10, Van Schaack's *Laws*, 28; 4 *New York Colonial Documents*, 127. That this was also true with respect to boroughs in England, see *Statute* 3 Geo. III, chap. 15; Cox, *Antient Parliamentary Elections*, chap. viii and ix.

That the New England colonies regarded themselves as corporations is shown by *Laws*, 1636, 11 *Plymouth Colony Records*, 7, Brigham, 37; *Laws*, 1658, *ibid.*, 107, 113; *Second Fundamental, Book of General Laws*, 1671, *ibid.*, 241, 258. Massachusetts was a "company" by its charter (1 *Massachusetts Colonial Records*, 10, 12,) "freemen of this jurisdiction" to elect officers (*Laws*, ed. 1660, 28; 1814, 105); "freedom of the commonwealth," (ed. 1660, 33; ed. 1814, 117; 1 *Massachusetts Colonial Records*, 87); "freedom of this body politick" (*ibid.*, 2 *Massachusetts Colonial Records*, 208). In Rhode Island "freemen of colony" (1 *Rhode Island Colonial Records*, 236); "free inhabitants of colony" (*ibid.*, 429). The second charter (2 *Rhode Island Colonial Records*, 8,) provided for election of officers out of the company by freemen. In New Haven the term "free burgesses" (1 *New Haven Colonial Records*, 20, 35, 46, *etc.*) seems to have been used as an equivalent to "freemen" (*ibid.*, 112); in Hartford, "freemen of this company" (1 *Connecticut Colonial Records*, 417); in Connecticut, "freemen of this corporation" (*Session Laws*, 40). These colonies possessed the elements of a corporation such as a common seal and perpetual succession.

[1] 9 Geo. I, Franklin ed., 1730, 131.   [2] *Session Laws*, 40.

[3] Plymouth, *Laws*, 1658, Brigham, 114; *Book of General Laws*, 1671, *ibid.*, 258; Connecticut, *Session Laws*, 40; Massachusetts, 4 *Colonial Records*, pt. ii, 143; Rhode Island, 1 *Colonial Records*, 125.

[4] 4 *Rhode Island Colonial Records*, 338.

of the southern colonies. But as these were either proprietary or directly under royal rule, there is reason to believe that the word was used in its literal significance of *free man*. Thus a Virginia statute, in limiting the elective franchise to free-holders, spoke in its preamble of the election of burgesses having been "by the votes of all persons who haveing served their tyme are ffreemen of this country."[1] Before this date (1670), all free men had possessed the privilege of electing burgesses.[2] On account of there being no evidence of anything like the technical freedom which existed, as has already been shown, in the New England colonies and in the English municipal corporations, it seems reasonable to infer that the word freeman had no technical meaning here, although the qualifying phrase "of this country" gives color to an opposite belief. In the Carolina charters, and commissions, the word *freemen* also occurs[3] in its literal meaning, although the contrast between the words *freeholders* and *freemen* in Locke's constitution, seems to imply a technical significance.[4] As only the former could vote, the question does not particularly concern us.

Penn's frame of government and the laws agreed upon in England speak of "freemen of the said province" who were to be capable of electing representatives or of being elected to the provincial council or assembly.[5] The charter of Philadelphia speaks of persons who were free denizens of the province being admitted as freemen of the city;[6] but this is the technical freedom of a corporation on which depended certain rights not connected with the suffrage. As the statutes and charters of this province and of Delaware fix

---

[1] 22 Car. II, 2 Hening, 280.   [2] See 1 Hening, 333, 403; 2 Hening, 356.

[3] See 1 *North Carolina Colonial Records*, 23, 80, 104, 166, 377; Rivers, *South Carolina*, Appendix, 347.

[4] 1 Cooper, 43, especially art. 94.   [5] 1 *Pennsylvania Colonial Records*, 37, 33.

[6] Miller's *Laws*, 10, 11.

the qualifications required of voters with great exactness, the use of this term is not so important from our point of view.

In the Maryland charter, which was drawn up in Latin, the terms *liberi tenentes*[1] and *liberi homines*[2] occur in such a connection as to lead to the inference that only *freeholders* could make laws.[3] But there seems to be a plain distinction between the words. All freeholders are freemen, but a freeman could not possibly be a freeholder, unless he owned a freehold in land. However, when the question came up for discussion, the charter was interpreted in such a manner as to destroy all distinction between the two terms and give the word *freemen*, in Maryland at least, a technical meaning. At one of the early assemblies when all persons were required to attend either in person or by proxy (which could be done by joining in the election of a representative), and a summons was sent to all delinquents, a "certain Thomas Weston being called, pleaded he was no freeman because he had no land or certain dwelling here, &c., but being put to the question it was voted that he was a Freeman, and as such bound to his appearance by himself or proxie, whereupon he took place in the house."[4] Subsequent Maryland laws gave the franchise to *freemen* with a certain amount of property in freehold or in personalty.[5] That even the statesmen of Rhode Island were not always perfectly clear as to the meaning of the term freeman is shown by the doubts which arose when the question of the interpretation of this word in the charter of 1664 came up.[6]

In the preceding pages I have attempted to give some

[1] § 8.   [2] § 37, see Bacon's *Laws*.

[3] See Bozman, *History of Maryland*, 48, note; McMahon, *History of Maryland*, 444.

[4] *Maryland Archives*, 1 *Proceedings and Acts of Assembly*, 170.

[5] *Maryland Archives*, 3 *Assembly*, 60.

[6] 2 *Rhode Island Colonial Records*, 29.

idea of the indefinite character which marked the qualifications required of electors in the early history of each colony. Gradually by means of legislative action, additional and more specific qualifications were imposed. The following sections will, therefore, aim to classify the tests required of electors at different times in the various colonies. Every statutory requirement which has come within the knowledge of the author has been included, although all of them may not have been in actual operation. Such, for instance, are those prescribed by constitutions like that of Locke or of the East Jersey proprietors which never went into effect, as well as those contained in statutes repealed by authority of the crown or of the proprietors. The qualifications imposed by the latter class of statutes were generally in force, however, until abrogated by the proper authority. Only by comparison of dates and examination of the references will it be possible for the reader to ascertain precisely what was the qualification required from a voter in any particular province at a given time. Indeed, the subject is not always free from doubt, because a new statute did not always in terms repeal a preceding one. A law might also fall into disuse through non-user, and we have the reports of very few concrete cases where questions involving the suffrage were decided by competent authority.

§ 1. *Ethnic.* Race qualifications were not prescribed by statute, except in the southern colonies. I know of no law that would prevent an Indian or a negro, if otherwise qualified, from voting in the northern colonies. It will be noted that the following provisions are all of a comparatively late date.

Thus, in Virginia[1] and North Carolina[2] no negro, mulatto,

[1] 3 Geo. III, chap. 1, § 7, 7 Hening, 519.

[2] *Laws* 1715, 2 *North Carolina Colonial Records*, 213.

or Indian could vote, while in the former colony this was declared to be so, even if such persons were freeholders. North Carolina also disfranchised Mustees.[1] In South Carolina[2] and in Georgia[3] the franchise was expressly restricted to white men. Notwithstanding these laws, negroes were sometimes permitted to vote even in South Carolina. A petition to the Lords Proprietors complains of this abuse being practiced in Berkeley county in 1701 and 1703,[4] when "free Negroes were received and taken for as good Electors as the best freeholders in the province."

§ 2. *Political.* Qualifications of this sort were rarely prescribed by statute. In Pennsylvania,[5] voters were required to be natural born subjects of England; in Delaware,[6] of Great Britain. Persons naturalized in England or in Pennsylvania could vote in either colony, while Delaware permitted persons naturalized within her own borders to vote.[7] Massachusetts[8] after 1664 required freemen to be Eng-

---

[1] *Laws* 1715. This law as printed in 2 *North Carolina Colonial Records,* 213, omits the word Mustees, which, as we have learned through the kindness of Mr. J. C. Birdsong, Librarian of the State of North Carolina, is to be found in the original act. A Mustee (or Mestee) is the offspring of a white and a quadroon (*Century Dictionary,* vol. iv.).

[2] Act 1716, no. 365, § xx, 2 Cooper, 683; Act 1717, no. 373, § i, 3 Cooper, 2; Act 1719, no. 394, § iv, 3 Cooper, 50; Act 1721, no. 446, § iii, 3 Cooper, 135; Act 1745, no. 730, 3 Cooper, 657.

[3] Act June 9th, 1761.

[4] This is given in Rivers, *South Carolina,* Appendix, 453, *et seq.* See also petition to the English House of Lords, *ibid.,* 462.

[5] 4 Anne, chap. 129, Franklin ed., 1742, 67.

[6] 7 Geo. II, chap. 61a, § 2, Franklin and Hall, ed. 1752, 118; Adams, Newcastle, ed. 1797, 147.

[7] See also act of 1700, chap. 28, referred to in Penn's Charter of Privileges. Recorded A., Vol. I., 15, published in Appendix B of the present work.

[8] 4 *Massachusetts Colonial Records,* pt. ii, 117, 167. Supplement to *Laws,* ed. 1660, Act 1664, 3; ed. 1814, 117.

lishmen,[1] while in North Carolina there was the peculiar provision that "no person inhabitant of this province, born out
of the allegiance of his majesty and not made free," could
vote.[2] The Pennsylvania frame of government of 1696 declared that electors must be free denizens of the government[3]
and thus anticipated the action of the English House of Commons which held in 1698 that no alien, (not being a denizen or
naturalized), had any right to vote for members of parliament.[4]

In this connection it may well be asked what was the
position of the Huguenots in South Carolina. Bancroft[5]
speaks of an act passed in 1696,[6] by which the suffrage was
given to all except Roman Catholics. How far this is true
the writer has been unable to ascertain. In 1691, however,
Governor Ludwell, acting under instructions from the proprietors, called an assembly in which six members were to
be returned from Craven county, which was settled almost
entirely by Huguenots. The journals of the assembly show
that the members returned from this district took the oath
of allegiance to William the Third.[7] The petition mentioned in the preceding section complains that in 1703
"almost every Frenchman in Craven and Berkeley counties
came down to elect" and was allowed to vote.[8]

§ 3. *Moral.* Moral qualifications were insisted on only in
New England, though Virginia denied the franchise to any
"convict or person convicted in Great Britain or Ireland

[1] Also New Hampshire, 1 *New Hamphire P. P.*, 396, but repealed.

[2] *Laws* 1715, 2 *North Carolina Colonial Records*, 213.

[3] 1 *Pennsylvania Colonial Records*, 49.

[4] 12 *Resolutions and Orders of the House of Commons*, 367.

[5] 3 *History of United States*, 17, 18.

[6] This is probably the act mentioned by Cooper (vol. ii, p. 130) and of which
it is stated that the original cannot be found. Although diligent inquiry has been
made, the writer has not been able to secure a copy of this act.

[7] Rivers, *South Carolina*, 160, 176, 181.   [8] *Ibid.*, 196, 462, 453, *et seq.*

during the term for which he is transported," even though such person might be a freeholder.[1] In the New England colonies moral delinquencies had a double effect. Evidence of a positive character was at one time necessary before a person could be admitted to the freedom of the colony, while the absence of correctness in moral behavior would, in certain cases, lead to the suspension of a freeman from his privileges or even to his total disfranchisement. . Under conditions of the former class, Plymouth refused to admit as a freeman "any opposer of the good and wholsome laws of this colonie," or "such as refuse to do the country service, being called thereunto."[2] Some years later a would-be freeman needed the testimony of his neighbors that he was of "sober and peaceable conversation."[3] Connecticut required a certificate as to this, and as to honest and civil conversation as well, from a majority of the freemen in the town where the candidate lived.[4] A later act made necessary a certificate from the selectmen of the town where the candidate resided, to the effect that he (the candidate) was of a "quiet and peaceable behaviour and civil conversation." That the selectmen might exercise due care in signing such certificates, they were liable to a fine of £5 in case the candidate turned out otherwise than was represented.[5] After 1664 Massachusetts required a certificate from the minister at the candidate's place of residence to the effect that he was not "vitious" in his life.[6] Rhode Island admitted as freemen all persons properly qualified in other respects, if they were " of civil conversation who ac-

---

[1] 3 Geo. III, § 7, 7 Hening, 519. [2] *Laws*, 1658, Brigham, 113.

[3] *Book of General Laws*, 1671, chap. 5, § 5, Brigham, 258.

[4] 1 *Connecticut Colonial Records*, 389.

[5] *Session Laws*, 40; *Laws*, ed. Cambridge, 1673, 26.

[6] 4 *Massachusetts Colonial Records*, pt. ii, 117, 167.

knowledged and are obedient to the civil magistrate."[1] This, as well as other provisions of a similar nature first required in the New England colonies about 1665, was probably due to the royal commission sent over at that time, and of which more will be said in the next section.[2]

In order to lose the freedom of Plymouth freemen must speak contemptuously of the laws of the general court or of the court itself, or be adjudged by the court to be "grossly scandalouse, or notoriously vitious, as common lyars, drunkards, sucarers or doth manifestly appear to be disaffected to this government."[3] The reason given for making this enactment was that "some corrupt members may creep into the best and purest societies." Connecticut was less severe, and a "scandalous" freeman could be disfranchised only till "good behaviour shall cause restoration of the privilege."[4] The code of 1650,[5] expressed the law on this point in the following forcible language: "It is ordered by this Courte and decreed, that if any person within these Libberties haue beene or shall be fyned or whipped for any scandalous offence, hee shall not bee admitted after such time to haue any voate in Towne or Commonwealth, nor to serue in the Jury, vntill the Courte shall manifest theire satisfaction." The Cambridge edition of the laws, as published in 1673, gave the court of assistants power to disfranchise freemen for scandalous walking.[6] In Massachusetts disfranchisement was authorized as an additional penalty upon conviction of

---

[1] 2 *Rhode Island Colonial Records*, 112; 16 Car. II, Franklin ed., 1730, 1744, 4.

[2] A similar rule as to moral qualifications was enacted in New Hampshire in 1680, but soon repealed. (1 *Provincial Papers*, 396).

[3] *Laws*, 1658, Brigham, 114; *Book of General Laws*, 1671, chap. 5, § 6, Brigham, 258.

[4] *Session Laws*, 40. [5] Title *Voates*, 1 *Connecticut Colonial Records*, 559.

[6] P. 26, title, *Freemen;* or this was done by superior court, *Session Laws*, 81.

fornication or any "shamefull and vitious crime." [1] There
was also a law that no one who was detected and convicted
in any court of "any evill carriage agnt ye gouernments or
churches, it being intended to be imediately doun" should
be allowed to vote until he was restored to liberty by the
court that convicted him. [2]

§ 4. *Religious.* In Massachusetts and also in the New
Haven colony freemen were required to be church members.
This was first ordered in the former colony as early as 1631.
"To the end that the body of the freemen may be preserved
of honest and good men, it is ordered," ran the statute, "that
henceforth no man shall be admitted to the freedom of the
commonwealth, but such as are members of some of the
churches within the limits of this jurisdiction." [3] In 1660,
the general court defined the meaning of this enactment to
be that "no man whosoever shall be admitted to the freedom
of this body politick but such as are members of some
church of Christ and in full communion." [4] That this law
enabled many persons to escape the liability of serving in an
official capacity was shown in 1643 by the court ordering that
all members of churches refusing to take their freedom should
be summarily dealt with. [5] This law was ineffectual, and
four years later it was enacted that all church members
should be liable for public service, and fined for delinquency
in that respect, just as if they had actually taken their freedom. [6] This law did not, however, at least in terms, give
these non-church members power to vote for general officers.
How fully this principle of church membership was carried

[1] 4 *Massachusetts Colonial Records*, pt. ii, 562.

[2] 3 *Massachusetts Colonial Records*, 110.

[3] *Laws*, ed. 1660, 33; ed. 1814, 117; 1 *Massachusetts Colonial Records*, 87.

[4] *Ibid.;* 4 *Massachusetts Colonial Records*, pt. i, 420.

[5] 2 *Massachusetts Colonial Records*, 138.

[6] *Ibid.*, 208; *Laws*, ed. 1660, 33; ed. 1814, 117.

out was curiously shown by the answer given to a query from Falmouth as to the best way in which the number of freemen could be increased. "It is the best expedient," said the general court, "to obteine the ends desired that those parts furnish themselues wth an able, pious & orthodox minister & comend that to them."[1]

The measures taken by Massachusetts to preserve the "honest and good" character of her freemen seem to have attracted the attention of the English government, and in 1662 a letter was addressed to the general court on this subject. The colony was requested to permit all persons with competent estates, not vicious in their conversation, and "orthodoxe in religion (though of different persuasions concerning church government)", to vote. In reply, the court declared the law of 1631 in reference to church membership to be repealed, and proceeded to lay down a series of qualifications, embodying the requirements of his Majesty's letter, as an alternative to the old rule of "full communion with some church among us." These alternative qualifications included a certificate signed by the minister of the place where a would-be freeman resided, to the effect that he was orthodox in religion and not vicious in his life. As will appear later, these qualifications were possessed by so few persons, that the practical effect of the new law was to leave the religious qualifications of Massachusetts voters where they were before.[2]

Soon after this, the royal commission above referred to made an investigation of the governments of the New England colonies, and, among other things, endeavored to secure a certain amount of uniformity in the qualifications for electors. Their instructions authorized them to see that

---

[1] 4 *Massachusetts Colonial Records*, pt. ii, 452 (1670).

[2] *Ibid.*, pt. ii, 117, 165, 166, 177; *Laws*, ed. 1660, 33; ed. 1814, 117.

"persons of good and honest conversations, who haue lieued long there may enjoy all the priuledges . . . . as to choose . . . . into places of government . . . . that differences of opinion doe not lessen their charity to each other, since charity is a fundamentall in religion."[1] In pursuance of their mission the commissioners wrote to the general court of Massachusetts. In reply they received a copy of the law of 1664, already mentioned. This was unsatisfactory, and so the Commission addressed the following letter to the colony:

"You haue so tentered the king's qualliffications as in making him only who paieth ten shillings to a single rate to be of competent estate, that when the king shall be enformd, as the trueth is, that not one church member in an hundred payes so much & y^t in a toune of an hundred inhabitants, scarse three such men are to be found, wee feare that the king will rather finde himself deluded than satisfied by your late act."[2]

The court did not, however, pay any attention to this remonstrance, and finally the commissioners requested that the phrase "none be admitted freemen but such as are members of some of the churches w^{ith}in the limitts of this jurisdiction, may be explained, and comphend such as are members of ye church of England." The writer has not been able to find that even this was done.[3] Non-church members, however, could still vote under the law of 1662, though they were required to pass through a long period of probation.[4] Under the Massachusetts charter of 1691 there was no rule limiting the exercise of the suffrage to church members.

New Haven also insisted upon all freemen being church members. This was decided at the first meeting of the

[1] 4 *Massachusetts Colonial Records*, pt. ii, 192.
[2] 1665, *ibid.*, 205.   [3] 4 *Idem*, 212.
[4] 1673, *ibid.*, 562; 5 *Massachusetts Colonial Records*, 385, repealed in 1682-3.

New Haven planters in 1639,[1] and again provided for by the constitution of 1643.[2] Milford had let in six free burgesses who were not members of "approved churches," and after some hesitation the general court seems to have allowed these six to retain their freedom upon being cautioned, but they were not allowed to vote for magistrates, "neither personally nor by proxi."[3] They might act in town-business "wherein the combination was not interested," and might vote for deputies to be sent to the general court, provided deputies were always church members. The royal commission of 1665 seems to have addressed the governments of both Rhode Island and Connecticut on the subject of electoral qualifications. In the former colony a law was passed requiring a profession of Christianity,[4] though Roman Catholics were debarred; while in Connecticut the request of the commissioners was noted in the records in language similar to that used in the first letter to Massachusetts, and accompanied only by the simple remark, "our order judged consonant."[5] New Plymouth at about the same time, and possibly because of this royal interference required freemen to be orthodox in the fundamentals of religion.[6]

In the South, Locke's constitution provided that "no man shall be permitted to be a freeman of Carolina . . . . that doth not acknowledge a God, and that God is publicly and solemnly to be worshiped."[7] In South Carolina a statute

---

[1] 1 *New Haven Colonial Records*, 15.   [2] *Ibid.*, 112.

[3] *Ibid.*, 110. These six free burgesses of Milford were specially exempted in the provisions of the constitution which required church membership as a qualification for voters. *Ibid.*, 112.

[4] 2 *Rhode Island Colonial Records*, 110–113; 16 Car. II, Franklin ed., 1730, 1744, 4. See p. 63, *post*.

[5] 1 *Connecticut Colonial Records*, 439.

[6] *Book of General Laws*, 1671, chap. 5, § 5, Brigham, 258.

[7] Art. 94, 1 Cooper, *South Carolina Laws*, 43.

enacted in 1716 required voters to profess the Christian religion.[1]

The foregoing pages include all the qualifications of a positive character, so far as the writer has been able to ascertain. Persons professing certain religions were in some cases denied the privilege of voting. For instance, Quakers were strictly debarred from becoming freemen in Massachusetts,[2] and in Plymouth.[3] In Rhode Island, the principles of religious toleration were practiced, and Quakers were admitted as freemen. The commissioners of the United Colonies tried to prevent this,[4] but their efforts were futile. This is shown by the king's commissioners, who reported in 1665 that all religions, even Quakers and Generalists, were admitted to this colony.[5]

Although Quakers were not in terms disfranchised in the other colonies, their scruples against taking oaths often debarred them from voting. In order to permit them to take part in elections, clauses enabling Quakers and others to affirm or declare the effect of the oaths required of voters[6] were frequently inserted in the statutes. "Ranters or any such corrupt persons," "manifest opposers of the true worship of God," "manifest encurragers" of Quakers "soe

[1] Act 1716, no. 365, § xx; 2 Cooper, 683.

[2] 4 *Massachusetts Colonial Records*, pt. ii, 88; *Laws*, ed. 1814, 107.

[3] *Laws*, 1658, Brigham, 113.   [4] 1 *Rhode Island Colonial Records*, 374 *et seq.*

[5] 2 *Rhode Island Colonial Records*, 128.

[6] So, for example, New York ("Quakers or one of Unitas Fratrum," 11 Geo. III, chap. 1490, Van Schaack's *Laws*, 620); Rhode Island (20 Geo. II, Franklin ed., 1752, 13); New Jersey (12 Geo. I, chap. 40, Allinson's *Laws*, 69, Nevill's *Laws*, 142); Pennsylvania (4 Anne, chap. 129, Franklin ed., 1752, 67); Delaware (7 Geo. II, chap. 61a, Franklin and Hall ed., 1752, 110, Adams ed., 1797, 147); Maryland (here Quakers were declared liable to affirm as to all oaths to be taken by others, but they were not to be debarred for not swearing: 1724, 10 Charles, Lord Baltimore, chap. 7, Bacon's *Laws*); Virginia (11 Will. III, chap. 2, 3 Hening, 172; 10 Geo. II, chap. 2, § vii, 4 Hening, 475); South Carolina (Act 1704, no. 227, § v, 2 Cooper, 249).

judgéd by the court," could not be freemen in Plymouth, although this colony did not in so many words require church membership.[1] "Apostates from the fundamentals of religion" could be disfranchised.[2]

In England the right of Quakers to vote upon declaring the effect of the elector's oath on their affirmation was recognized by the statute of 10 Anne, chap. 23, § 8. In 1690, however, the House of Commons had decided that the refusal to take the oath rendered Quakers incapable of voting for knights of the shire.[3] Just before yielding to the royal commands, under the pretense of permitting non-church members to become freemen, Massachusetts, in furtherance of her laudable desire to preserve the "good and honest character" of her freemen, had passed a law which recounted the dangers she had found by experience to exist within her boundaries from those of her inhabitants who were "enemies to all government, civil and ecclesiastical, who will not yield obedience to authority, but make it much of their religion to be in opposition thereto," and who carried out their designs by electing wicked persons, and so forth. In consequence of all these evils, it was enacted, that "all persons, quakers or others, which refuse to attend upon the public worship of God established here; that all such persons, whether freemen or others, acting as aforesaid" should be incapable of voting "during their obstinate persistency in such wicked ways and courses, and until certificate be given of their reformation." This law, it may be remarked, was not repealed[4] while the colonial charter remained in force.

It seems to have been the rule in most of the American colonies that Roman Catholics could not vote. They were spe-

---

[1] *Laws*, 1658, Brigham, 113.   [2] *Book of General Laws*, 1671, Brigham, 258.
[3] 10 *Resolutions and Orders of the House of Commons*, 396.
[4] 1663, 4 *Massachusetts Colonial Records*, pt. ii, 88; *Laws*, ed. 1814, 105.

cifically disfranchised by the statutes of New York[1] and
Maryland.[2] In these two governments persons suspected of
popish beliefs were required, before being permitted to vote,
to take the oaths of supremacy and allegiance, and to sign
the test and association. Popish recusants were disfranchised
in New York[3] and Virginia.[4] An early law of New Hampshire, which was repealed immediately after it was enacted,
required freemen to be Protestants.[5] In the absence of
further information the writer does not feel justified in
asserting that Roman Catholics were debarred from voting
in all the colonies. The laws just cited were enacted during the eighteenth century, and were confined to four provinces. The provisions in regard to church membership
in Massachusetts during the government under the charter of
1628, would doubtless have excluded Roman Catholics.
On the other hand, the religion of the Baltimores and the
general character of their government would seem to justify
the belief that before the royal régime commenced in 1689
papists could vote in Maryland. On general principles it
would seem that every man could vote, unless he was specifically debarred by statute. Possibly there never were enough
Roman Catholics outside of the colonies mentioned to make
special legislative action necessary. Nothing can be assumed from the analogy of England, for the writer has there
found no law depriving papists of the suffrage. They could
not, it is true, hold office,[6] possess, inherit or purchase

---

[1] 13 Will. III, chap. 94, Van Schaack's *Laws*, 40. See also Leisler's illegal
election in New York City, "by Protestant freeholders" (3 *New York Colonial
Documents*, 675), which took place ten years before the statute of 13 Will. III.

[2] 3 Charles, Lord Baltimore, chap. 1, § 3 (1718) Bacon's *Laws;* "Profest Papists."

[3] 13 Will. III, chap. 94, § 1, Van Schaack's *Laws*, 40.

[4] " Recusants convict," 11 Will. III, chap. 2, 3 Hening, 172; " recusant," 3
Geo. III, chap. 1, § 7, 7 Hening, 519.

[5] 1 *New Hampshire Provincial Papers*, 396.

[6] *Statute* 30 Car. II, Stat. 2, chap. 1.

land,[1] and they were forbidden the king's or queen's presence;[2] but it does not necessarily follow from those facts that they could not vote for members of the House of Commons. They might not have been permitted to exercise their suffrage if they had tried, but that does not mean that they were disfranchised.

There has been a great deal of discussion in regard to the statute of Rhode Island which debarred Roman Catholics. The first printed edition of the laws, published in 1719, contained the phrase "all men *professing Christianity* though of differing judgements in religious affairs (*Roman Catholicks only excepted.*)"[3] The marginal note states that this law was passed in 16 Charles II. As a matter of fact neither the original copy of the statute enacted at that time, nor the letter from the King of England, in consequence of which that law was passed, contains the words italicised in the above extract.[4] If we believe that the inhabitants of Rhode Island acted consistently with their second charter, there can be no doubt that they would not have dared to pass a law abridging the exercise of a particular religion. It is therefore generally believed, at the present time, that the words in regard to religious tests were interpolated at some later date, possibly not till 1719 when they first appear and then perhaps with the hope of currying favor with the home government. The clause in regard to Roman Catholics again appeared in the editions and digests published in 1730, 1745 and 1767. As the law was not repealed until 1783, there can be no doubt that persons professing this religion could not vote during the greater part of the eighteenth century. At

[1] 11, 12, 13 Will. III, chap. 4, § 4; 1 Geo. I, Stat. 2, chap. 55.

[2] 30 Car. II, Stat. 2, chap. 2.   [3] Page 3.

[4] 2 *Rhode Island Colonial Records*, 110–113.

any rate the founders of the colony seem to be exculpated from the charge of inconsistency.[1]

The writer has found in two colonies evidence tending to prove that Jews could not legally vote. The first authority is the decision of the New York assembly, when it settled the contested election case of Philipse *vs.* Van Horne, in 1737. The language employed by the house in rendering its decision, indicates that Jews were debarred from voting in England also.[2] The petition of the South Carolina assemblymen, which has already been referred to, complains that Jews were illegally permitted to vote.[3] The absence of further mention of the Jewish race is perhaps sufficiently accounted for by the conjecture that its numbers were few in the American colonies.

§ 5. *Age.* It may be stated as a general proposition that electors were required to be twenty-one years of age.[4] That

[1] The whole subject is treated exhaustively in S. S. Rider, *An inquiry concerning the origin of the clause in the laws of Rhode Island (1719–1783) disfranchising Roman Catholics* (1889). W. E. Foster, Esq., Librarian of the Providence Public Library, furnishes the following additional references on the subject : Chalmers, *Political Annals,* 276 *et seq.;* 1 Arnold, *Rhode Island,* 488 *et seq.;* Walsh, *Appeal from the Judgments of Great Britain,* 430; *Proceedings of the Rhode Island Historical Society,* 1872–3, 64; 2 Douglass, *Summary,* 83; 3 *Narrative and Critical History of America,* 379–80; 2 *Rhode Island Colonial Records,* 36 note.

[2] " Resolved that it not appearing to this House that Persons of the Jewish Religion have a right to be admitted to Vote for Parliament men in Great Britain, it is the unanimous Opinion of this House that they ought not to be admitted to vote for Representatives in this colony. Die Veneris, Sept. 23, 1737. 1 *Journal New York Assembly,* 712; 6 *New York Colonial Documents,* 56.

[3] Rivers, *South Carolina,* 206, 453 *et seq.,* 462.

[4] Plymouth : *Laws,* 1671, Brigham, 258; Connecticut : 1 *Connecticut Colonial Records,* 382; 4 *Connecticut Colonial Records,* 11; *Session Laws,* 40; New York : 11 Will, III, chap. 74, § 9, Van Schaack's *Laws,* 28, "No infant under twenty-one shall elect;" Pennsylvania : Frame of Government, 1696, 1 *Pennsylvania Colonial Records,* 49, *Laws* 1700, chap. 28, referred to in Charter of Privileges; chap. 129, 4 Anne, Franklin ed., 1742, 67; Delaware : 7 Geo. II, § 2, Franklin and Hall, ed. 1752, 118; Adams, 1797, 147; Virginia : "infants under 21 " disquali-

minors did sometimes vote, though illegally, appears from the account of an eye-witness of an election in North Carolina about 1708.[1] In England by the statute of 7 & 8 William III, chap. 25, § 8, minors were forbidden to vote for members of Parliament. To this rule there are very few exceptions. The act of Massachusetts which provided a substitute for the one single qualification of church membership declared that freemen must be at least twenty-four years old.[2] This was copied in an early, New Hampshire law.[3] In Rhode Island the only statement in regard to an age qualification was that made in 1665 in reply to the letter of the royal commission. After mentioning an oath to be taken by freemen, and stating that if they did not take it, they could not vote for officers, the records go on to say that the oath was taken by all housekeepers aged eighteen or more. This does not, however, necessarily mean that persons of that age could vote.[4] Plymouth had a peculiar law that " in reference to military concernments—noe single persons under twenty years of age either children or servants shall voate as to that accompt."[5]

§ 6. *Sexual.* There seems to have been no women's rights party in the colonies; it was thus not found necessary to expressly debar women from the privilege of voting, except in Virginia. In that colony it was enacted that " no woman, sole or covert," even though a freeholder, should have a

---

fied, 7 Geo. III, chap. I, § 7, 7 Hening, 519; North Carolina: 33 Geo. II, chap. I, § 4, Davis ed., 1773, 247; South Carolina: Act 1716, no. 365, § 20, 2 Cooper, 683; Act 1745, no. 730, 3 Cooper, 657; Georgia: Act June 9th, 1761.

[1] Pollock's Letter Book, 1 *North Carolina Colonial Records*, 696; 2 Hawks, *History of North Carolina*, 511.

[2] 4 *Massachusetts Colonial Records*, pt. ii, 117, 166; ed. *Laws*, 1814, 117.

[3] 1 *New Hampshire Provincial Papers*, 396.

[4] 2 *Rhode Island Colonial Records*, 112.

[5] *Laws*, 1667, Brigham, 151.

voice in the election of burgesses.[1] In New England the restriction of the suffrage to freemen of a colony would necessarily debar women. In a statute prescribing the qualification of voters from the town of Wilmington, North Carolina, the word *man* was several times used in describing an elector.[2]

§ 7. *Residential.* In the early history of each colony there was, as has already been explained, very little definiteness in regard to the qualification of voters. The warrants or the royal commissions by virtue of which the earlier elections were held are full of such expressions as the "freeholders of the province,"[3] "the freeholders in thy bailiwick,"[4] "freeholders of your county,"[5] "inhabitants,"[6] or "freemen inhabiting" a certain place.[7] Such phrases, vague as they may seem, undoubtedly imply residence in an elector. The writer conceives it to be true, though he cannot show a great deal of authority, that residence within the government, province or territory, was generally required.[8]

[1] 11 Will. III, chap. 2, 3 Hening, 172; 3 Geo. III, chap. 2, 7 Hening, 519.

[2] Act 1740, Davis and Swann ed., 1752, 114.

[3] 3 *North Carolina Colonial Records*, 68.

[4] Pennsylvania, 1682, 1 Proud, *History of Pennsylvania*, 234.

[5] N. Y., 1683, *Introduction to Journal of Legislative Council*, xiv.

[6] Virginia, 1621, 1 Hening, 110; North Carolina, 1667, 1 *North Carolina Colonial Records*, 80.

[7] *Maryland Archives*, 1 *Assembly*, 27, 28.

[8] In support of this view may be cited the expressions: those that " do cohabit within this jurisdiction," as expressed in the first American constitution, that of Hartford in 1638 (1 *Connecticut Colonial Records*, 21); the limitation to those "cohabiting upon the island" at Newport, before the formation of the Confederacy (1 *Rhode Island Colonial Records*, 125), and "inhabitants within the colony," afterward (Franklin ed., 1730, 1); "every planter and inhabitant dwelling and residing within the Province" (East Jersey *Concessions*, 1683, Leaming and Spicer, 153); "inhabitants, freeholders or proprietors resident upon the said province" (West Jersey *Concessions*, chap. 32, Leaming and Spicer, 385; also Pennsylvania *Laws*, 1682, 1 *Pennsylvania Colonial Records*, 37); "freemen of

In four colonies the length of residence within the government was defined. This was two years in Pennsylvania,[1] and Delaware,[2] and six months in Georgia.[3] In North Carolina, a full year's residence in the government was at one time necessary,[4] but before 1734 this was reduced to six months' residence within the precinct.[5] Other provinces had more specific provisions on this subject. Thus, in Rhode Island, no person could vote except in the town where he lived,[6] and New Jersey under the royal government, required a residence of one whole year in the county, city, or town,[7] where the voter was polled. In South Carolina the necessity for a period of residence as a qualification for voters seems to have been fully appreciated. In 1693, the proprietors disallowed an act giving the privilege of electing representatives to persons worth £10. One of the reasons for their action was because "these act not mentioning how long any person worth ten pounds must have been an Inhabitant of the Country before he be admitted to vote for members of the assembly, it is so loose that by this act, all the Pyrates that were in the Shipp that had been pilundering on the Red Sea had been qualified to vote for representatives, which being of dangerous

this province" (*Maryland Archives*, 3 *Assembly*, 60); "settled inhabitants in this jurisdiction" as used in Massachusetts (4 *Massachusetts Colonial Records*, pt. ii, 117, 167; *Laws* ed., 1814, 117 [also in Plymouth, *Laws*, 1667, Brigham, 151]) and New Hampshire (1 *New Hampshire Provincial Papers*, 396).

[1] Frame of Government of 1696, 1 *Pennsylvania Colonial Records*, 149; *Laws* 1700, chap. 28, referred to in Charter of Privileges; 4 Anne, chap. 129, Franklin ed., 1742, 67.

[2] 7 Geo. II, chap. 61a; Franklin and Hall ed., 1752, 118; Adams, 1797, 147.

[3] Act June 9th, 1761.

[4] *Laws*, 1715, chap. 10; 2 *North Carolina Colonial Records*, 213.

[5] 8 Geo. II, chap. 2; 17 Geo. II, chap. 2, Davis and Swann ed., 1752, 177. For the first act see appendix B.

[6] Hall's *Code*, 1767, Title *Elections*, 78.

[7] 12 Geo. I, chap. 40, Nevill's *Laws*, 142.

consequence to the Inhabitants we have dissented."[1] In
1704 a personal residence in the county and precinct
for three months next preceding the date of the writs for
the election was required,[2] possibly with a view of remedy-
ing the abuses at a recent election, when it is said, strangers
and sailors had been allowed to vote.[3] Twelve years later
this was replaced by six months' residence in the province and
parish,[4] and seafaring and other transient men, not owning
freeholds or liable to pay taxes on personal property, were
debarred from voting. In 1721 the time of residence was
finally fixed at one year within the county.[5] In New York
and Virginia the laws appear to be silent as to general residence qualifications, but persons voting in New York City
and Albany in their capacity of freemen must have resided
there three months,[6] while in Williamsburg, Virginia, holders
of the town franchise must have had an actual residence of
twelve months.[7] The former provision was probably aimed
at the practice, which seems to have existed, of giving freedoms to sailors and other non-residents, in order to let them
vote for assemblymen.[8] In some colonies the elector voted
solely by virtue of his freehold, and in such cases residence
was not considered of any importance. Thus New Hampshire passed a law enabling property holders, though non-

---

[1] April 10th, 1693, Rivers, *South Carolina*, Appendix, 437.   This is probably the
act mentioned in 2 Cooper, 73, act no. 78, of which it is stated the original is lost;
this act was, however, to be temporary.

[2] Act 1704, no. 227, 2 Cooper, 149.

[3] Rivers, *South Carolina*, Appendix, 462, 453 *et seq.*

[4] Act 1716, no. 365, § xx, 2 Cooper, 683; Act 1717, no. 373, §§ i, ii, 3 Cooper, 2.

[5] Act 1721, no. 446, § iii, 3 Cooper, 135.

[6] 11 Will. III, chap. 74, § 10, Van Schaack's *Laws*, 28.

[7] 15 Geo. II, chap. 26, § 11, 5 Hening, 204.   The act of 4 Anne, chap. 2, 3 Hening, 236, required an elector to be a resident of the county in which he voted.

[8] 4 *New York Colonial Documents*, 127-9.

residents, to vote,[1] and in New York a complaint against the sheriffs for conspiring to hold all the elections on the same day, so as to prevent freeholders having estates in several counties from voting in each, shows that it was a common practice for non-resident freeholders to exercise the elective franchise.[2] In 1737 this was decided by the legislature in the contested election case of Philipse *vs.* Van Horne to be a legal usage.[3] The writer has found no trace of a system of plural voting in any other colony.

In England the question of residence was treated as early as 1413, by the statute of 1 Henry V, chap 1, (3). This enacted that "the knights and esquires and others which shall be *choosers* of these knights of the shires, be also resident within the same shires in manner and form as aforesaid;" that is, "at the day of the date of the writ of the summons of the parliament."[4] The laws requiring electors to reside within the counties in which their freeholds were situated, were repealed in 1774.[5]

§ 8. *Property*. A. THE COUNTY FRANCHISE. The property qualification in the American colonies is a subject of great importance. The qualifications mentioned in the preceding sections were for the most part confined to particular portions of the continent. For example, the religious

---

[1] 1 Geo. II, chap. 107, § 2; Fowle ed., 1771, 166.

[2] 4 *New York Colonial Documents*, 127-9.

[3] 6 *New York Colonial Documents*, 56.

[4] Troward, *Elections,* London, 1790, 5; Cox, *Antient Parliamentary Elections*, 109, quotes this statute and uses the word *chosen* instead of *choosers;* Gneist, *History of the English Constitution*, vol. ii, chap. 25, 5 (p. 35), says that by this act electors were to be resident in the county. This seems more reasonable as the word *chosen* would merely repeat another clause of the same act in slightly different language. The question was, however, settled in favor of residence within the county where the freehold lay, by the statutes of 8 Henry VI, chap. 7, and 10 Henry VI, chap. 2.

[5] *Statute* 14 Geo. III, chap. 58.

and moral qualifications, which were predominant during
the seventeenth century, were practically limited to the
colonies most directly under Puritan influence. When
Massachusetts and Plymouth lost their independent status
by their union under the charter of 1691 property replaced
religion as the main test of a man's right to vote. In
every province, whether royal or proprietary, there was
introduced, beginning in the latter part of the seventeenth
century, some sort of property qualification, and the tendency during the middle of the eighteenth century, was
toward a certain amount of uniformity in this respect
throughout the colonies. In Rhode Island there were, as
we shall see, violent fluctuations in the property qualification, and at one time the enormous sum of four hundred
pounds or twenty pounds a year, was required.

In considering the history of the property qualification in
this country it will be well to examine at the outset the
development in the oldest of the colonies, namely, Virginia.
By the constitution and ordinance of 1621, as issued by the
treasurer and company in England, all inhabitants of the
colony were to have a vote in the choice of burgesses.[1]
For upwards of thirty years this was the rule, until in 1655
a law was passed limiting the franchise to " all housekeepers,
whether ffreeholders, leaseholders or otherwise tenants." [2]
But in less than a year this statute was repealed, because,
said the house of burgesses, "we conceive it something
hard and unagreeable to reason that any persons shall
pay equall taxes and yet have no votes in elections." [3]
It was not long, however, before the harshness of this rule
was lost sight of, and the house of burgesses in 1670 dis-

[1] Art. iv, 1 Hening, 112.

[2] 5-6 Commonwealth, Act vii, 1 Hening, 411.

[3] 6 Commonwealth, Act xvi, 1 Hening, 403.

covered that the voting "of all persons, who haveing served their tyme are ffremen of this country, who haveing little interest in the country doe oftner make tumults at the election to the disturbance of his majesties peace, then by their discretions in their votes provide for the conservasion thereof, by making choyce of persons fitly qualifyed for so greate a trust." Besides this, they remembered that "the lawes of England grant a voice in such election only to such as by their estates, real or personall have interest enough to tye them to the endeavour of the publique good." Therefore, they enacted that only "ffreeholders and house keepers who are answerable to the publique for the levies, shall hereafter have a voice in the election of any burgess in this country."[1] That the people did not look with unmixed satisfaction upon this limitation of the suffrage is shown by the action of the assembly called during Bacon's revolt in 1676, which repealed the law of 22 Charles II, and admitted all freemen to a share in the choice of burgesses.[2] When the rebellion was put down this act was repealed, and as far as Virginia was concerned, non-freeholders were permanently deprived of the privilege of voting.

Turning now to England, we find that the history of the county franchise, which corresponds to what we are at present considering in the American colonies, was similar to the development in Virginia. We have the authority of that learned scholar, William Prynne, for the statement that originally " every inhabitant and commoner in each county had a voyce in the election of knights whether he were freeholder or not, or had a freehold only of one penny, sixpence or twelvepence by the year."[3] But early in the fifteenth century the famous statutes of 8 Henry VI, chap. 7, and 10 Henry VI, chap. 2,[4] were enacted, and in accordance with

[1] 22 Car. II, Act iii, 2 Hening, 220.   [2] 2 Hening, 425.
[3] *Brevia Parliamentaria Rediviva*, 187.   [4] 1430 and 1432.

their provisions the elective franchise was limited to holders
of "free land or tenement to the value of forty shillings by
the year, at the least, above all charges." Notwithstanding
the statement in the preamble of the Virginia statute just
quoted, a freehold was necessary to qualify county electors
in England all through the colonial period, and no amount
of personal property would serve as a substitute.

In America the forty shilling freehold franchise was recognized in Massachusetts by the charter[1] of 1691, as well as in
Rhode Island,[2] and Connecticut.[3] In all of these colonies,
however, the forty shilling freehold was merely an
alternative qualification. In New England, as in Virginia,
there was no property qualification required at first, and
the writer is of the opinion that with the possible exception
of Connecticut its introduction was due solely to the
interference of the Crown, already mentioned under the
subject of religious qualifications.[4] In support of this
view it can be shown that upon receipt of the royal
mandate that electors should be "men of competent estates"[5] some sort of property qualification was adopted or
declared by the general courts of the four colonies affected.
Thus Plymouth[6] allowed holders of "twenty pounds rateable estate, at the least, in the government" to be made freemen, and Massachusetts embodied in the qualifications
offered as an alternative to church membership, a clause
giving the suffrage to freeholders, "for their own proper estate (without heads of persons), rateable to the country in a
single country rate, after the usual manner of valuation in the

---

[1] 1 Ames and Goodell, 11.

[2] 4 Geo. I, Franklin ed., 1730, 131; Hall, *Code*, 1767, Title *Elections*, 78.

[3] *Session Laws*, 40.   [4] See p. 57 *ante.*

[5] 4 *Massachusetts Colonial Records*, pt. ii, 166; 2 *Rhode Island Colonial Records*, 110; 1 *Connecticut Colonial Records*, 439.

[6] *Book of General Laws*, 1671, chap. 5, § 5, Brigham, 258.

place where they live to the full value of ten shillings," and who were householders as well.[1] When these two colonies were united the qualification of voters was fixed by the charter in the following language:

"Noe Freeholder or other person shall have a vote in the Eleccon of Members to serve in any Greate and General Court or Assembly to be held as aforesaid who at the time of such Eleccon shall not have an estate of freehold in Land within Our said Province or Territory to the value of Forty Shillings per Annū at the least, or other estate to the value of Forty pounds Sterl'."[2]

In accordance with the proposals of the crown, Rhode Island in 1665 enacted simply that electors should be men of "competent estates."[3] The property qualification remained thus indefinite until 1723 when it was decided that a "freeman must be a freeholder of Lands Tenements or Hereditaments in such towns where he shall be admitted free, of the value of one hundred pounds or to the value of 40 shillings per a."[4] In 1730 the requirement was raised to two hundred pounds or ten pounds a year,[5] and in 1747 it was still further increased to four hundred pounds or twenty pounds a year.[6] In 1767 the real estate of a freeman must be worth forty pounds or

[1] 4 *Massachusetts Colonial Records*, pt. ii, 117, 167; *Laws*, ed. 1814, 117.

[2] 1 Ames and Goodell, 11. There has been considerable doubt as to whether forty or fifty pounds is the correct version of the last clause. It appears from the report of the Attorney General and the acceptance of the Colonial agents, as contained in the minutes of the Plantations committee of the Privy Council that fifty is correct, but it is said that the copy of the charter sent to Massschusetts contained the word forty. The Boston government seems to have acted on the latter assumption and the home government on the former, for it disallowed several laws because they contained the word forty, which was the qualification in New York and in Rhode Island. In the printed editions of the acts, the word forty is mentioned three times, and fifty occurs four times. See 1 Ames and Goodell, 249, 282, 315, 363.

[3] 2 *Rhode Island Colonial Records*, 112.

[4] 9 Geo. I, Franklin ed., 1730, 131.

[5] 3 Geo. II, Franklin ed., 1730, 206.

[6] 20 Geo. II., Franklin ed., 1752, 13.

else must bring in a yearly rental of forty shillings.[1] Rhode Island was the only American colony which permitted a man to vote by virtue of his birth. This franchise was given in 1723 to the eldest son of a freeman,[2] and it seems to have existed for a number of years. If a freeman, who was such by virtue of his being the eldest son of a freeholder qualified to vote, died with issue, the second son of the freeholder was not to be made a freeman because of his father's freehold.[3] This franchise was doubtless derived from the English rule permitting the heir apparent of a peer or of a freeman to vote.[4]

In 1658, just before the royal interference, Connecticut had prescribed a qualification of thirty pounds proper personal estate, (those who had held office were exempt from this qualification,) and in 1662 had changed this to "twenty pounds estate beside the person in the list of estate," so that the request of the royal commissioners was dismissed with the words "our order judged consonant."[5] If the qualification of 1662 was meant to be realty—and in the light of a subsequent enactment,[6] the writer believes it was not—the "order" of Connecticut could hardly be "consonant." The Cambridge edition of the Laws of Connecticut speaks of the property qualifications of freemen as being "willed by our Royal Soveraign" to be "twenty pownd Estate in Housing or Land, besides their personal Estate in the Common List."[7] In 1675 a statute provided that in addition to "these other qualifications

---

[1] Hall's *Code*, 1767, Title *Elections*, 78.

[2] 9 Geo. I, Franklin ed., 1730, 131; also 209, 252; Hall's *Code*, 1767, Title *Elections*, 78.

[3] Hall's *Code*, Title *Elections*, 78.

[4] See Troward, *Elections*, 76, 167; *Statutes* 9 Anne, chap. 5; 3 Geo. III, chap. 15.

[5] 1 *Connecticut Colonial Records*, 331, 389, 439.

[6] 2 *Connecticut Colonial Records*, 253.   [7] Title *Freemen*, 26.

expressed in the former law" a freeman must have in the " List
of Estates ten pownd estate in land beside their personal estate."[1] In 1689[2] a freehold estate of forty shillings in county
pay was prescribed, while the session laws finally placed the
property qualification at a " freehold estate to the value of
forty shillings per an., or forty pounds personal estate."[3]
The first provision in regard to property qualifications in
New Hampshire is found in a law passed by the first Assembly, but soon repealed.   This simply provided for " a ratable
estate of twenty pounds without heads of persons."[4]   An act
of 1691 probably copied the Massachusetts charter when it
required voters to be freeholders of the value of forty pounds
a year, or worth fifty pounds in personal estate.[5]   After 1729
only freeholders with an estate of fifty pounds in the town, parish
or precinct in which they voted could elect representatives.[6]
In New York the first Charter of Liberties declared that
all freeholders in the province had a voice in the election of
representatives, and a freeholder was defined to be " every
one who is so understood according to the laws of England."[7]
The second charter explained that a freeholder was a person
who had forty shillings a year in freehold.[8]   A later general
act limited the county franchise to persons holding " Land
or Tenements, improved to the Value of Forty pounds in
Freehold, free from all encumbrances."[9]
    When we come to consider the more southern colonies we

----

[1] 2 *Connecticut Colonial Records*, 253. The royal proposals as expressed to
Massachusetts certainly required voters to be freeholders, and the quotation just
given from the Cambridge edition of the laws bears out this view. The language
of the law of 1675 seems to imply that no estate in land had been required before
this time. So, on the whole, the meaning of the earlier enactments seems doubtful.

[2] 4 *Connecticut Colonial Records*, 11.   [3] *Session Laws*, 40.

[4] 1680, 1 *Provincial Papers*, 396.   [5] 11 Will. III, 3 *Provincial Papers*, 216.

[6] 1 Geo. III, chap. 107, Fowle ed., 1761, 142; ed. 1771, 166.

[7] 2 Brodhead, *History of the State of New York*, 659.   [8] Bradford ed., 1710, 1.

[9] 11 Will. III, chap. 74, § 1, Van Schaack's *Laws*, 28.

find that the general criterion for determining the amount of the real estate qualification was not so much its value as its area. So in East Jersey,[1] Pennsylvania,[2] Delaware,[3] Maryland,[4] North Carolina,[5] and Georgia,[6] fifty acres was the required amount of land. Of these fifty acres East Jersey required ten acres to be cultivated; in Pennsylvania the same number must have been "seated and cleared," though after 1700 twelve acres must be "cleared and improved;"[7] while Delaware required the whole tract of fifty to be cleared.[8] In Pennsylvania the voter, instead of having land, might be worth "fifty pounds lawful money of the government, clear estate."[9] In Delaware,[10] and also in Maryland, a personal estate of forty pounds value would enfranchise an elector.[11] The laws made by Penn in England offered the privilege of voting to every purchaser of one hundred acres of land or upwards, his heirs and assigns; to every person paying his passage and taking up one hundred acres of land at a penny an acre and putting ten of them under cultivation; and also to every

[1] *Concessions*, 1683, iii, Leaming and Spicer, 153, 1 *New Jersey Archives*, 397.

[2] *Frame of Government*, 1696, 1 *Pennsylvania Colonial Records*, 49.

[3] 7 Geo. II, chap. 61a, Franklin and Hall ed., 1752, 118; Adams, 1797, 147.

[4] Act 1678, *Maryland Archives*, 3 *Proceedings and Acts of the Assembly*, 60; 4 Anne, chap. 35; 1715, chap. 42, Baskett ed., 1723, 131.

[5] 8 Geo. II, chap. 2; 17 Geo. II, chap. 1, § iii; Davis and Swann ed., 1752, 177.

[6] Act June 9th, 1761.

[7] 1700, chap. 28, referred to in charter of 1701; 4 Anne, chap. 129, Franklin ed., 1742, 67.

[8] 7 Geo. II, chap. 61a, Franklin and Hall, 1752, 118; Adams, 147.

[9] Frame of Government, 1696, 1 *Pennsylvania Colonial Records*, 49; 1700, chap. 28, referred to in Charter of Privileges, 1701, 1 Proud, *History of Pennsylvania*, 444, "Lawful money of this province;" 4 Anne, chap. 129, Franklin ed., 1742, 67; 6 Geo. III, chap. 8, Hall and Sellers ed., 1775, 323.

[10] 7 Geo. II, chap. 61a, § 2, Franklin and Hall ed., 118; Adams, 1797, 147.

[11] Act 1678, *Maryland Archives*, 3 *Proceedings and Acts of the Assembly*, 60; 2 Charles Lord Baltimore, chap. 11, § 3, Bacon's *Laws*.

person who had been a servant or a bondsman and was free by his service and had taken up his fifty acres of land and cultivated ten of them.[1] In New Jersey under the royal government, a freeholder having one hundred acres of land in his own right, or worth fifty pounds current money of the province in real and personal estate, could vote.[2]

Virginia had limited the elective franchise to freeholders, in 1670,[3] but in 1736 on account of the practice of conveying " small and inconsiderable parcels of land upon feigned considerations," it was found necessary to define a freehold. Accordingly the amount of land to be possessed by an elector was fixed at one hundred acres, if uninhabited, or twenty-five acres with a house and a plantation.[4] In case the uninhabited estate lay in two or more counties the owner could vote in the county where the greater part was situated, though that part might not amount in itself to a hundred acres. Some years afterward it was enacted that fifty unsettled acres would qualify a freeholder. There must have been a house twelve feet square on the settled plantation of twenty-five acres, and if the estate was in several counties the elector could vote only in that county in which the house was situated.[5] All sorts of property qualifications seem to have been required at different times in South Carolina. Locke's constitution provided that only freeholders could vote and that these must possess fifty acres.[6] In 1692 an act was passed permitting all persons who would swear that they were worth ten pounds to vote for members of the assembly. The proprietors disallowed this, because they

[1] 1 *Pennsylvania Colonial Records*, 37.

[2] 7 Anne, chap. 4, § 1, Nevill's *Laws*, 7; Allinson's *Laws*, 6. " Current money of Great Britain," 8 Geo. III, Allinson's *Laws*, 306.

[3] 22 Car. II, Act iii, 2 Hening, 280. See page 71 *ante*.

[4] 10 Geo. II, chap. 2, § 11, 4 Hening, 475.

[5] 3 Geo. III, chap. 1, § 4, 7 Hening, 519.   [6] Art 72, 1 Cooper, 43.

were of opinion that only freeholders should be permitted to vote.[1] In 1704 the qualification of an elector was a freehold of fifty acres or else ten pounds in money, goods, chattels or rents.[2] Twelve years afterwards personal property to the value of thirty pounds "current money of this province" would qualify a voter.[3] In 1717 the franchise was given to holders of fifty acres in land, and to persons liable to pay taxes for the sum of fifty pounds.[4] This personal qualification was changed in 1721 to a tax of twenty shillings for the year of the election or the year preceding.[5] In 1745 a freehold estate in a settled plantation or three hundred acres unsettled for which taxes had been paid the previous year was demanded,[6] while in 1759 only one hundred acres were required, or in lieu of this, the payment of a tax of ten shillings "proclamation money"[7] during the preceding year. The rule requiring the payment of taxes on the land for the previous year was probably borrowed from England where it had been made a condition precedent to the exercise of the forty shilling franchise.[8]

At the beginning of this section it was noted that the connty franchise in England was confined to freeholders. Governor Berkeley of Virginia was instructed in 1676 to "take care that the members of the assembly be elected only by freeholders as being more agreeable to the custom of England to which you are as nigh as conveniently you can to conform yourselfe."[9] We have seen that this had

[1] Rivers, *History of South Carolina*, Appendix 437. There was an act on this subject in 1696-7, of which the writer has been unable to procure a copy. See 2 Cooper, 130.

[2] Act 1704, no. 227, 2 Cooper, 249.   [3] Act 1716, no. 365, 2 Cooper, 683.

[4] Act 1717, no. 373, 3 Cooper, 2.   [5] Act 1721, no. 446, 3 Cooper, 135.

[6] Act 1745, no. 730, 2 Cooper, 657.   [7] 33 Geo. II, no. 885, 4 Cooper, 98.

[8] 10 Anne, chap. 23; 18 Geo. II, chap. 18; 20 Geo. III, chap. 17.

[9] 2 Hening, 425.

been done in Virginia even before he arrived. We have also found that but four other colonies, *viz.* : Rhode Island, New York, North Carolina and Georgia, confined the elective franchise strictly to freeholders. In two of the constitutions which never had a real influence on the colonies for which they were framed, *viz.* : that of East Jersey and that of the Carolinas, we have seen that strict freehold suffrage was provided for. New Hampshire ultimately seems to have debarred all but freeholders. Everywhere else, though freeholders could always vote if they pleased, there was some provision permitting the holder of a certain amount of property, personal in its nature and not always of great value, to cast a vote counting for just as much as that of the largest freeholder. Though this was the sign of a democratic tendency opposed to the landed interests which predominated in England, the British crown seems to have permitted it, despite the protests that were raised. For example, when Lord Cornbury took possession of New Jersey, he was instructed by the royal government, at the special request of the retiring proprietors, to have the members of the assembly from the counties chosen by freeholders.[1] Some years after his arrival an act was passed which after stating that the instructions of Lord Cornbury were inconvenient, proceeded to lay down a money qualification for electors.[2] This action drew forth a spirited protest from the late proprietors.

"For certainly," they petitioned the Crown, "those persons are fittest to be intrusted with choosing and being Legislators who have a fixed valuable and permanent interest in Lands, and must stand and fall with their country ; but money is an uncertain Interest and if it be admitted a qualification equal to Land, an assembly may be packed of Strangers and Beggars who will have little regard to the

---

[1] Leaming and Spicer, 599, 623.
[2] 7 Anne, chap. 4, 1; Nevill's *Laws*, 7, Allinson's *Laws*, 6.

Good of the Country from whence they can remove at Pleasure and may oppress the Landed Man with heavy Taxes."[1]

This provision, they wrote to the Lords of Trade, was contrary to the instructions of the governor,

"Which was intended to be a standing and unalterable part of the constitution as most agreeable to the constitution of England where the electors of knights by the counties must have a certain fixed freehold—but the alteration now made was intended to put the election of representatives into the meanest of the people, who being impatient of any superior will never fail to choose such from among themselves, as may oppress and destroy our rights."[2]

That the objectionable qualification was not repealed is shown by an act passed in 1767,[3] which reaffirmed the rule laid down by the statute of 7 Anne.

1) *Class of Estate Required.* The question as to what class of estate would be necessary to qualify an elector seems to have arisen only in those colonies which limited the county franchise strictly to freeholders. The end sought by the rules that were adopted appears to have been to prevent one and the same estate from qualifying two different persons. Thus in Rhode Island an estate in fee simple, fee tail, or an estate in reversion which qualified no other person, or an estate for one's own life, was sufficient. An admission as freeman in right of a wife's dower, or an estate in reversion which qualified another person, or a house on lands not belonging in fee simple, fee tail, or for life, but belonging to another, was null and void.[4] The other colonies were more liberal. Thus in New York[5] and Virginia[6] an estate for one's own life or for the life of his wife would qualify an elector. North Carolina also permitted a man to vote in right of a

---

[1] Leaming and Spicer, 658.   [2] Smith, *History of New Jersey*, 341.
[3] 8 Geo. III, Allinson's *Laws*, 306.   [4] Hall's *Code*, 1767, Title *Elections*, 78.
[5] 13 Will. III, chap. 94, § 2, Van Schaack's *Laws*, 40.
[6] Resolution of the House of Burgesses, 36 Car. II, 3 Hening, 26.

life estate,[1] while both this colony[2] and Virginia[3] declared
that an estate for the life of another, or an estate of greater
dignity, was sufficient.[4] The privilege of voting in right of
an estate for the life of one's wife was recognized also in
England, where it was enacted that a man might vote in
right of his wife's dower from a former husband, even
though the dower had not been assigned or set out by
metes and bounds.[5] New York required freeholds to be
free from all encumbrance,[6] although an exception seems to
have been recognized in the case of persons who had mort-
gaged their lands, but were still in possession and in receipt
of the income or profits.[7] In the case of Philipse *vs.* Van
Horne, the Assembly rendered a decision to the effect that
" a grantor of a mortgage in fee forfeited, who has been in
possession several years, could not vote by virtue of said mortgage." [8] The meaning of this decision is not perfectly clear,
but it appears to be based on the theory that the grantee of
a piece of property, conveyed upon foreclosure of a mortgage,
did not hold the fee absolutely so long as there existed an
equity of redemption. An English statute[9] held in the analogous case of the property qualification of a member of Parliament that seven years' possession was necessary in order
to extinguish the equity of redemption. The rule in Rhode
Island was that no person whose estate was under mortgage
could vote after the mortgage had expired and the mortgagee
had come into possession. The mortgagee, if he was in

---

[1] 17 Geo. II, chap. 1, § iv; Davis and Swann ed., 1752, 177.   [2] *Ibid.*

[3] Resolution of the House of Burgesses, 36 Car. II, 3 Hening, 26.

[4] Also 4 Anne, chap. ii, § 6, 3 Hening, 236.

[5] 20 Geo. III, chap. 17, § 12.

[6] 11 Will. III, chap. 74, § 1, Van Schaack's *Laws,*, 28.

[7] 13 Will. III, chap. 94, § 3; Van Schaack's *Laws*, 40.

[8] 6 *New York Colonial Documents*, 56; 1 *Journal New York Assembly*, 716.

[9] 9 Anne, chap. 5, 4thly.

possession, could vote.[1]   In England, in the case of lands
under mortgage or held in trust, the mortgagor or *cestui que
trust* could vote, unless the trustee or mortgagee was in
actual possession or in receipt of the rents or profits.[2]
With reference to joint estates, there was a peculiar provision in Virginia.   Joint tenants or tenants in common had
but one vote between them, unless the quantity of land was
sufficient to give each of them the number of acres required
to qualify a single voter.[3]   A subsequent enactment provided
that if there was only property enough to qualify for a single
vote, that was not to be given unless the owners were agreed.[4]
In all matters of property, the common law favored possession rather than ownership.   Therefore, as will be seen when
we come to treat of the town franchise in North Carolina, the
tenant   rather   than   the   owner   was   permitted   to   vote.[6]
Georgia gave a vote to a person "legally possessed in his
own right of fifty acres of land,"[6] and Connecticut required
no more than possession.[7]   Virginia on the contrary recognized ownership.   Persons could vote who had freeholds in
their own possession or in the possession of their tenants for
"term of years, at will or suffrance."[8]   After 1760 copy-
holders were disfranchised in England,[9] but whether this
tenure would qualify a voter in America does not appear to
have been decided.

2) *Length of Possession Required.*   In order to put a stop
to conveyances made on purpose to qualify an elector,
several of the colonies required freeholders to have been in

---

[1] Southwick ed., 1772, 29.   [2] 7 and 8 Will. III, chap. 25, § 7.

[3] 10 Geo. II, chap. vi, § 6; 4 Hening, 475.

[4] 3 Geo. III, chap. 15, 7 Hening, 519.   [5] Davis and Swann ed., 1752, 99, 114.

[6] Act June 9th, 1761.   [7] *Session Laws*, 40.

[8] 10 Geo. II, chap. ii, § 11, 4 Hening, 475; 3 Geo. III, chap. 1, §4, 7 Hening,
519.

[9] *Statute* 31 Geo. II, chap. 14.

possession of their estates a certain length of time before an election. In New York this period was put at three months before the test of the writs,[1] while in North Carolina it was three months before the elector offered to vote.[2] A freemen voting as a freeholder in New Jersey must have been such for one year.[3] In Virginia no person could vote "in respect or in right of any lands, or tenements, whereof he has not been in possession for one whole year, next before the test of the writ for such election: unless such lands or tenements came to such person within that time, by descent, marriage, marriage settlement or devise."[4] Just before the revolution the length of possession was reduced to six calendar months.[5] The law on this point in Virginia appears to have been taken from two English statutes,[6] which required holders of the county franchise to have paid charges and received rents during the year preceding an election, with the exceptions allowed in Virginia and also for lands acquired by presentation to some benefice in the church or by promotion to some office, to which such freehold was affixed.

3) *Proof of Property Qualification.* The general rule was that a voter must declare his qualifications upon oath if he was required to do so.[7] This power to examine voters as to their

---

[1] 11 Will. III, chap, 74, § 1, Van Schaack's *Laws,* 28.

[2] 8 Geo. II, chap. ii, 17 Geo. II, chap. I, § v; Davis and Swann ed., 1752, 177.

[3] 13 Geo. I, chap. 40, § 1; Nevill's *Laws,* 142, Allinson's *Laws,* 69.

[4] 10 Geo. II, chap. ii, § 4, 4 Hening, 475. 3 Geo. III, chap. I, § 6, required either possession or a legal title for a year, 7 Hening, 519.

[5] 10 Geo. III, chap. i, § 4, 8 Hening, 305.

[6] 10 Anne, chap. 23, § 2, and 18 Geo. II, chap. 18.

[7] See Massachusetts, *Laws* 1693-4, chap. 14, § 8, 1 Ames and Goodell, 148; Rhode Island, 16 Geo. II, Franklin ed., 1730, 252; New York, 11 Will. III, chap. 74, § 5, Van Schaack's *Laws,* 28; New Jersey, 12 Geo. I, chap. 40, Nevill's *Laws,* 142; Virginia, 10 Geo. II, chap. ii, 4 Hening, 475; North Carolina, 17 Geo. II. chap. I, Davis and Swann ed., 1752, 177; 33 Geo. II, chap. I, ed. 1772, 247; Georgia, Act June 9th, 1761. See appendix A, *post.*

qualifications under oath was established in England by the statute of 8 Henry VI, chap. 7. Perjury and subornation were punished there,[1] as well as in New York[2] and Virginia,[3] under the Statute of Perjuries of 5 Elizabeth. The laws of Rhode Island were especially explicit on this subject. Deeds must be recorded and produced in open town meeting at the time of voting. In case of dispute as to the value of a freehold, three persons chosen by the town meeting were to appraise the property in question. Town clerks were permitted to search the records and certify as to a freeholder's qualifications. Persons were required to vote in the town where they lived, but in case the estate for which they voted was not at their place of residence, they were required to produce a certificate, dated within ten days, from the clerk of the town in which the estate was situated. If a person was challenged as to his qualification, he could take the oath and vote on that occasion only. In future, he must have a certificate of the value of his freehold from the appraisers.[4] In New Hampshire, qualifications were proved by the last lists of rates and assessments which the selectmen were required to bring to the place of election,[5] although later the moderator seems to have decided the matter.[6] Massachusetts required that the property qualification of those who were not church members should be certified by the majority of the selectmen of the town where they resided.[7] This was at one time the law in Connecticut, but ultimately,[8]

---

[1] 7 and 8 Will. III, chap. 25.

[2] 11 Will. III, chap. 74, § 9, Van Schaacks *Laws*, 28.

[3] 10 Geo. III, chap. ii, § 7, 4 Hening, 475.

[4] 20 Geo. II, Franklin ed., 1752, 13, 24; Hall's *Code*, 1767, Title *Elections*, 78.

[5] 11 Will. III, 3 *Provincial Papers*, 216.

[6] 1 Geo. II, chap. 107, Fowle ed., 1761, 142; ed. 1771, 166.

[7] *Massachusetts Colonial Records*, pt. ii, 117, 167.

[8] 4 *Connecticut Colonial Records*, 11; *Session Laws*, 40.

the value of a person's estate was computed by the tax-list of the year in which he desired to be admitted as a freeman.[1]

In Pennsylvania the Quakers preserved their conscientious scruples by leaving the matter of estimating the value of freeholds to election officers chosen for that purpose, and aided by tax lists, as well as by the oaths and affirmations of the voters.[2] There seems to have been a similar reluctance to commit perjury in Virginia. Accordingly we find that the sheriffs were required to put in a separate poll list, the votes of such electors as had any scruple about taking the oath, because they did not feel qualified to judge of the value of their freeholds. If the House of Burgesses made a scrutiny of the poll such votes were to be counted as good.[3] At one time in South Carolina a number of parishes had been occupied by the Indians, and it was provided that the inhabitants who still held lands could vote in whatever parish they pleased. In such cases, however, they were required to prove to the electors of parishes that they had not parted with their property.[4] How such proof was to be adduced is not clear.

A great deal of fraud was perpetrated by means of conveyances made in order to qualify electors, in order that they might vote for some particular person. To prevent this, the oaths taken by electors frequently contained a clause declaring that the estate by which the voter was qualfied had not been conveyed for this purpose.[5] In Rhode Island the

---

[1] 5 *Connecticut Colonial Records,* 129; *Session Laws,* 149.

13 Geo. I, chap. 284, Franklin ed., 1742, 346.

[3] 3 Geo. III, chap. i, § 14, 7 Hening, 519.

[4] Act 1716, no. 365, §§ xi, xii, 2 Cooper, 683.

[5] New York (11 Will. III, chap. 74, § 4, Van Schaack's *Laws,* 28); New Jersey (12 Geo. I, chap. 40, Nevill's *Laws,* 142); Virginia (10 Geo. II, chap. ii, 4 Hening, 475); North Carolina (33 Geo. II, chap. i, Davis ed., 1773, 247); Georgia (Act June 9th, 1761). See appendix A of this work. Similar oaths were required in England. *Statutes,* 10 Anne, chap. 23; 18 Geo. II, chap. 18.

grantee of an estate had to take a similar oath, and persons convicted of giving or receiving fraudulent conveyances were forever disfranchised.[1] In New Jersey fraudulent conveyances to multiply votes or to qualify voters were taken as free and absolute against the grantors if there was an agreement to reconvey, while collateral securities for defeating the estate were declared void. Persons making such conveyances, or voting by color of them, were liable to a fine of ten pounds.[2] In Virginia estates created or conveyances made to qualify voters were null and void; persons voting by color of such conveyances, or who being privy to the purpose of their creation should aid in drawing them up, were liable to a fine of forty pounds.[3]

B. THE TOWN AND BOROUGH FRANCHISE. As towns began to spring up, it became necessary, in those colonies where the qualifications of electors were determined not so much by the value of the real property they held, as by its area, to provide some special test for those voters who resided in towns and hence did not own fifty or a hundred acres, as was required in the counties at large. This franchise must be distinguished also on the one hand from that possessed by persons voting for assemblymen in right of their freedom in a municipal corporation, as, for instance, New York and Albany,[4] and on the other hand from the right to vote for local officers in a New England town meeting or for municipal officers, by virtue of the ownership of a freehold within the city limits.[5] We shall see that this franchise was generally conferred by the act incorporating a particular town, while the want of it in Georgia, where the possession

---

[1] Hall's *Code*, 1767, Title *Elections*, 78.

[2] 12 Geo. I, chap. 40, § 1, Nevill's *Laws*, 142. This was the law in England, as laid down by 7 and 8 Will. III, chap. 25, and 10 Anne, chap. 23.

[3] 10 Geo. II, chap. 1, § iii, 4 Hening, 475.

[4] 11 Will. III, chap. 74, § 10, Van Schaack's *Laws*, 28.

[5] New York, 11 Geo. III, chap. 1490, Van Schaack's *Laws*, 620.

of fifty acres of land was required of electors, is said to have disfranchised many freeholders in towns whose estates might be greater in value and liable for heavier taxes than several hundred acres in the country.[1] It may be supposed that in Virginia this franchise was indicated by the shortlived law of 1655, which limited the suffrage to "all housekeepers, whether ffreeholders, leaseholders or otherwise tenants,[2] and also by the statute of 22 Charles II, which finally gave the elective franchise to freeholders and housekeepers.[3] The former act allowed but one person in a family to avail himself of this privilege. This is in line with the ancient English custom which regarded the burgess-ship as the absolute right of all free inhabitant-housekeepers,[4] and admitted but one voice to a house.[5] The act of 1736 which defined the number of acres to be possessed by freeholders in the counties expressly exempted from its operation all freeholders resident in cities or towns incorporated by act of assembly, and confirmed them in their privilege of voting in right of a house and lot, or of a house and part of a lot. In case the interest in such house and lot was divided, but one voice could be admitted for the same house and lot.[6] A later statute required such town houses to be at least twelve feet square.[7] The burgess from the college of William and Mary was returned by the president and the masters or professors.[8] The charter of Williamsburg gave the right to return one burgess, first to all the freeholders of the city who owned a lot of land in the city with a house built thereon according to law; in the second place, to all actual residents who

[1] I Stevens, *History of Georgia*, 412.

[2] 5–6 Commonwealth, Act vii, 1 Hening, 411.

[3] 2 Hening, 280.　　　　[4] Cox, *Antient Parliamentary Elections*, 177, 189.

[5] 7 and 8 Will. III, chap. 25.　[6] 10 Geo. II, chap. ii, 4 Hening, 475.

[7] 3 Geo. III, chap. 1, § 4, 7 Hening, 519.

[8] 4 Anne, chap. ii, § vii, 3 Hening, 241. See Appendix A, *post*.

had a visible estate of fifty pounds current money, and, lastly, to all persons who had served five years at any trade within the city, and should at the end of that time be actually house-keepers and residents. A certificate in regard to the apprenticeship must be obtained from the court of Hustings. On the lot owned by a freeholder there must be a house of certain dimensions required by law for "saving" such lot in tenantable repair at the time of voting. Servants, whether they were bound by indenture, covenant or other form of obligation, could not vote. Twelve months residence was required of all electors. Joint tenants and tenants in common had only one vote between them, and that was to be given only in case the parties could agree.[1]

By the Fundamental Constitutions of East Jersey the possessor of a house and three acres in a borough was enfranchised; also the tenant of a hired house and land, provided he could prove that he had fifty pounds in stock of his own.[2] Under the royal government two representatives were returned by the inhabitants-householders of Burlington in West Jersey and two by the inhabitants-householders of Perth Amboy in East Jersey.[3] In Philadelphia two representatives were returned by those of the inhabitants who had a freehold estate or were worth fifty pounds clear, personal estate, within the city.[4] In South Carolina a freeholder of "houses, lands or town lots or parts thereof to the value of £60 proclamation money in Charlestown or any other town for which he paid tax the precedent year" was permitted to vote for assemblymen.[5] As soon as a town in North Carolina had sixty families it returned a member to the assembly.[6] As

---

[1] 15 Geo. II, chap. 26; 5 Hening, 204.

[2] *Concessions* 1683, § iii, Leaming and Spicer, 153.   [3] *Ibid.*, 623.

[4] 4 Anne, chap. 129, Franklin ed., 1742, 67.   [5] Act 1745, no. 730, 3 Cooper, 657.

[6] 2 Hawks, *History of North Carolina*, 176.

the early laws required only the payment of one year's levy and residence in the province a full year preceding an election, there was no need of a separate qualification for residents of towns.[1] In 1723 the law of 1715 was supplemented by an act defining the qualifications of holders of the town franchise. Every elector must own a "saved lot" in the town and constantly keep a house thereon in repair. The house and lot could not be let to or tenanted by a "person capable of voting in the town, though not residing therein." If, however, a person who had paid the preceding year's "levy or pole tax," rented and lived "in and on such house and lot, in the said town not tenanted," he could vote. "But if the tenant by law have not a right to vote, then the owner thereof, and not the tenant, shall have the vote."[2] The act incorporating the town of Edenton[3] gave a vote to the owner of a "saved" lot who had held it for six months before the election. In Wilmington the borough franchise was given to the tenant of a brick, stone or frame house twenty feet long by sixteen wide, who inhabited said house on the day of election and had done so for three months previously. If there was no tenant qualified to vote, then

---

[1] *Laws* 1715, 2 *North Carolina Colonial Records*, 213.

[2] These vaguely worded provisions are taken from the original copy, now preserved in the North Carolina State Library, of chap. ii, *Laws* of 1723, "An act intituled an additional Act relating to biennial and other assemblies and regulating Elections and divers other things relating to Towns." See Appendix B, *post*. It is quoted as obsolete in Davis and Swann ed., 1752, 53, and ed. 1773, 30. There is also another act, chap. ii, *Laws* 1727, "an Act regulating towns and election of Burgesses," Davis and Swann ed., 1752, 67; ed. 1773, 37. This is given only by title in the statute books, and the writer is informed by Mr. J. C. Birdsong, the State Librarian, that the original manuscript laws of the State from 1723 to 1743 are supposed to have been destroyed by fire about 1830. It has consequently, been impossible to secure a copy, although Dr. Hawks (*History of North Carolina*, 177) apparently refers to it.

[3] 14 Geo. II, chap. xii, Davis and Swann ed., 1752, 107.

the person seized in his own right in fee simple, fee tail or for life had the franchise. A vote in the choice of the representative from ˚Wilmington was also given to every "man" who inhabited a brick house, thirty feet by sixteen, " between the bounds of that town upwards and South Creek, and within 120 Poles of Cape Feare River," unless such person was a servant.[1] In Brunswick the voter must be the tenant, or if there was none, the owner of a stone or habitable house within the town of the " Dimensions of Twenty feet by Sixteen with one or more Brick or Stone Chimney or Chimnies."[2] In other respects the qualifications were the same as in Wilmington. The preference given the tenant as against the owner in North Carolina is worthy of note. This doubtless was due to the common law presumption in favor of possession.

§ 9. *Miscellaneous.* There were a few minor qualifications required at various times, which do not fall conveniently under any of the preceding heads. Thus, New Jersey's first concession and agreement, as well as that of Carolina, declared that all persons who were " subjects to the King of England and swear or subscribe allegiance to the King and faithfulness to the Lords," should be freemen. The inhabitants who were freemen or chief agents to others should elect the representatives.[3] In West Jersey proprietors were allowed to vote,[4] though in South Carolina both they and their deputies were debarred.[5] The latter provision was doubtless derived by analogy from England, where a peer of the realm had no voice in the choice of a member of

---

[1] Acts 1739, 1740, Davis and Swann ed., 1752, 99, 114.

[2] 33 Geo. II, chap. 1, § xiii, Davis ed., 1773, 247.

[3] New Jersey, 1664, 1 *New Jersey Archives*, 30, Leaming and Spicer, 12 *et seq.*; Carolina, 1665, 1 *North Carolina Colonial Records*, 80, 166.

[4] Leaming and Spicer, 385.　　　　　[5] Act 1704, no. 227, § xi, 2 Cooper, 249.

parliament.[1] Persons under guardianship could not vote in
Rhode Island.[2] A statute enacted in 1717 declared that
"no apprentice or other covenanted servant for term of
years, whether by indenture or custom of the county,
could be an elector" in South Carolina.[3] The petition,
already quoted, to the lords proprietors, of Carolina, complained, that, at the Berkeley county election in 1701, a
great number of servants, and also poor and indigent persons
voted promiscuously with their masters and creditors.[4]
This would lead to the inference that neither debtors nor
servants could legally be electors in South Carolina.[5] During the interval between the efforts to introduce the constitution of Locke and the final adoption of a property
qualification,[6] North Carolina required of voters the payment of the levy for the year preceding the election.[7] The
laws drawn up by Penn in 1682, declared that every inhabitant, artificer or other resident who paid scot and lot to the
government could vote.[8]

In New York persons refusing to take upon tender of the
sheriff the oaths appointed by law to be taken instead of the
oaths of allegiance and supremacy, and to sign the test and
association could not vote.[9] New Hampshire in the earlier
part of her history as a separate province, seems to have
required the oath of allegiance from all electors.[10] By the
Hartford Constitution of 1638 all those who had taken

---

[1] Troward, *Elections,* 21.   [2] Hall's *Code,* 1767, Title *Elections,* 78.

[3] Act 1717, no. 373, § xi, 3 Cooper, 2.

[4] Rivers, *South Carolina,* Appendix, 453, *et seq.*

[5] Probably this was also true in Virginia. 21 Car. I, Act xx, 1 Hening, 333.

[6] 17 Geo. II, chap. 1, Davis and Swann ed. 1752, 177.

[7] *Laws,* 1715, 2 *North Carolina Colonial Records,* 213.

[8] 1 *Pennsylvania Colonial Records,* 37.

[9] 13 Will. III, chap. 94, Van Schaack's *Laws,* 40.

[10] Belknap, *History of New Hampshire,* 177; 1 *Provincial Papers,* 396.

the "oath of Fidellity and doe cohabitte within the jurisdiction (haueing been admitted inhabitants by the major
part of the town where they live)" were allowed to vote for the
magistrates of the colony.[1]   In general it may be stated that
whenever the suffrage was exercised only by persons duly
admitted as freemen, the taking of the prescribed oath became a condition precedent to the right of voting.

§ 10. *Admission of Freemen.*   It has already been mentioned that in New England the right of voting was inherent
in persons admitted to the freedom of a colony.   To obtain
this freedom, and thus become a freeman and incidentally an
elector, certain prescribed steps had to be taken.   Before
going into a detailed account of the methods that were
followed in admitting the freemen of the different colonies, it will perhaps be well to state the general rules on the
subject.   Freemen could originally be admitted only at one
of the general courts.   The court could probably exercise
a certain amount of discretion as to who should be admitted, and it usually insisted that the names of candidates
should be proposed a certain length of time before enrol-
ment.   Freemen became such upon taking the oath and having their names enrolled.   Ultimately freemen were allowed
to be admitted in their own towns, and in such cases the
town clerk was required to send their names to the secretary
of the colony for enrollment.   The writer, for reasons elsewhere explained, believes that the principle of allowing the
freedom of a colony to stand as the sole qualification of a
voter did not exist outside of the five Puritan colonies.[2]

Beginning with the Plymouth colony, we find that in 1658
a law was passed requiring those who desired to be admitted
as freemen to have their names "propounded" at the June
court, and in that case they could be admitted at the corres-

---

[1] 1 *Connecticut Colonial Records*, 21.   [2] See p. 49, *ante.*

ponding court twelve months later, " if the court shall not see cause to the contrary." [1] We may imagine that this discretion given to the court was the earliest form of an electoral qualification. In 1674, as a condition precedent to proposal in the general court, candidates had to be approved by the majority of the freemen of their town, and that approval communicated to the general court through the deputies under the town clerk's hand. The names of the freemen in each town were required to be kept on the town record.[2] Later when qualifications were required, persons could only be admitted at the court of election in open court, and then not until after they had been proposed for a year. Persons " generally known and approved, or of whom the court may make present improvement," were not required to serve a term of probation.[3] In Massachusetts, as in Plymouth, the power to admit freemen rested with the general court. But in 1664, in order to save newly-admitted freemen the trouble of coming to Boston in order to take the oath, it was provided that they could be sworn by a county court. For this purpose the Secretary of the colony was authorized to make out from the records of the general court a list of those who had been admitted to the freedom of the colony, and give it, with a copy of the freeman's oath, to an agent of the persons admitted, who should deliver it to the clerk or recorder of the county court where they were to be sworn.[4] The names of those desiring to receive the freedom of the colony were propounded and put to vote in the general court for acceptance " by the suffrage of the major part."[5] From 1673 to 1683 candidates who were not church members were required to have their names entered

[1] *Laws,* 1658, Brigham 108.   [2] *Laws,* 1674, Brigham, 170.

[3] *Book of General Laws,* 1671, Brigham 258.

[4] 4 *Massachusetts Colonial Records,* pt. ii, 134, 299.   [5] *Ibid.,* 117, 167.

" from tyme to tyme with the Secretary at the court of election, and read over before the court sometime that session, and not put to vote " till the court of election next following.[1] For a short time there existed a law forbidding the admission of freemen on the day of the court of election.[2] Under the royal government after 1691 the freedom of the colony did not exist.

Rhode Island seems to have recognized a distinction between the freedom of the colony and the freedom of a town. This was most probably due to the fact that Rhode Island was a confederacy of several towns of equal size, rather than a colony whose towns were created under acts of a general court, as was the case in Plymouth and Massachusetts.[3] Before the first charter Portsmouth decided that none could be admitted as inhabitants or as freemen without the consent of the body.[4] At first the freedom of the colony in Rhode Island as well as elsewhere was conferred only by the general court.[5] About 1665 we find it stated that persons with " sufficient testimony of their fitness and qualifications, as shall be deemed satisfactory by the assembly, or by the chief officer of the town where they lived," should be proposed and admitted " upon their express desire declared to the assembly either by themselves or the chief officer of their town." They could not vote until they had been admitted by the assembly and sworn, and their names entered on the general records of the colony.[6] The towns were given power to admit freemen soon afterward, and the

[1] 5 *Massachusetts Colonial Records*, 385.

[2] 4 *Massachusetts Colonial Records*, pt. ii, 86; repealed, *ibid*. 134.

[3] 1 *Rhode Island Colonial Records*, 236, 4 *Rhode Island Colonial Records*, 338. The latter reference is the repeal of a law which was in force for a short time, and which restricted the choice of deputies to freemen of the colony.

[4] 1 *Rhode Island Colonial Records*, 53, 85.   [5] *Ibid.*, 104, 108, 263, *etc.*

[6] 2 *Rhode Island Colonial Records*, 113, 516.

clerk was required to send a list of those admitted to the general assembly in May of each year.[1] The assembly did not lose its power to admit freemen.[2] The names of candidates for admission were proposed for three months in town meeting,[3] an exception, however, being made in the case of those entitled to be freemen by virtue of their birth. Freemen removing from one town to another were admitted in their new place of residence upon presentation of a certificate, without being propounded.[4] No one could be made free on election day.[5]

In the New Haven colony freemen were admitted at a meeting of the general court,[6] and this was also true in Hartford,[7] though at first freemen had to take the oath of fidelity and be admitted inhabitants by the majority of the residents of the town where they lived.[8] They were presented at the October general court in "an orderly way, to prevent tumult and trouble," and admitted at the May court.[9] After 1689 freemen were admitted and sworn by any assistant or commissioner, who was required before the next general sessions to send the names of those he had admitted to the secretary of the colony for enrollment.[10] Finally freemen were admitted in town meetings, as was ultimately the case in Rhode Island. The town clerk administered the oath and enrolled the names in a book provided

---

[1] 18 Car. II, Franklin ed, 1744, 9; 6 *Rhode Island Colonial Records*, 323.

[2] 6 *Rhode Island Colonial Records*, 256.   [3] 20 Geo. II, Franklin ed., 1752, 13.

[4] Hall's *Code*, 1767, Title *Elections*, 78.   [5] 2 *Rhode Island Colonial Records*, 190.

[6] 1 *New Haven Colonial Records*, 35, 40, *etc.*

[7] 1 *Connecticut Colonial Records*, 417.   [8] *Ibid.*, 21.

[9] *Ibid.*, 331, 389.

[10] 4 *Connecticut Colonial Records*, 17, *Session Laws*, 40; 4 *Connecticut Colonial Records*, 483, provided that an assistant or a justice of the peace could administer the oath.

for the purpose.[1]   The penalty of disfranchisement was inflicted by the superior court.

In addition to the freedom of the Puritan colonies it is necessary to consider the rules governing the admission of freemen of the cities in the province of New York, inasmuch as such persons could vote for assemblymen. Thus, the Dongan charter gave to the Mayor, Recorder and Aldermen of New York the privilege of making free citizens under their common seal. As a condition precedent to the freedom of the city, persons must be natural born subjects of the king or else have been naturalized by act of assembly, or by letters of denization from the lieutenant governor. The use of any " Art trade Mystery or Manual Occupation " within the limits of the city, was restricted to freemen of the corporation and as we have already seen,[3] they possessed the privilege of voting at the elections of members of the assembly. The Montgomery charter contained similar provisions. The common council fixed the fee for freedoms at five pounds.[4] The provisions in regard to freemen under the Dongan charter of Albany are similar to those with respect to New York.[5] In Philadelphia the freedom of the corporation could be bestowed on free denizens of the province twenty-one years of age who were inhabitants of the city with an estate of inheritance or of freehold, or who were worth fifty pounds in money or other stock, and who had been residents within the city for the space of two years, or who should purchase their freedom from the Mayor and commonalty.   This does not, however, specially concern

---

[1] 3 Geo. II, chap. 47, *Session Laws*, 370; 7 *Connecticut Colonial Records*, 260.

[2] *Session Laws*, 1750, 81.   [3] See p. 47, *ante*.

[4] See *New York Historical Society Collections*, 1885, 48, 481. The complete rolls of the freemen of the city, as well as of the holders of the Burgher rights in Dutch times are published in this volume.

[5] 1686; Weise, *History of Albany*, 200.

us, for the freedom of Philadelphia did not in itself entitle a person to vote for assemblymen. Besides this, the qualifications required of freemen were practically the same as those required of electors in general.[1]

In England, toward the close of the colonial era, two statutes were enacted with a view to putting a stop to the numerous abuses which appear to have developed on the subject of freedoms. On being refused admission, a person could compel the officers to grant him a certificate, by means of a writ of *mandamus* from the Court of King's Bench, and he could recover his costs from the delinquent corporation. Freemen must have held their freedom for twelve months before they could vote for members of Parliament, and corporate officers were fined £500 for antedating the admission of a freeman. During certain hours of the day, and upon payment of a nominal fee, books and papers bearing on the subject were open to the inspection of candidates or of their agents, or of any two freemen.[2]

---

[1] Miller ed., 1762, 10.   [2] 3 Geo. III, chap. 15; 12 Geo. III, chap. 21.

CHAPTER III.   THE MANAGEMENT OF ELECTIONS.

When we come to consider the subject of the management of elections we find the colonies divided into three
great classes.   The first group comprised the four colonies
founded under Puritan influence and situated in the territory
which we call New England.   Just as these developed the
principle of requiring voters to be freemen of the colony, and
inclined, so long as they were left to themselves, toward religious and moral rather than property qualifications for
electors, so did they develop and possibly originate the system of nominating candidates for the office of assistant, and
the proxy method of voting.   These two features, peculiar to
New England elections, were developed contemporaneously
in the four Puritan colonies, and reached in Rhode Island
and Connecticut the final stage which would doubtless have
been attained in Massachusetts and Plymouth had it not
been for the interference of the English government which
resulted in the charter of 1691.

The second group of colonies includes those which elected
the members of their legislatures in a manner almost precisely similar to that employed in choosing members of the
House of Commons .in England.   In this class we
would place New York, Virginia, Georgia, Maryland, and
New Jersey after 1704.   The system in vogue was due to
the fact that these colonies were most closely under royal
rule, and. that Maryland, although she had a proprietary
government, avowedly followed the English practice.[1]

[1] See Act 1678; *Maryland Archives*, 3 *Proceedings and Acts of Assembly*, 60.

The third group includes colonies proprietary in their origin, just as those of the first were corporate, and those of the second, royal provinces. In the present group we would place the two Jersey colonies, Pennsylvania and Delaware, and the two Carolinas. In all of these the proprietors tried to introduce systems of government, original in many respects, but so visionary that they worked badly in practice. For several of these colonies some remarkable methods of conducting elections were designed, and these in time received many modifications, so that they finally occupied a position midway between those of the colonies in the first two classes and embracing many of the salient characteristics of each.

It is noteworthy that the first and the third class from the beginning of their history used the ballot, an institution which was not introduced in English parliamentary elections until 1872. The form of the ballot differed considerably, but secrecy was the chief end desired by the Puritans, especially in the election of assistants. In the Carolinas, however, the secret ballot seems to have reached a high state of development, although, as we shall see, North Carolina went back to the English method in 1760.[1]

§ 1. *The Calling of an Election.* Two methods appear to have been employed by the colonial governments in calling an election. The first was by a statutory or constitutional provision fixing certain days as those on which elections should take place. The best example of this method is found in the Puritan colonies. In each of these the election

---

[1] Mr. Douglas Campbell in his recent work, *The Puritan in England, Holland and America*, makes the statement (vol. ii, 440) that the ballot did not appear in the colonies south of Pennsylvania. With all deference to Mr. Campbell, I believe this statement to be erroneous, because, as will be shown in a subsequent section, the ballot in the Carolinas was as fully developed in the direction of secrecy as in those colonies under the influence of Puritan ideas.

of the governor and other general officers took place at specified sessions of the general courts usually held in the spring. When assembled for the choice of magistrates it was known as the General Court of Election, and was originally attended by all the freemen, but afterwards by their representatives.

The second method prevailed in the colonies which were more directly controlled by the English government, and where the only elected officers of a general character were the members of the legislative assembly. The elections of these, like the election of the members of the House of Commons, were called by means of writs prerogative in their character, and therefore issued by or under authority of the royal governor as representive of the crown. The only limitation on the power to issue writs of election was that established by statutes similar to those in England,[1] and requiring assemblies to be elected at least once in certain fixed periods. The power to call assemblies was usually conferred by the commissions or instructions of the royal governors.[2] The maximum period for which assemblymen were elected in New Jersey was fixed by statute at seven years[3]; in Maryland[4] and Virginia,[5] (perhaps also in New Hampshire[6]) at three

---

[1] 6 Will. and Mary, chap. 1, "triennial;" 1 Geo. I, chap. 38, " septennial."

[2] For example, New Hampshire, commission of President Cutts (Fowle ed, 1771, .4); New York, Governor Dongan, 1682–3 (3 *New York Colonial Documents*, 317, 330, and 624); New Jersey, Lord Cornbury, 1702 (Leaming and Spicer, 623, 647). Penn called his assemblies by virtue of his own authority as Proprietor, conferred by his charter (§4, 1 *Pennsylvania Colonial Records.* 19; Chalmers, *Political Annals*, 645; 1 Proud, *History of Pennsylvania*, 206). So did Lord Baltimore through his representative in Maryland (*Maryland Archives*, 1 *Assembly*, 1, *etc.*). So also the Carolinas (1 *North Carolina Colonial Records*, 181, 235, 333), and under royal rule by Governor Burrington's commission (1729–30, 3 *North Carolina Colonial Records*, 68).

[3] 8 Geo. III, Allinson's *Laws*, 306, 307.

[4] *Maryland Archives*, 1 *Correspondence Governor Sharpe*, 68. See p. 34 *ante*.

[5] 3 Geo. III, chap. 1, § 3, 7 Hening, 519.   [6] 4 *Provincial Papers*, 114.

years; while North Carolina had biennial elections,[1] as had South Carolina during a portion of her history.[2] By Penn's Charter of Privileges it was provided that assemblies should be elected annually.[3]

In addition to these two systems we shall find that one or two colonies not only fixed a certain date on which elections were to be held, but also provided that a writ should be issued in anticipation of the appointed day.[4] We find that in Pennsylvania in 1688–9 the question of issuing writs in such cases was decided in the negative. It seems that the governor asked his council whether it were useful or needful for him to issue writs or warrants for summoning the freemen to elect representatives on the appointed day. The council in reply resolved that the freemen would observe the day " of course " without writs or warrants.[5]

The New England court of election was held annually at the capital of each colony, the date being fixed by law. In the Plymouth Colony, until 1636, it was held at Plymouth on January 1st,[6] though in the latter years of this period the persons elected did not take office until after March 27th.[7] From 1636 till 1658, the first Tuesday in March was fixed as the day of election,[8] but in the latter year the date was changed to the corresponding Tuesday in June, " nothing extraordinary preventing."[9] The last general court of elec-

---

[1] 1715; 2 *North Carolina Colonial Records*, 213.

[2] 3 Cooper, 135, "triennial;" 3 Cooper, 692, "biennial;" 3 Cooper, 656, "annual." See p. 43, *ante*.

[3] 1 Proud, *History of Pennsylvania*, 444.

[4] West Jersey, Leaming and Spicer, 423; Carolinas, 1 *North Carolina Colonial Records*, 181, 376, 696, *etc.*

[5] 1 *Pennsylvania Colonial Records*, 240.

[6] 1 *Plymouth Colony Records*, 5.   [7] *Ibid.*, 21.

[8] *Laws*, 1636; 11 *Plymouth Colony Records*, 7, 10; Brigham, 37, 40.

[9] *Laws*, 1658, Brigham, 108.

tion was held June 2nd, 1691.[1]   After 1691, associates were elected in the county courts on the last Wednesday in June.[2]

The Massachusetts election took place at Boston. The date prescribed by the charter of 1628 was the last Wednesday of Easter Term.[3]   In April 1629, Governor Endicott was elected in London, and another election appears to have been held in October of the same year.[4]   In October, 1678, a special court of election was held,[5] while after 1632 the regular election took place on the second Wednesday in May.[6]   This continued to be the practice until 1686, when the last election before the forfeiture of the charter took place."[7]

Newport, before the charter of Providence Plantations was granted, held her courts of election on March 12th of each year.[8]   Under the charter the first court of election was held at Portsmouth, May 19th, 1647, and it was resolved to hold it thereafter on May 15th of each year " if wind and weather hinder not."[9]   Subsequent elections appear to have been held in rotation at each of the four towns.[10]   The charter of 15 Charles II, provided that the court of election should be held every year on the first Wednesday of May, at Newport or elsewhere " if urgent."[11]

In New Haven until about 1647 the court of election was held during the last week of October.[12]   Then the date was

---

[1] 6 *Plymouth Colony Records,* 264.   [2] Brigham, 237.

[3] 1 *Massachusetts Colonial Records,* 12, 277.   [4] *Ibid.,* 59.

[5] 5 *Massachusetts Colonial Records,* 195.

[6] 1 *Massachusetts Colonial Records,* 95.

[7] 5 *Massachusetts Colonial Records,* 513.

[8] 1640, 1641; 1 *Rhode Island Colonial Records,* 98, 100, 112, 123.

[9] 1 *Rhode Island Colonial Records,* 147, 149.

[10] *Ibid.,* 149, 216, 220, 235, 241.   Two rival elections each purporting to be for the colony, *Ibid.,* 244, 262, 264, 278, 303, 336, 363, 386, 407.

[11] 2 *Rhode Island Colonial Records,* 11.

[12] 1 *New Haven Colonial Records,* 20, 114.

changed to the last Wednesday in May.[1]   The Hartford constitution of 1638 fixed the date for the election of Governor as the second Thursday in April,[2] but in 1646 this was changed to the third Thursday in May.[3]   As provided by the charter of 14 Charles II, the date of the election of Governor and other general officers for the colony of Connecticut was the second Thursday in May.[4]   Plymouth passed a law ordering that the court of election should be held in his " Majesties name of England," and that the Governor through the constables should warn the freemen to attend.[5]   The other colonies do not seem to have provided for any further notice of the court of election beyond that implied by the statute fixing the day on which it should be held.[6]

In the Puritan colonies, as has been mentioned, deputies were chosen by each town to represent the freemen at the general election.[7]   When the proxy system was introduced, those freemen who did not attend the general court of election handed in their proxies at the town elections when the deputies were chosen.[8]   It came to be a matter of importance to fix properly the dates of those town meetings, for ultimately, both in Rhode Island and Connecticut, all the votes had to be cast in the towns, freemen being prohibited from voting in person at the general court. Usually each town was allowed to fix the date on which it would elect its deputies, provided, it may be assumed, that this was done a sufficient time before the meeting of the gen-

---

[1] 4 *New Haven Colonial Records*, 383; 2 *New Haven Colonial Records*, 567, 568.

[2] 1 *Connecticut Colonial Records*, 21.   [3] *Ibid.*, 140.

[4] 2 *Connecticut Colonial Records*, 5.

[5] *Laws*, 1638, Brigham, 40; 11 *Plymouth Colony Records*, 10.

[6] 1 *New Haven Colonial Records*, 129; 2 *Connecticut Colonial Records*, 131.

[7] See pp. 4, 5, 10, 14, 15 *ante.*

[8] See Plymouth, *Laws*, 1652; Brigham, 94.

eral court.   Such was the rule in New Haven, where deputies
were separately chosen for the legislative courts which met
in April, and for the election courts which met in October.[1]
In Rhode Island deputies were chosen for the October court
at a town meeting held on the last Tuesday of August, and
for the May court (of election when proxies were to be delivered) on the first Tuesday of March.[2]   In 1744 the date
of the spring election was changed to the third Wednesday
in April.[3]   Hartford, like Rhode Island and New Haven, required deputies to be elected semi-annually, *viz:* before the
April court of election and before the September legislative
court.   The constables of each town were to be notified by
the secretary or by the governor of the colony one month
before the date of the semi-annual courts, and fourteen days,
or less, before the meeting of special courts.   The democratic character of the Hartford government as established
by the constitution of 1638 is shown by the provision that
freemen could petition the governor if courts were not called
as often as seemed necessary, and if he refused to order an
election the freemen could empower the constable to hold one.[4]
Under the Connecticut charter the date on which the deputies to the October court were chosen was the third Tuesday
in September, and for the May court the last Tuesday in
April.   The law also provided that on both days the election should begin at nine o'clock in the morning.[5]   Some
years later the Monday next following the first Tuesday in
April[6] became the legal date of the spring election.

In some of the proprietary colonies, where there were no
general courts of election, assemblymen were chosen on a

---

[1] 1 *New Haven Colonial Records*, 51, 58, 69, 114, 129.

[2] 16 Geo. II, Franklin ed., 1744, 255.   [3] 17 Geo. II, *Ibid.*, 287.

[4] 1 *Connecticut Colonial Records*, 21.

[5] 2 *Connecticut Colonial Records*, 131; 4 *idem*, 223; *Session Laws*, 30.

[6] 8 *Connecticut Colonial Records*, 297.

day fixed by law. East Jersey, for example, held elections on March 26th of each year,[1] and West Jersey on March 4th for commissioners,[2] and October 1st for deputies.[3] Writs were to be issued if necessary,[4] and in 1682 the date was changed to the fourteenth day of the second month.[5] Pennsylvania originally selected as the date of her elections the twentieth day of the twelfth month,[6] but later changed it to the tenth day of the first month.[7] The thirteenth day of the third month was the date for sheriff and coroner elections.[8] After 1705, October 1st was the day on which both representatives and county officers were elected.[9]

Locke's Constitution designated the first Tuesday in September of each alternate year as the day on which the freeholders of the precincts should elect representatives to the Carolina Parliament.[10] Writs were issued,[11] and the steward was required to give thirty days' notice in case the election was to be held at other than the customary place. North Carolina also selected the first Tuesday in September as the date for elections.[12] An early statute of New Hampshire, and one that was disallowed, because it was said to be copied from the laws of Massachusetts, required the constables of the towns

---

[1] Constitution of 1683, arts. i, ii, Leaming and Spicer, 153; 1 *New Jersey Archives*, 395.

[2] Concessions and Agreements, Art. iii; Leaming and Spicer, 385.

[3] *Ibid.*, Art. xxxii.   [4] Leaming and Spicer, 423.

[5] *Laws*, 1682, chap. 10; Leaming and Spicer, 455; later changes, *Ibid.*, 533.

[6] Frame of 1682, 1 *Pennsylvania Colonial Records*, 33.

[7] Act of Settlement of 1682, Colden, *History of the Five Nations*, 245.

[8] Frame of 1682, § 16, 1 *Pennsylvania Colonial Records* 42; Markham's Frame, 1696, 1 *Pennsylvania Colonial Records*, 49.

[9] 4 Anne, chap. 129, Franklin ed., 1742, 67.

[10] Art. 75, 1 Cooper, 43; 1 *North Carolina Colonial Records*, 199.

[11] 1 *North Carolina Colonial Records*, 181, 377, 696, *etc.*

[12] *Laws*, 1715, chap. 10; 2 *North Carolina Colonial Records*, 213.

to hold elections of representatives on the first Monday in February.[1]

In England the lord chancellor, lord keeper, or lords commissioners of the great seal issued writs for a parliamentary election. They were ordered to act "with as much expedition as the same may be done."[2] In the American colonies these officials did not exist, so that the power of issuing prerogative writs was usually vested in the governor as the legal representative of the crown. Thus in Massachusetts Bay a statute provided that writs should be signed by the governor and addressed to the sheriffs of the several counties.[3] This was also the rule in New Hampshire,[4] where we find that the secretary was allowed a fee of five shillings for every writ sent to a sheriff or marshal. The marshal was allowed a fee of ten shillings for his services.[5] In Virginia the secretary was allowed a hogshead of tobacco for each writ, and was liable to a fine for neglect to deliver the writ to the sheriff.[6] The governor of New York signed the writs;[7] but the earliest statute on the general subject of elections in the last named colony provided that the secretary or the clerk of the crown should issue the writs with as much expedition as possible, and deliver them under the seal to the sheriff of each county.[8]

In Maryland writs were issued in the name of the lord

---

[1] Act 1680, 1 *New Hampshire Provincial Papers*, 396; 1 Farmer, *New Hampshire Historical Collections*, 203.

[2] *Statute* 7 and 8 Will. III, chap. 25.

[3] *Laws*, 1692–3, chap. 38; 1 Ames and Goodell, 89.

[4] 1 Geo. II, chap. 107, Fowle ed., 1761, 142; ed., 1771, 166.

[5] 3 *New Hampshire Provincial Papers*, 213, 215.

[6] 14 Car. II, Act 83, 2 Hening, 105, 203.

[7] Gov. Dongan's Commission, 3 *New York Colonial Documents*, 331.

[8] 11 Will. III, chap. 74, Van Schaack's *Laws*, 28.

proprietor by his representatives,[1] while under the royal government from 1689 to 1715, this was done by the governor in the name of the crown.[2] In Virginia the method of calling an election was prescribed in detail. Writs must be signed by the governor or commander-in-chief of the dominion for the time being, and the seal of the colony affixed. They were then to be delivered to the secretary forty days before the date set for the meeting of the assembly. The secretary within ten days after receiving them must transmit them to the sheriffs in the counties.[3] Georgia required the governor to obtain the consent of his council before he issued the writs. They were then to be directed to the provost marshal, the official who had control of elections in this province.[4] Writs are also mentioned in New Jersey[5] and South Carolina, and in the latter colony they were issued[6] "by Governor and Council."[7]

The form to be used in writs for the election of assembly-men was sometimes prescribed by statute. Examples of these and also of the writs used for calling the first elections in several of the colonies are given in the first appendix to this work. It is said that the writs issued in 1680 by President Cutts, of New Hampshire, in calling the first assembly of that province, mentioned by name the persons who were to vote in each town.[8] This was also done in the early history of Maryland, where general writs were issued naming the freemen who were to vote in a particular district; and

---

[1] Act 1678, *Maryland Archives*, 1 *Assembly*, 60; 2 Charles Lord Baltimore, chap. 11 (1716), Bacon's *Laws*.

[2] 4 Will. and Mary, chap. 76; 4 Anne, chap. 42; 8 Geo. I, chap, 42.

[3] 4 Anne, chap. ii, 3 Hening, 236.   [4] Act June 9th, 1761.

[5] 12 Geo. I, chap. 40; Nevill's *Laws*, 142.

[6] Act 1704, no. 227, 2 Cooper, 249.   [7] Act 17 16, no. 365, 2 Cooper, 683.

[8] See 1 Belknap, *History of New Hampshire*, 177.

also special writs citing gentlemen mentioned by name to appear in person at the assembly.[1]

The period of time which must elapse between the signing or test of the writ and the day on which it was to be returned, was generally forty days.[2] In Virginia the sheriff was required to hold his court of election at least twenty days after receiving his writ,[3] while in Maryland the date was fixed at not less than ten days after making proclamation,[4] although an act of 1678 had provided that the election must take place within a reasonable time after the proclamation.[5] An English statute passed soon after the colonial period, required the election to begin between the tenth and sixteenth day after proclamation.[6]

The place at which an election was to be held was not usually described definitely in the laws. Thus, in New York it was provided that it should be " at the most public and usual place of election where the same has most usually

---

[1] See *Maryland Archives*, 1 *Proceedings and Acts of Assembly*, especially Act 1638–9, page 74.

[2] New York " between teste and return of summons " (11 Will. III, chap. 74, Van Schaack's *Laws*, 28); Maryland (2 Charles Lord Baltimore, chap. 11, Bacon's *Laws*); Virginia forty days " before the day of return" (14 Car. II, Act 83, 2 Hening, 105); South Carolina " before session" (Act 1716, no. 365, 2 Cooper, 683); Georgia (Act June 9th, 1761). This was also the English rule (*Statute* 7 and 8 Will. III, chap. 25). In Massachusetts, writs were issued thirty days (*Laws*, 1692–3, chap. 38; 1 Ames and Goodell, 89), and in New Hampshire, fifteen days in advance of the date fixed for the assembly (1 Geo. II, chap. 107, Fowle ed., 1761, 142; ed., 1771, 166. Ten days seem to have been proposed as the limit, 4 *Provincial Papers*, 114). Governor Dongan was instructed to send out his writs thirty days before the meeting of the first New York assembly (3 *New York Colonial Documents*, 331).

[3] 4 Anne, chap. 2, 3 Hening, 236.

[4] 2 Charles Lord Baltimore, chap. 11, Bacon's *Laws*.

[5] *Maryland Archives*, 3 *Assembly*, 60.

[6] *Statute* 25 Geo. III, chap. 84; see also 7 and 8 Will. III, chap. 25, § iii.

been."[1]   Sometimes, however, the precise place was indicated.[2]   In Orange county, New York, because of the difficulty in crossing the mountains which intersected it, two polling places were provided.   By the law of 1748 the sheriff was required to begin the election at one of the places designated, and then adjourn to the other for not more than six nor less than ten days.[3]

For special elections to fill vacancies, the general rule was that writs should be issued by the governor upon address of the assembly.[4]   A law enacted in Virginia in 1763 seems to give the sheriff power to hold a special election on his own motion.[5]   In Pennsylvania it was at first the law that the proprietor or his representative should send out writs for special elections.[6]   Finally, however, the secretary issued them upon order of the speaker.   If the order was not complied with in two days, the speaker could issue writs under his own hand and seal, but in the name of the governor. The sheriff was required to hold special elections within five days after receipt of the writ.[7]   In Maryland special elections

---

[1] 11 Will. III, chap. 74, Van Schaack's *Laws*, 28; compare English Statute, 7 and 8 Will. III, chap. 25, 3; New Jersey, "most public place" in county (12 Geo. I, chap. 40, Nevill's *Laws*, 142); Virginia, "in those places where county courts are held" (20 Car. I, Act i, 1 Hening, 299; 4 Anne, chap. ii, 3 Hening, 236).

[2] See for Westchester county, New York, "Presbyterian meeting house" (25 Geo. II, chap. 911; Van Schaack's *Laws*, 305, also 281); Philadelphia (6 Geo. III, chap. 8, § 12; Hall and Sellers ed., 1775, 323); North Carolina (*Laws*, 1715, 2 *North Carolina Colonial Records*, 213; 8 Geo. II, chap. ii, Appendix B of this work.)

[3] 21 Geo. II, chap. 875, Van Schaack's *Laws*, 281.

[4] South Carolina, Act 1716, no. 365, § xviii, 2 Cooper, 683); Georgia (Act June 1761); *Semble*, Virginia (11 Will. III, chap. ii, 3 Hening, 172).

[5] 3 Geo. III, chap. 1, § 17, 7 Hening, 519.

[6] *Laws*, 1700, chap. 28, incorporated by reference in Penn's Charter of Privileges, and published in Appendix B of the present work.   Also Frame of Government, 1696.

[7] 4 Anne, chap. 129, Franklin ed., 1742, 67.

were called by writs issued by the speaker, without regard to the time between the test and the return, provided the ordinary notice was given in counties and a notice of four days in cities and boroughs.[1] In New Jersey under Carteret's rule, the governor was empowered, in 1664 to issue writs for special elections to fill vacancies caused by the death of members.[2] Under the royal government of the last named province, a law was passed declaring that any member by accepting an office of profit from the crown or the governor vacated his seat, and a new writ issued just as if he were actually dead. In such a case, however, he could be rechosen.[3] This is an English custom in existence at the present day.

In regard to the calling of special elections the English practice was as follows: In case a seat in the House of Commons became vacant during a recess of Parliament, the speaker issued a warrant to the clerk of the crown and the latter sent out a writ.[4] If a vacancy occurred during a session of Parliament, an address of the House to the king was necessary.

§ 2. *Publication of the Writ.* In order to give the voters due notice of the time and place of an election, various methods of publishing the writs were employed. Thus the Hartford Constitution of 1638 provided that immediately on receipt of his warrant for the election of deputies, the constable of each town should go from house to house and give distinct notice, or else should publish his writ in some assembly.[5] No summons was needed for the general court of election at Hartford.[6] In Massachusetts under the royal

---

[1] 3 Charles Lord Baltimore, chap, i, § 2, Bacon's *Laws.*

[2] Leaming and Spicer, 19.

[3] 3 Geo. II, chap. 2, Allinson's *Laws,* 83; Nevill's *Laws,* 195.

[4] See *Statute* 10 Geo. III, chap. 41.

[5] 1 *Connecticut Colonial Records,* 21.   [6] *Session Laws,* 30.

government the sheriffs sent out precepts to the selectmen of the towns in their counties, commanding them to assemble the voters and proceed to the election of representatives.[1]

The method to be followed in New York was prescribed more in detail. Each sheriff endorsed upon the writ the day of its receipt. Within six days thereafter he was required to give public notice of the time and place of the election. He also gave six days' notice to each constable in his bailiwick, and the latter was required to publish his precept at the most frequented place of each town.[2] This method of publishing a writ by means of precepts addressed by the election officer to the local officials of his district, also prevailed in England.[3] Notice was given in New Jersey at least twenty days before the election, by the sheriff of each county posting advertisements at three of the best known places in his bailiwick;[4] while in Georgia a notice of ten days must be given by affixing proclamations in one or more "noted" places in each parish, district, town or village returning a member.[5]

For special elections in Pennsylvania and Delaware, an effective method of publication was provided, in order, we may suppose, to compensate for the short notice of two days that was permitted. The writ was to be read by the sheriff or his deputy in the capital town, or in the most public place in his bailiwick, between the hours of ten in the morning and two in the afternoon. Immediately upon receipt of the writ, notices were posted upon some tree or house in the way leading from each township or precinct to the place of election, and upon every court house and "fixed meeting

[1] *Laws*, 1692–3, chap. 36, 1 Ames and Goodell, 80; 1692–3, chap. 38, *ibid*, 89.

[2] 11 Will. III, chap. 74, Van Schaack's *Laws*.

[3] *Statute* 7 and 8 Will. III, chap. 25.

[4] 12 Geo. II, chap. 40, Nevill's *Laws*, 142.

[5] Act June 9th, 1761, which is published in Appendix B of the present work.

house for Religious worship " in the county. Every constable was to receive due notice and was required to promulgate the same immediately.[1]

In Virginia the original custom was for the sheriff to give six days' notice of an election by going about from house to house within ten days after he received his writ.[2] Strange as it may seem, the method of summons was found to be defective, and in 1662 a more thorough system was provided. Within three days after receiving his writ, each sheriff delivered a copy of the same, endorsed with the time and the place of the election, to the minister or the reader of every parish in his county. According to the provisions of the law, the writ was then read to the people in every church and chapel after divine service, and the reading was repeated weekly until the time appointed for the election. The ministers must return their copies to the sheriff with an attestation that they had performed the duty required. Heavy fines were imposed for neglect.[3] In Maryland election proclamations were read and posted in all churches, chapels, and other public places,[4] while in North Carolina they were made on three successive Sundays immediately after divine service.[5] Publication was effected in South Carolina by the managers posting a notice in writing on the door of a church, or if there was no church, at some public place, three Sundays before an election.[6] This method of giving notice is instructive as showing that the Southern colonists seldom came together except on Sunday, and then for religious purposes.

[1] *Laws* 1700, chap. 28, published in Appendix B of this work; 4 Anne, chap. 129, Franklin ed., 1742, 67.

[2] 20 Car. I, Act. i; 5–6 Com., Act vii; 1 Hening, 299, 411.

[3] 14 Car. II., Act 50, 2 Hening, 82; 4 Anne, chap. ii, 3 Hening, 236.

[4] 8 Geo. I, chap. 42; 2 Charles Lord Baltimore, chap. 11, Bacon's *Laws.*

[5] 33 Geo. II, chap. i, § vi, Davis ed., 1773, 247.

[6] Act 1716, no. 365, § xv, 2 Cooper, 683.

When a writ was issued for a special election in Virginia, it became the duty of the sheriff to send a notice of the time and place to every freeholder in his county, and the election must be held as soon as possible after the receipt of the writ.[1]

§ 3. *Hours of Election.* In England, a statute of 23 Henry VI[2] had provided that county courts for the election of knights of the shire must be held " betwixt the hour of 8 and the hour of 11 before noon." This practice of requiring an election to be held within certain hours of the day prevailed to some extent in this country. Thus in Connecticut I find that the semi-annual elections of deputies in the towns were held at nine o'clock.[3] In Massachusetts, however, certain hours were fixed for the nomination of assistants; and in 1680 a law was enacted requiring the courts of election to begin at eight in the morning.[4] No enactments except those of Massachusetts have been found which tend to prove that it was customary in New England to begin the sessions of the general courts of election at any particular hour of the day. In West Jersey, we find that elections were to begin at nine o'clock,[5] and in New Jersey at any time between the hours of ten and twelve.[6]

In Pennsylvania and Delaware,[7] the hours of ten in the morning and two in the afternoon were made the limits of time within which an election must be held. In North Carolina it was customary to have a morning session, beginning before ten o'clock and lasting until one, and then in the afternoon the polls were open from half past two until

---

[1] 11 Will. III, chap. 2; 4 Anne, chap. 2, § viii, 3 Hening, 172, 236.

[2] Chap. 14.

[3] *Session Laws*, 30.

[4] 5 *Massachusetts Colonial Records*, 292.

[5] Leaming and Spicer, 385.

[6] 12 Geo. I, chap. 40; Nevill's *Laws*, 142.

[7] 4 Anne, chap. 129, Franklin ed., 1742, 67.   7 Geo. II, chap. 61a, Franklin and Hall ed., 1752, 118; Adams ed., 1797, 147.

sunset, unless the candidates consented to have them closed before that time.[1]

For a time two sessions of the court of election were held in South Carolina, namely: from eight to twelve in the morning and from two until six in the afternoon, for two consecutive days.[2] After 1716 there was but one session, and the polls were, according to successive enactments, to remain open from sunrise till sunset,[3] from seven a. m. till seven p. m.,[4] and, finally, from nine till four.[5] In Georgia the hours were from nine in the morning until six in the afternoon, although the poll might be concluded two hours after the last voter appeared, or at any other time if the candidates present consented.[6] In the last named province, adjournments were permitted at convenient hours, and, unless a scrutiny were demanded, elections were not to continue for more than ten days.

§ 4. *Election Officers.* In considering the topic of election officers, it may be laid down as the general rule that, outside of New England, the sheriff, by virtue of his capacity as head of the county, acted as the presiding and returning officer at all elections.[7] The provost marshal was the manager of elections in Georgia,[8] and for a while in North Carolina.[9] In South Carolina the size of the counties was so great that electors were forced to travel long distances in order to vote.

---

[1] 17 Geo. II, chap. i, Davis and Swann, 177; 33 Geo. II, chap. i, Davis ed., 1773, 247. This last act seems to require the polls to be kept open until sunset.

[2] Act 1704, no. 227, 2 Cooper, 249.   [3] Act 1716, no. 365, 2 Cooper, 683.

[4] Act 1719, no. 394, 3 Cooper, 50.   [5] Act 1721, no. 446, 3 Cooper, 135.

[6] Act June 9th, 1761.

New York: 11 Will. III, chap. 74, Van Schaack's *Laws*, 28; New Jersey: 12 Geo. I, chap. 40, Nevill's *Laws*, 142; Maryland: *Maryland Archives*, 3 Assembly, 60; Virginia: 14 Car. I, Act xix, 1 Hening, 227, *etc;* North Carolina: 17 Geo. II, chap. i, Davis and Swann ed., 1752, 177; South Carolina: Act 1704, no. 227, 2 Cooper, 249.

[8] Act June 9th, 1761.   [9] 2 *North Carolina Colonial Records*, 213.

Accordingly the parish was constituted the election district, and the whole management was placed in the hands of the church-wardens, although the governor could appoint substitutes for them. Surveyors were ordered to settle disputes, by laying out the boundaries of the parishes. The repeal of this law by the proprietors caused the revolution of 1719, and it was natural that it should be revived by the royal assembly of 1720.[1] We find in those New York manors, which were represented in the assembly, that a returning officer was vested with the powers of a sheriff in the matter of elections,[2] while in Maryland like powers were exercised by the mayor, recorder and aldermen of cities and boroughs.[3] In the latter province, elections were held in full county court,[4] and " in such manner and form as the laws of England and this province doe direct and provide." For this purpose the sheriff was empowered to summon four or more commissioners of his county, who, with the clerk, were to be members of the court.[5] Some years later the court consisted of three or more justices of the peace, "whereof one to be of the quorum," together with the clerk of the county court.[6] In Pennsylvania, Delaware and North Carolina if the sheriff was unable to attend, the coroner was authorized to act as manager of elections.[7] In Pennsylvania the sheriff and his deputy or the coroner and his appointee, and in case of the failure of all these, two freeholders elected by the majority

---

[1] Act 1716, no. 365, 2 Cooper, 683; Act 1719, no. 394, 3 Cooper, 50.

[2] 8 Geo. II, chap. 607, Van Schaack's *Laws*, 183.   [3] 8 Geo. I, chap. 42.

[4] " Electionem tuam in pleno comitatu tuo factam," as required by English statute of 7 Henry IV, chap. 15.

[5] Act 1678, *Maryland Archives*, 3 *Assembly*, 60.

[6] 8 Geo. I, chap. 42, 2 Charles Lord Baltimore, chap. 11, Bacon's *Laws*.

[7] Pennsylvania: 4 Anne, chap. 129, Franklin ed., 1742, 67; Delaware: 7 Geo. II, chap. 61a, Franklin and Hall ed., 1752, 118; Adams ed., 1797, 147; North Carolina: 12 Geo. III, Davis ed., 1773, 505.

of the electors present, were constituted judges of the election.[1]

Besides the judges already mentioned, Pennsylvania and Delaware provided officers known as inspectors, whose chief duty was to judge of the qualifications of voters. At first these inspectors were nominated by a majority of the electors,[2] and their names were successively proposed by the judges at the place of election until a certain number[3] had been chosen by a fair majority of votes. The inspectors were put under oath and were required to duly attend the election throughout its continuance. Besides judging the qualifications of electors it was their duty " to well and truly and faithfully assist the sheriff, coroner and other person who shall by virtue of the before recited act, officiate as judge of the said Elections; to prevent all Frauds and Deceits whatsoever of Electors or others in the management or carrying on of the same, and in causing the poll or votes at such elections to be taken and cast up according to law."[4] In order to insure a satisfactory performance of their duties, it was necessary that the inspectors should be thoroughly acquainted with the circumstances of all the voters, and for this reason the statutes required that care should be taken to secure inspectors from different parts of the county.

But as a matter of fact this was not done, and in 1739 it was found necessary to so change the method of selecting these officers so that the desired result might be attained.

----

[1] 4 Anne, chap. 129, Franklin ed., 1742, 67; Delaware; 7 Geo. II, chap. 61a, Franklin and Hall ed., 1752, 118; Adams ed., 1797, 147. In Delaware, the justices of the peace seem to have been judges in case of the failure of the coroner or sheriff to act; 12 Geo. III, chap. 207, Adams ed., 1797, 500.

[2] 4 Anne, chap. 129, Franklin ed., 1742, 67.

[3] Eight for Philadelphia, six for Philadelphia county, and four for each of the other two counties.

[4] 13 Geo. I, chap. 284, Franklin ed., 1742, 346.

For this purpose each justice of the peace was required to divide his county into eight parts or hundreds, as nearly equal in size as was possible. On receiving official notice of the division, it became the duty of the sheriff to inform the constable of each town. The freeholders met in their towns on September 25th of each year, at a place appointed by the constable, or in case of his failure to act, by the overseer of the poor, and proceeded to ballot for inspectors to serve at the regular election which took place on the 1st of October. At these elections, which were held between the hours of nine in the morning and two in the afternoon,[1] the constables and freeholders acted as judges. One "able and discreet freeholder, who may be supposed to be best acquainted with the Estates and Circumstances of the Inhabitants," was chosen from each township to act as inspector. The names of all so chosen were to be returned to the sheriff of the county before nine o'clock on the day of the regular election.[2] Upon receiving the reports of the the several constables, the sheriff was required to call in four freeholders, and in their presence write the names of all the nominees on " papers cut and folded, &c., as near as may be of equal size and bigness." Those returned from each district of the county were placed in a separate box, and then, "some indifferent person" drew a name from each receptacle. The persons whose names were drawn, if they were present at the election, served as inspectors and were proclaimed as such to the assembled voters. In Philadelphia a similar course was pursued by the inhabitants of each ward. The names of four

---

[1] Nine and three: 16 Geo. II, chap. 351, Franklin ed., 1742, 546. A later act fixed September 27th as the day, and from twelve till five as the hours in the counties, and from ten till four in Philadelphia. 6 Geo. III, chap. 8, Hall and Sellers ed., 1775, 323.

[2] October 1st.

persons were drawn on the day of election, and they were
the inspectors for the districts, while the six persons whose
names remained in the boxes were the inspectors for Philadelphia.[1]

A similar system prevailed in Delaware,[2] where the inspectors were judges concurrently with the sheriff or coroner, as
the case might be, although in case of an equal division of
opinion the latter had a double vote.[3] As was originally the
rule in Pennsylvania, the Delaware inspectors were at first
chosen at the county elections. It was not until about 1766
that they were elected in the towns. The time appointed for
that purpose was the fifteenth of September, or the following
day, if the fifteenth fell on Sunday. The collector or the
overseer of the poor, assisted by two freeholders, acted as
judges of these town or hundred elections, which took place
between the hours of twelve o'clock noon and six o'clock in
the afternoon. Ten days' notice was given by putting up
advertisements throughout the hundreds. The collector, or
overseer, as the case might be, together with the judges,
issued certificates of election to the persons chosen, and
these were presented to the sheriff before ten o'clock in the
morning of the day appointed for the election of representatives. The sheriff publicly proclaimed the names of those
chosen for inspectors, and if any of them failed to appear,
their places were filled by the votes of the freeholders
attending the election from the hundred whose inspector was
absent.[4]

The personal knowledge of these inspectors does not ap-

---

[1] 12 Geo. II, chap. 345; 16 Geo. II, chap. 351, Franklin ed., 1742, 514, 546:
19 Geo. II, chap. 2; 6 Geo. III, chap. 8; 13 Geo. III, chap. 13, Hall and Sellers
ed., 1775, 202, 323.

[2] 6 Geo. III, chap. 188; Adams ed., 1797, 429.

[3] 12 Geo. III, chap. 207, § 1; Adams ed., 1797, 500.

[4] 6 Geo. III, chap. 188; Adams ed., 1797, 429.

pear to have been relied on as much as the language of the statutes would seem to indicate. They had power to examine voters on oath in regard to their qualifications, and were also assisted by separate alphabetical lists of the names and rates of all the taxables taken from the last assessment of each town, ward or district. These lists were to be furnished to the sheriff at least one day before the election by the commissioners of the county, at a compensation of half a crown for each list, but under penalty of fifty pounds for failure to deliver them.[1]

In some of the colonies inspectors were appointed in the interest of the candidates rather than in that of the government. Thus in New York, New Jersey and the Carolinas, each candidate was empowered to nominate and the sheriff to appoint as many inspectors as there were clerks to take the poll.[2] Such was also the custom in England.[3]

When a poll was required the sheriff was usually authorized to employ clerks appointed and sworn by himself. It was usually left to the discretion of the sheriff to designate the number of clerks, although in New Jersey[4] the candidates seem to have had power to appoint them; while at one time in Pennsylvania[5] the inspectors decided on the number. A later statute[6] in the last named province required the sheriff to appoint two or more clerks of the age of twenty-one

---

[1] 6 Geo. III, chap. 8, § 8, Hall and Sellers ed., 1775, 223.

[2] New York: 11 Will. III., chap. 74, § 5, Van Schaack's *Laws*, 28; New Jersey: 12 Geo. I, chap. 40, Nevill's *Laws*, 142; North Carolina: Act 1715, 2 *North Carolina Colonial Records*, 213; 17 Geo. II, chap. 1, Davis and Swann, 177; 33 Geo. II, chap. 1, Davis ed., 1773, 247. This last act seems to allow but two inspectors, who were to be appointed by the candidates collectively, or on their refusal to do so, by the sheriff.

[3] 7 and 8 Will. III, chap. 25.   [4] 12 Geo. I, chap. 40, Nevill's *Laws*, 142.

[5] 4 Anne, chap. 129, Franklin ed., 1742, 67.

[6] 6 Geo. III, chap. 8, §§ 1, 3, Hall and Sellers ed., 1775, 323.

years.[1] That the candidates themselves also had a certain amount of official capacity at elections is shown by the fact that their consent was sometimes necessary in order to close or adjourn the poll.[2]

For the election of deputies and the collecting of proxies in New England, the town was the unit; and this was possibly due to the lack, at an early date, of an efficient county organization. The duties of an election officer were therefore performed by the constable of each town.[3] In Rhode Island the chief officer of the town[4] was perhaps the town clerk,[5] but at a later date the whole management of elections in Rhode Island was placed in the hands of a grand committee of both houses of the legislature.[6] Under the royal government of Massachusetts Bay writs were issued to the sheriffs of the counties, but the direct management of elections was in the hands of the constables and selectmen of the several towns.[7]

§ 5. *Nomination of Candidates.* In a few of the colonies we find that a more or less thorough system of nominating candidates for offices of a general character prevailed. There was nothing resembling the modern method of nomination by opposing parties, but the plan followed seems to have been practically a preliminary election for the purpose

---

[1] See also New York, 11 Will. III, chap. 74, § 5, Van Schaack's *Laws*, 28. (In this and other respects this law was modelled on the English statute of 7 and 8 Will. III, chap. 25.) Virginia, 11 Will. III, chap. 2, 3 Hening, 172.

[2] New York, 11 Will. III, chap. 74, § 7, Van Schaack's *Laws*, 28; Georgia, Act June 9th, 1761.

[3] Massachusetts, see Title *Election*, *Laws*, ed., 1660, 27, ed., 1814, 105; Connecticut, 1 *Connecticut Colonial Records*, 21, *Session Laws*, 30.

[4] 1 *Rhode Island Colonial Records*, 150.

[5] 4 *Rhode Island Colonial Records*, 208; Franklin ed., 1730, 1.

[6] Hall's *Code*, 1767, Title *Elections*, 78.

[7] *Laws*, 1692-3, chaps. 36, 38, 1 Ames and Goodell, 80, 88, 89.

of reducing the whole number of eligible candidates by a process of exclusion.

The first definite trace of such a system appears in the Hartford Constitution of 1638, in which it was provided that no person could be newly chosen magistrate unless his name had been proposed at the general court in September and voted upon at the regular court of elections in April. For these purposes each of the towns, through its deputies, nominated two persons, while the court added as many as it judged requisite.[1] Something similar appears to have been done in New Haven, for there is a provision in the statute book which was prepared about 1648, to the effect that " when any man of what Plantation soever, shall be first proposed for Magistracy within this jurisdiction, reasonable notice shall be first given to all the Plantations of such a purpose or desire, that all the Freemen may duly consider or informe themselves."[2] This law was amended by an act of 1662, providing that in case no nominations were made in time from the towns, "as an addition to those now in trust," the freemen present at the election could nominate and choose the magistrates.[3] The records of the New Haven jurisdiction prior to 1653 are lost, and this accounts for the fact that no further mention of the law as given in the statute book, has been found. The act of 1662 is declared to be " an addition to ye printed law for ye nomination of magistrates."

Under the Connecticut charter the Hartford practice appears to have been continued, and we find that candidates were nominated " by papers" at the October court, in order to be voted upon at the court of election in May."[4] In 1689

---

[1] 1 *Connecticut Colonial Records*, 21.

[2] 2 *New Haven Colonial Records*, iv; *Laws*, ed., 1656, *ibid.*, 567, 8.

[3] *Ibid.*, 439, 479.   [4] 2 *Connecticut Colonial Records*, 141.

a different method was introduced, which was practically a double election in that the freemen both selected the nominees and voted for the persons nominated when these were finally put up for election. At nine o'clock in the morning of the third Tuesday in March of each year, the freemen gathered at the meeting houses of their respective towns. Each voter there gave the .names of twenty persons whom he judged qualified to stand for election in the following May to the local commissioner, justice of the peace, constable or some townsman, whose duty it was to seal them in a package and deliver them to the constable of the county town. The latter was required to take the ballots himself or else send them to Hartford by a person appointed for that purpose by the constables of the county. The messengers from all parts of the colony met in the chamber of the general court on the last Tuesday in March, and were sworn as canvassers by an assistant or by the secretary of the colony. The ballots were then compared and the names of the twenty persons who had the most votes were returned to the towns as the nominees from whom the governor, deputy governor and assistants were to be chosen.[1]

Three years afterwards the old method was restored and the nominations were made by the general court.[2] In 1696 we find twenty-four persons were nominated as assistants.[3] In 1697 a law was passed requiring the constable, without awaiting special orders, to call the freemen together on the third Tuesday in September, and after electing deputies, have them hand in the names of twenty persons " fairly written upon a piece of paper." Instead of a separate canvass by representatives of the counties as in 1689, it was provided that the names of the persons voted for, and the number of votes received by each, should be entered by the election

---

[1] 4 *Connecticut Colonial Records,* 11.   [2] *Ibid,* 81.   [3] *Ibid.,* 175.

officer " upon office oath," and a copy of such entry sent
sealed, to the general court at its October meeting, by means
of the representative of the town. There the votes were
canvassed and the twenty persons having the highest
number were declared to be nominated. Their names were
sent to the towns by the secretary of the colony, together
with the laws passed by the general court, although afterwards
he was ordered to have the list of names, as well as the laws,
prepared by the public printer for distribution.[1]   Until after
1707 the governor and deputy governor as well as the magistrates could be chosen only from the persons nominated.[2]
It will be seen that under this system electors had at least
six months within which to decide for what candidates they
should vote.

Massachusetts was the only other colony which developed
a successful method of nominations, and it was there
applied only to candidates for the office of assistant. As
early as 1631 we find a faint suggestion of nominations in
the order of the general court that the commons should propose persons whom they desired to have chosen as assistants, and "if it be doubtfull weth^r it be the great^r pte of
the comons or not, it shalbe putt to the poll."[3]   In May,
1640, a method was introduced similar to that provided by
the Hartford Constitution two years before. The towns were
requested, when electing deputies, to give in the names of
those whom they wished to have chosen as magistrates, and
the deputies were required to " set downe the names of such
as shalbee nominated & the certaine number of votes which
every man so named shall have & shall make a true returne
of the same at the next General Court." The magistrates

---

[1] 4 *Connecticut Colonial Records*, 223; *Session Laws*, ed. 1715, 30; ed. 1750,
ed. 1754, ed. 1764, 45.

[2] 5 *Connecticut Colonial Records*, 39; *Session Laws*, 1715, 133.

[3] 1 *Massachusetts Colonial Records*, 87.

and the deputies canvassed the votes and returned to the towns the names of those who had received the largest number. Only persons so nominated could be voted for at the court of election.[1]

Four years after this a system very much like the modern State convention was introduced. Delegates from each of the towns of the colony met at Salem in April and agreed upon a certain number of the " most able and fit men," whose names were certified to the·colonial secretary as the persons to stand for election as assistants.[2]

In 1649 another method was devised which, with a few modifications, remained in use until the surrender of the charter, and which, as we have seen, was used in Connecticut from 1689 till 1692. The freemen of the various towns were called together by the constables during the last week of the ninth month (November) in order to give their votes on separate pieces of paper for the twenty persons whom they wished to have nominated. But one vote could be cast for each candidate by any one person. After the voting was over, the ballots were carried to the shire town by a person selected by the freemen. On the " last fourth day of the week in the first month (March)," at twelve o'clock, the deputies from the several towns met and appointed one of their number to carry the votes of the entire shire to Boston " on the second third day of the second month (April)." These commissioners from the several shires, together with the magistrates, " opened and perused" the ballots. The twenty persons having the most votes were then declared the nominees, and their names were certified in writing by the commissioners to the several constables, and by them to the freemen.[3]

[1] 1 *Massachusetts Colonial Records,* 293.   [2] 2 *Massachusetts Colonial Records,* 21.

[3] 3 *Massachusetts Colonial Records,* 177; 4 *Massachusetts Colonial Records,* pt. i, 326.

The needless precaution of having the nominations in the towns take place in November and lie over till the following March, was done away with in 1652 by an order of the court which fixed as the date of town meetings the second week of the first month (March).[1] Six years later another order required that but fourteen persons should be nominated, on account of "some inconveniences in the annual choice due to the large number of twenty."[2]

The final form of the nomination system was that the town meetings should be held on the second Tuesday in March due notice and warning having been given to the freemen. Each elector could vote for twenty persons whose names might be "on one list clearly distinguished," and "in distinct papers," while no person could be voted for twice, except under a penalty of ten pounds for each offense. There were to be two commissioners instead of one for each shire, and they were to serve under oath. At the canvass all lists containing more than twenty names, or with the name of the same person occurring more than once, were to be rejected, and the twenty-six persons receiving the most votes were to be nominees.[3]

In the elaborate series of fundamental constitutions drawn up in 1683 for East Jersey, there was a provision for the nomination of candidates by a method that combined in a singular manner the Greek notion of election by means of the lot and the more modern idea of election by the free choice of the voters. The third clause of this constitution provided that, "for the full prevention of all indirect means" the names of those persons in each county that were eligible to the great council should be placed on pieces of parchment,

---

[1] 3 *Massachusetts Colonial Records*, 280, *Laws*, chap. xl, § 3, ed., 1660, 27; ed., 1814, 105.

[2] 4 *Massachusetts Colonial Records*, pt. i, 347.

[3] 1680, 5 *Massachusetts Colonial Records*, 292.

prepared the day before the election by the sheriff and his clerk. On the day appointed, these pieces of parchment were put into a box and a boy under ten years of age drew out fifty of them. The fifty so drawn were then put back in the box and twenty-five of them drawn out. The twenty-five tickets remaining in the box contained the names of the nominators. In case the county in question was entitled to three members on the council board, the nominators were, by a plurality of votes, to select twelve persons from the twenty-five whose names had been drawn, and these were to be the candidates to be voted for at the next election. If the county were entitled to but two members, only eight persons were to be selected. Before proceeding to their task, the twenty-five nominators were to solemnly declare before the sheriff that they would not name any one "known to them to be guilty for the time, or to have been guilty for a year before, of adultery, whoredom, drunkenness, or any such immorality, or who is insolvent or a fool."[1] The East Jersey method of nomination was probably derived from the "lot and suffrage" system proposed in Harrington's *Oceana.* The English philosopher used the lot to determine who should propose the competitors, and the suffrage to decide which of them should be elected.[2]

With these exceptions the writer has found no trace of anything like a system of regular nominations. In the laws of those colonies where the English method of elections was closely followed, the word *candidate* is frequently used. In Georgia the act of 1761 speaks of a "person presented or presenting himself as a candidate," and from this language it might be inferred that a method of nomination by petition may have been in vogue. The same quotation also shows

[1] Fundamental Constitutions, iii, Leaming and Spicer, 153; 1 *New Jersey Archives*, 397.

[2] *Oceana*, 80, 106, Harrington's works, ed. Toland, 1771.

that a person could nominate himself. There is no positive authorization of a hustings platform on which the candidates sat and from which they addressed the assembled voters, after having been nominated by one elector and seconded by another, as was the custom in England.[1]

§ 6. *Manner of Voting.* (*Personal or by Proxy.*) The five older New England governments which have been classed in the present work under the general title of the Puritan colonies, developed a method of voting which they called the proxy system. Unlike the method of nomination and the means employed in the election of the assistants, which were peculiar to one or two of these colonies, the proxy system was common to them all, and is found only in this group. Though it originated in Massachusetts it spread rapidly and was developed on the same general lines in the other New England jurisdictions. Still, as each colony followed its own peculiar methods in regard to the details of the process, it will be necessary to study the history of all five with reference to this subject.

In the preceding pages it has been mentioned that at first all freemen were required to attend in person at the general courts, whether they were held for legislative purposes or for the election of magistrates. It has also been shown that it became necessary in the course of time to permit the freemen to be represented by deputy on all matters except the annual election of officers, which was regarded as a privilege too precious to be delegated.[2] As the settlements increased in number and the colonies in extent of territory, it became more and more necessary to devise some plan, in order to save the freemen the inconvenience and trouble required by a journey to the capital town, and at the same time permit

[1] See 2 De Franqueville, *Le Gouvernment et le Parlement Brittanique*, 417. The modern method of nomination by petition is described in 423 *et seq.*

[2] See pp. 4, 5, 10, 14, 15, *ante.*

them to retain their right to vote at the general court of election. It was for these purposes that the proxy system was devised, and by this means the identical ballots of the freemen were still cast at the general court. Because it was desired to preserve the character of the general court of elections in Massachusetts as the one and only place where votes could be legally cast for the officers of the colony, the simpler method of counting the votes cast in the towns, and merely reporting the totals to the general court, was never introduced, although we have seen that such a plan was used in Connecticut for the nomination of magistrates.[1] Freemen were still allowed, and even encouraged, to cast their votes in person, although, as may be imagined, the increasing number of voters caused such a proceeding to become very disorderly and inconvenient. The natural result, therefore, was to abolish the practice of personal voting, and cause all ballots to be handed in at the " proxings," which took place in the towns. Massachusetts in 1641, and again in 1663, made an unsuccessful move in this direction.[2] Had not her charter been taken away, she would doubtless ultimately have prohibited freemen from voting at the general court of election except by proxy. This result Connecticut reached in 1750,[3] and Rhode Island not till 1760.[4]

Although, as we shall see in due course, the absence of a provision requiring a voter to sign his name to his proxy in one or two colonies brought about a secret ballot, yet the writer believes that this result was only incidental. Secrecy was the end especially desired and attained by the corn and beans ballot of Massachusetts and the balls and boxes of West Jersey. That the proxy system was really a subter-

---

[1] See pp. 122, 123, *ante.*

[2] 1 *Massachusetts Colonial Records*, 333; 4 *Massachusetts Colonial Records*, pt. ii, 86.

[3] *Session Laws*, 1750.   [4] 6 *Rhode Island Colonial Records*, 256.

fuge and was not strictly legal is shown by a report of Lord Bellmont on the condition of Rhode Island in the early part of the eighteenth century. He complained of the proxy as a violation of the charter, which he construed to mean an election of all freemen present in the assembly,[1] a point on which the colonists themselves were not free from doubt.[2] The exercise of a public franchise by proxy was illegal at common law.

In the following pages, the history of the proxy system will be followed out wherever it existed, commencing with Massachusetts, where it was first introduced, and concluding with Connecticut, where it reached its final development.

Among the records of the general court of the Boston colony, as early as 1635–6, we find an order that certain towns should have "libertie to stay soe many of their free-men att home for the safety of their towne as they judge needful, & that the said ffreemen that are appoyncted by the towne to stay att home shall have liberty for this court to send their voices by pxy."[3] This law, which affected only a few towns, was made general the following year, when, on account of the "great danger and damage that may accrue to the State by all the freemens leaveing their plantations to come to the place of elections," it was ordered:

"That it shalbe free & lawfull for all freemen to send their votes for elections by proxie the next Generall court in May, and so for hereafter, wᶜʰ shall be done in this manner: The deputies wᶜʰ shalbee chosen shall cause the freemen of their townes to be assembled & then to take such freemens votes as please to send by pxie for every magistrate & seale them ꝟp, severally subscribing the magistrates name on the backside & soe to bring them to the court

---

[1] 3 *Rhode Island Colonial Records*, 385 *et seq.*
[2] 2 *Rhode Island Colonial Records*, 29, 39, 62.
[3] 1 *Massachusetts Colonial Records*, 166.

sealed, wth an open roule of the names of the freemen that so send by pxie."[1]

The method thus prescribed was followed in general terms by all the Puritan colonies, although, as we shall see, further elaborations were made in regard to details.

"It being found by experience that the court of elections had neede to be brought into some better order, the freemen growing to so great a multitude as will be overburdensome to the country & the day appointed for that service will not afford sufficient time for the same, and the way of p'xies (as it is called) is found subject to many miscarriages and lorse of opportunities for advice in the choyse :"— for these reasons a substitute for the proxy system was proposed in 1641. The freemen of each town which sent a deputy regularly to the general court were to hold a meeting upon the day of election, and choose one delegate for every ten of their voters. Each of these delegates was to go to Boston with power to vote on behalf of those joining in his election, and "in this way to bee at liberty whether they will joyne altogether or vote severally, so as every one that hath ten votes shall be an elector, and ma^trats and elder^s to put in their votes as other free-men."[2] This plan did not meet with the approval of the towns, and the former method was continued.[3] Some years later the means to be employed in collecting the proxies at the towns received further elaboration. The freemen were to deliver them in the presence of the deputy and constable, and these officers sealed them up "in distinct papers." In small villages that were not represented at the general court the constable and two or three of the leading freemen were empowered to collect the proxies and deliver them, sealed up, to the deputy of the nearest town, whose duty it was to

[1] March, 1636–7, 1 *Massachusetts Colonial Records*, 188.   [2] *Ibid.*, 333.
[3] See also 2 Winthrop's *New England*, 311.

carry them to the court of election. In addition, it was provided that only those made free at the court of election should deliver their votes "at the dóres."[1]

Another attempt was made in 1663 to put an end to the proxy system. The constable was ordered to call the freemen together in their town meetings as before, but no one could hand in the proxy of another freeman unless the latter were present or sent his proxy "sealed up in a note directed to the Deputy or Townsmen met together for that work." This shows in effect that a system of sub-proxy existed. By means of this it was possible for the elector to vote, although he might be absent from the town meeting, as well as from the general court. According to the law at present under consideration, no one who was not a member of the general court would be allowed to vote in person at the general court of election. This provision, however, was found unsatisfactory, and it was repealed within a year after its adoption.[2]

Again in 1679–80 a law was passed with a view of saving confusion on election day. The proxies were to be collected in the towns on the second Tuesday in April. The ballots cast for each officer were separate and distinct, except that the names of the twenty assistants were to be put on a single sheet of paper "cut almost asunder betwixt each name." The latter would seem to indicate a crude form of the modern perforated ballot. All proxies were to be taken to Boston on the Monday before the general election, and at one o'clock in the afternoon of that day they were opened

---

[1] 2 *Massachusetts Colonial Records*, 220; *Laws*, ed. 1660, 27; ed. 1814, 106. In this as in many other instances the language of the records differs from that employed in the statute books. It is frequently a difficult matter to find the authority among the records for the year in which the foot-notes of the statute books declare that a particular law was enacted. Many of the statements in regard to Massachusetts during the course of the present work are the result of a combination of the matter derived from the several sources quoted.

[2] 4 *Massachusetts Colonial Records*, pt. ii, 86, 134.

and sorted in the presence of all the officers of the colony by tellers who were under oath.   When the canvass had been completed the proxies cast for each person were sealed up in separate packages, endorsed "on the backside" with the name of the candidate and the number of proxies cast for him.   Freemen who so desired could still vote in person at the regular court of election held the following Wednesday.[1]

The system prescribed by this law does not appear to have been successful, although it would seem that it made personal attendance still possible, and at the same time greatly simplified the procedure at the court of election.   In October, 1680, a law was passed requiring that town meetings should be held on the Wednesday before election, and reviving in substance the system originally introduced by the general orders of 1636–7 and 1647.[2]   We may accordingly conclude that in spite of all its disadvantages,[3] Massachusetts, after trying a number of plans, came to the conclusion that rather than debar the freemen from their privilege of voting in person it was better to keep up the unwieldy proxy system and endure the confusion that resulted on the election day.

The first appearance of the proxy system in the Plymouth colony was in 1647, when it was provided that "for the avoiding of travel and charge, the freemen of the towne of Rehoboth" should be permitted to send their votes by proxy, provided these were given in at a town meeting and immediately sealed up.   They were to be carried to the court of election by the committees or by the grand jurymen. Still " Rehoboth's Liberty" was not absolute, for on " weighty occasions" the personal attendance of the freemen might be required by special warrant.[4]

[1] 5 *Massachusetts Colonial Records*, 262.   [2] *Ibid.*, 292.

[3] "Fraud and Deceit;" May 1673, 4 *Massachusetts Colonial Records*, pt. ii, 553.

[4] 2 *Plymouth Colony Records*, 118; Brigham, 89.

It was not, however, until 1652 that the proxy system was extended throughout the colony. It was done at that time because " in regard of age, disabillitie of body, vrgent occasions and other inconveniences that doe accrew, sundrey of the freemen" were hindered from putting in a personal appearance. The method to be followed was similar to that first introduced in Massachusetts, except that the proxies were collected at the town meeting in which the deputies were chosen rather than on a special occasion, as was the custom in Massachusetts. The deputies were required to take a list of those who had not given their proxies, as well as of those who had.[1] All the votes for each officer (that is, for governor, assistant, *etc.*), were sealed up in separate packages at the town meetings. Just before Plymouth was annexed to Massachusetts Bay, associates or county magistrates were elected by the freemen of each county. The election took place at the county town. The proxy system was used and votes were collected at special town meetings held " seasonably before," and taken to the county seat by commissioners appointed for that purpose.[2]

As no general officers were elected under the provisional government of Massachusetts Bay, nothing like a proxy system was needed. County treasurers were chosen, however, by a course of procedure analogous to the method employed in the election of Plymouth associates, except that personal attendance at the county seat was not permitted. All votes were cast in town meeting, sealed up by the constables, and delivered by them to the justices of the county at the next quarter sessions, when they were counted.[3] It seems strange that even under the royal government the

[1] 11 *Plymouth Colony Records*, 59; Brigham, 94, 108, 258.
[2] *Laws*, 1691; Brigham, 237.
[3] *Laws*, 1692–3, chap. 27, § 1; Ames and Goodell, 63.

more simple method of counting the votes in each town, and reporting the number cast for every candidate to the court of quarter sessions, was not adopted.

Long before the Rhode Island charter was granted, the principle of voting by proxy was recognized at Newport, as is proved by the law of 1639–40, permitting those " necessarily detained" to send their votes, sealed up, to the judge who presided at an election.[1]　When the confederacy was organized in 1647, it was provided that " forasmuch as many be necessarily detained that they cannot come to the General court of Elections that then they shall send their votes sealed up unto the said Court, which shall be as effectual as their personal appearances."[2]　But a proviso was soon added that " None shall bringe them any voates but such as they receive from the voaters' hands, and that all voates presented shall be filed by the recorder in the presence of the Assembly."[3]

When the charter of 15 Charles II was received there was considerable doubt as to whether it would be constitutional to continue the proxy method.　Accordingly, it was resolved, pending a reference of the question to the authorities in England, to allow only those present in person at the general court to vote.[4]　But the question was taken up again, and it was decided to be " a kind of necessity to admitt of voting by proxy from such as are not present or cannot conveniantly ther come."[5]　It was therefore enacted that any freeman could vote by proxy, " provided this order noe may prejudice or discorradge any who desire to be personally present."　Proxies must be in writing and delivered, sealed up, to a magistrate " in the face of a town meeting" lawfully called, upon due notice for that purpose.　The names of the

[1] 1 *Rhode Island Colonial Records*, 98.

[2] *Ibid.*, 149.

[3] *Ibid.*, 217.

[4] 2 *Rhode Island Colonial Records*, 29.

[5] *Ibid*, 39.

persons voting or voted for (the language of the statute does
not clearly state which) " must be written at length on the
backside or the bottom," and all votes must be delivered to
the assembly. A system of sub-proxy like that which existed in Massachusetts seems to have been in use, for in
case of sickness and necessary absence from the town meetings an elector could send his vote to a magistrate, and the
latter was required to place it in the hands of the governor
or the deputy governor at the court of election.[1]

Whatever may have been the meaning of the statute just
quoted, an act was passed in 1715, requiring that every freeman should write his name " at length on the back side of
his proxy," and all proxies found wanting in this particular
were to be thrown out when the canvass took place.[2] Some
years after this a law was passed providing that proxies
should be collected at the regular town meetings for the election of deputies on the first Tuesday in March, and that
no proxies could be put in on any other day.[3] The following
year the date was changed to the third Wednesday in April,
and it was enacted that " no Person Proxing at said Meeting
should have Liberty of withdrawing his Proxy at the General
Election."[4]

The elector was compelled after 1747 to write the names
of all the officers he wished to vote for on a single piece of
paper, and when the ballot was cast, to sign it on the back with
his own name.[5] Until 1760 freemen were permitted to vote
either in person or by proxy as they preferred. Then it was
at last recognized that their presence at Newport was " very
injurious to the interest and public weal of the colony and

---

[1] 2 *Rhode Island Colonial Records*, 64; 16 Car. II, Franklin ed., 1730, 1744, 1.
[2] 4 *Rhode Island Colonial Records*, 195, 208.
[3] 16 Geo. II, Franklin ed., 1744, 255.
[4] 17 Geo. II, Franklin ed., 1744, 287.   [5] 20 Geo. II, Franklin ed., 1752, 13.

occasions a very great loss of people's time at a season of the year when their labor is abundantly necessary for preparing the ground and planting the seed: on which the produce of the whole season must depend; and as all the ends of voting for general officers may be as fully attained by the freemen's putting in their proxie votes at the town meeting in their own towns, appointed by law for that purpose agreeable to the ancient and laudable custom of the prudent freemen." So, in future, all freemen must vote at their town meetings, unless they were members of the assembly, in which case they were still permitted to cast their votes at the general court. The moderator was ordered to deliver all the ballots to the town clerk, who counted the number given for each candidate and sent a certificate of the total to Newport. As was the case before, the names of the officers voted for were placed on a single ticket signed on the back by the elector at the time the ballot was cast. Before sealing them up in a package for transportation to Newport, the town clerk compared the names on the ballots with a list of those voting which he had previously made. A person who had recently been admitted as a freeman in his town, could vote at the town meeting, and in case the assembly admitted him to the freedom of the colony, his proxy would be received and counted good. If he was rejected his proxy would be thrown out.[1]

Though it would seem that the character of the proxy as a power of attorney enabling one freeman to exercise the franchise of another, would require that such instruments should be signed, yet Rhode Island was the only colony where this was done. It seems to the writer that the Rhode Island rule is further evidence that the proxy system was introduced for another purpose than that of providing a more

[1] 6 *Rhode Island Colonial Records*, 256; Hall's *Code*, 1767, Title *Elections*, 78.

secret ballot. In fact, votes cast by the electors in person at the general court were secret, because unsigned.[1] It seems to have been customary, in Rhode Island at any rate, to preserve the proxies sent in from the towns, for in 1767 a law was passed ordering that those on hand should be burned.[2]

There is no very satisfactory evidence in possession of the writer as to a proxy system in Hartford before the charter of 14 Charles II. The language employed in the Constitution of 1638 seems to assume that personal attendance was necessary.[3] About the year 1660 we find mention of "ye remote planta[s] : (y[t] vse to send Proxies at y[e] Election by their Deputies," and this seems to show that proxies were used to a limited extent.[4]

In New Haven the evidence that a proxy system existed is more conclusive. The Fundamental Orders of 1643 provided for a course of procedure similar to that already described, and required that "votes be sealed up in the p[rs]ence of the free burgesses themselves that their severall libertyes may be preserved and their votes directed according to their owne perticular light."[5] Even before this date there is evidence of a proxy system.[6] The earliest edition of the laws printed in London in 1656, provided in addition to the order just quoted, that if a freeman " proposing to be present at the election, when the other votes were sealed up, should after be hindered, and then want opportunity to seal up his vote in the presence of the major part of the freemen ; in such case he may seal it up in the presence of two such freemen as know he sent no vote before, and (upon their

---

[1] 4 *Rhode Island Colonial Records,* 208; see p. 148, *post.*

[2] 7 *Rhode Island Colonial Records,* 18.

[3] " Every p'son present and qualified shall bring in to the persons deputed to receive the—." 1 *Connecticut Colonial Records,* 21.   [4] *Ibid.,* 340.

[5] 1 *New Haven Colonial Records,* 114.   [6] *Ibid.,* 111.

testimony or certificate) it shall be accepted, that so the liberty of the freemen shall be preserved and they may have means to attend their duty and their votes may be directed according to their own particular light."[1]

Under the Connecticut charter proxies do not appear to have been authorized until 1670, when the court became "sencible of the great charge, difficulty and expence of time the freemen of this colony are at by reason of their great numbers and remoatness from Hartford, the place of election, and considering the many inconveniences that otherwayes may arise upon the yearly day of election, and that the worke of that day may be the more orderly, easily and speedily issued."[2]

As in Plymouth and Rhode Island, the proxies were collected in the town meetings, at which the deputies were chosen. These took place at the meeting houses on the last Tuesday in April (the election was on the second Thursday in May), commencing at nine o'clock. The method of procedure was similar to that employed at the general court of election, and the secrecy of the ballot was thereby preserved. The meetings were first called to order, and after the freeman's oath and the penalty for disorderly voting had been read, the names of the persons nominated at the general court of the preceding October were announced. Each voter then brought to the constable the name of his choice for governor "fairly written upon a piece of paper." These ballots were sealed up in a package which was endorsed with the name of the town and the words: " These are the votes for the Governour." The votes for Deputy Governor, Secretary and Treasurer were then collected in like manner and sealed up in packages appropriately labeled. The assistants were voted for in the peculiar manner which was employed at the

[1] 2 *New Haven Colonial Records*, 567.
[2] 2 *Connecticut Colonial Records*, 131.

general court, and which will be considered in that connection. The proxies were sent to Hartford, accompanied by a list of the names of those who had cast them.[1]

Though there were occasional changes in the days appointed for the town meetings,[2] no alteration appears to have been made in the method of voting by proxy until after the Revolution. The proxies were handed in on the Monday following the first Tuesday in April. It would seem that freemen were no longer allowed to attend the court of election in person,[3] for no provision is made in the statutory revision of 1750 for their presence. The ballots cast in the towns were still regarded as proxies and sent to Hartford as before. In fact, this extremely ridiculous custom of having the votes cast at the town meetings in April kept secret and not counted till the middle of May, was continued until 1819, when it was at last abolished.[4]

Outside of New England the writer has found but a single instance of anything resembling the proxy system. The authority for this statement is found in a letter of instructions from the lords proprietors to the governor of South Carolina in September, 1683. The passage bearing on the point in question is as follows:

"Wee are informed that there are many undue practices in the choyce of members of Parl^mt, and that men are admitted to bring papers for others and put in their votes for them, wh is utterly illegal & contrary to the custome of Parliaments & will in time, if suffered, be very mischeevious: you are therefore to take care that such practices be not suffered for the future, but every man must deliver his own vote & noe man suffered to bring the votes of another,

---

[1] 2 *Connecticut Colonial Records,* 133; 4 *Connecticut Colonial Records,* 11; *Session Laws,* 1715, 30.

[2] 8 *Connecticut Colonial Records,* 277, 279.

[3] Election to be by "Proxy of the Freemen," *Session Laws,* 1750, 45.

[4] *Public Acts,* 1819, chap. 2, 312.

& if the sheriffs of the counties shall presume to disobey herein, you are to commissionate eight other sheriffs in their Roomes."[1]

Whether or not the threat contained in the last sentence of this letter was sufficient to stop the practice complained of, the writer cannot say. Certain it is that a law passed some years later expressly forbade any absentee from voting by "proxy, letter or otherwise."[2] As has been elsewhere noted,[3] election laws were passed in 1692 and 1696, of which the writer has not been able to obtain a copy. Beyond this no evidence has been found of anything like voting by proxy, and the common law doctrine of the illegality of the exercise of a public franchise by proxy should, it would seem, be an effectual bar to anything of the sort in the provinces more directly under royal control.[4]

§ 7. *Method of Taking the Vote.* A. NEW ENGLAND. 1) *Election of General Officers.* As has already been stated, the general officers of the New England governments were chosen at the annual meeting of all the freemen of the colony assembled in general court of election.[5] The introduction of the proxy system did not put an end to this custom, for all freemen were present in theory, even though they voted by proxy. As long as freemen were permitted to attend the general court of election, the character of the proceedings was not changed. It may be assumed that the governor, by virtue of his office, presided over the general court of of election. The court was usually held, not in the open air, but in a building of some sort, sometimes the meeting house, sometimes the residence of a private person.[6]

---

[1] Rivers, *South Carolina*, Appendix, 406. See also p. 160 *post*.

[2] Act 1704, no. 227, 2 Cooper, 149.   [3] See footnotes, pp. 53, 68, 78, *ante*.

[4] 21 Car. I, Act xx, 1 Hening, 333 (Virginia), seems to insist particularly on personal attendance at the election.   [5] See pp. 2 *et seq;* 101 *et seq, ante*.

[6] See 1 Winthrop's *New England*, 81; 3 *Rhode Island Colonial Records*, 30, 271; also p. 145, *post*.

In Massachusetts, the governor, as well as the other officers, were at first chosen by " ereccion of hands,"[1] which was the method employed in England, if no poll was demanded. But we have the authority of Governor Winthrop for the statement that in 1634 and thereafter, "the governor and deputy were elected by papers wherein their names were written."[2] Some years afterwards it was enacted that such "papers" must be "open, or once folded, not twisted or rolled up, that they may be the sooner perused."[3] Under the proxy system ballots were cast in the towns and sent in a package to the general court of election, where they were counted together with those cast by the freemen voting at the court in person.[4] A list of the names of those voting accompanied each package, but whether or not the names of all the freemen of the colony were read before the court and each voter present deposited his ballot in his turn, cannot be clearly made out from the laws.[5] The ballots cast at the court of election do not appear to have been signed, and therefore possessed all the elements of secrecy. Under the law of 1679–80, the proxies were counted and sorted into separate packages on the Monday preceding the Wednesday of election, so that it was a comparatively simple matter to add the ballots cast by the freemen attending on the latter day to the total number of proxies cast for each candidate, as previously ascertained.[6] But this law was in force less than a year. By the order of October, 1680, the colony

[1] 1 *Massachusetts Colonial Records,* 37j, 59, 95, 104.

[2] 1 Winthrop's *New England,* 65, 81. It is said that the written ballot was firs used in America at the election of the officers of the Salem church in 1629. See 2 Campbell, *The Puritan in Holland, England and America,* 431, *et seq.,* where a history of the ballot is given.

[3] 2 *Massachusetts Colonial Records,* 220; *Laws,* ed. 1660, 27; 1814, 105.

[4] 5 *Massachusetts Colonial Records,* 262, 292.

[5] 1 *Massachusetts Colonial Records,* 188. [6] 5 *Massachusetts Colonial Records,* 262.

returned to the old practice, it being declared that the governor and deputy governor should be elected and proclaimed before the election of the assistants.[1]   All ballots which were brought in for either nomination or election must be deposited at the court of election either by the person voting or by the deputy or constable of the town where the voters whose proxies were brought resided.

No further details are given in regard to the manner of voting for the governor and other general officers.   The election of assistants was, however, considered to be of such "great concernment"[2] that not only was a method of nomination by ballot required, but the election proper was conducted in a peculiar manner.   In 1630 assistants were first chosen by the freemen.   The following year the freemen were permitted to propose those whom they desired chosen, and "if it be doubtfull wheth[r] it be the great[r] pte of the comons or not, it shalbe putt to the poll."[3]   When the ballot was first used in 1634, a special form of procedure was employed in the election of assistants.   Governor Winthrop informs us that they "were chosen by papers without names, *viz.*, the Governor propounded one to the people when they all went out and came in at one door, and every man delivered a paper into a hat—such as gave their vote for the party named gave in a paper with some figure or scroll in it, others gave in a blank."[4]   This was substantially the form adopted for the election of assistants in Connecticut.[5]   When the method of nominations was introduced, it was expressly stipulated that those of the eighteen nominees who had been magistrates during the previous year, should be

---

[1] 5 *Massachusetts Colonial Records*, 292.

[2] 3 *Massachusetts Colonial Records*, 177.

[3] 1 *Massachusetts Colonial Records*, 79, 87.

[4] 1 Winthrop's *New England*, Savage ed.,|1790, 81.   [5] See page 150, *post.*

first proposed for election.[1]   This was an important matter inasmuch as the voters balloted not upon all the eighteen names at once, but upon each of the nominees as he was separately put up.

In 1643, assistants were no longer voted for by means of "papers," but by "Indian beanes, the white beanes to manifest election, the black for blanks."[2]   The language of the statute books required that Indian corn should be used to designate election, and beans the contrary, and imposed a penalty of ten pounds upon freemen who put in more than one grain for any officer.[3]   The result of the course of procedure followed in Massachusetts, was that each nominee was either accepted or rejected by each voter, and following the analogy of the Connecticut rule, it may be presumed that those receiving more affirmative than negative votes were elected.[4]   It is not perfectly clear what result the introduction of the proxy had on the corn and bean system. The act of 1647, required the town officers to seal up in distinct packages the votes of such freemen as remained at home, and send them to the court of elections, "all the assistants to be chosen by Indian corn as aforesaid."[5]   The most reasonable interpretation of this, and one that is borne out by the language of the records,[6] seems to be that the freemen were to vote in their town meetings by corn and beans, and that the identical grains of corn and beans so used, were to be sealed up and taken to Boston and deposited in the hat when the name of the person voted for was proposed. This explanation is in accord with the

---

[1] 3 *Massachusetts Colonial Records,* 177; 5 *Massachusetts Colonial Records,* 291; *Laws,* ed., 1660.

[2] 2 *Massachusetts Colonial Records,* 42, 220.

[3] *Laws,* ed. 1660, 27; ed. 1672, 47; ed. 1814, 105.

[4] *Connecticut Session Laws,* 30.

[5] *Laws,* ed., 1814, 106.   [6] 2 *Massachusetts Colonial Records,* 220.

theory of the proxy system which was instituted for the express purpose of enabling the identical ballots cast in the towns to be deposited at the general court of election in Boston. That the bean ballot was not soon abolished, is shown by the statute books of 1660[1] and of 1672.[2]

In 1679–80, however, a law was passed which seems to have suspended this method of voting for one year at any rate. According to this order the names of the twenty assistants were to be placed on one sheet of paper "cut almost asunder betwixt each name," and the rule seems to have applied to the votes cast at the general court of election, as well as to the proxies handed in at the towns. The system of separately proposing each nominee was also abolished, for it was specified that the eighteen receiving the largest number of votes should be assistants for the ensuing year.[3] As under this law all the proxy ballots had been counted and sorted on the Monday preceeding the Wednesday of election, the ballots cast on the latter day by the freemen attending in person were simply added to the number of proxies given for each candidate as previously ascertained.

But under the authority of the statute passed in October, 1680, the former method of procedure was revived. After the other general officers had been voted for in the town meetings by means of the Indian corn ballot, twenty assistants were chosen out of the twenty-six persons in nomination, and the ballots cast for these were carried to Boston. There the freemen who were present in person at the court of election voted, and the eighteen nominees receiving the largest number of votes were declared elected. Why twenty names were voted for in the towns and only eighteen at the general court does not appear. Although the assistants were still chosen by corn, there is nothing in the statute

---

[1] Page 27.   [2] Page 47.

[3] 5 *Massachusetts Colonial Records*, 262.

which would tend to support the presumption that the system of separate nomination was revived.[1]

The general court of election for Massachusetts was not always held at Boston. In 1637 it took place at Newton (now Cambridge), in the open air.[2] In 1644 the deputies voted that the next election should be held at Salem, but on account of the dissent of the magistrates this was not done.[3] Because of Indian troubles in the spring of 1635–6, some of the more distant towns were permitted to keep a number of their freemen at home for purposes of defence. This, as we have seen,[4] was the occasion when the proxy system was first introduced. In order to provide for the safety of those who attended the election court in person that year, each of the towns nearest to Boston was ordered to send ten of their freemen "completely armed with musketts, swords, shotts, &c."[5]

---

[1] 5 *Massachusetts Colonial Records*, 292; *Supplement to Laws and Orders of 1672*, dated October 13th, 1680; *Laws*, ed. 1814 109.

[2] Coffin, *History of Newbury* 22; 1 *Massachusetts Colonial Records*, 194.

[3] 3 *Massachusetts Colonial Records*, 5.   [4] See p. 129, *ante*.

[5] 1 *Massachusetts Colonial Records*, 166. Since the foregoing pages were written, my attention has been called to a contemporaneous description of the Massachusetts court of election about the year 1640. It is found in Lechford's *Plaine Dealing, Newes from New-England* (pp. 24, 25, London, 1642), and is worthy of insertion in this connection:

"The manner of elections is this: At first the Chiefe Governour and Magistrates were chosen in *London* by erection of hands of all the *Freemen* of this *Society*. Since the transmitting of the Patent into *New-England*, the election is not by voices, nor by erection of hands, but by papers, thus: The generall court Electory, sitting where are present in the church or meeting house at *Boston*, the old Governour, Deputy and all the Magistrates and two Deputies or Burgesses for every town or at least one; all the *Freemen* are bidden to come in an one doore and bring their votes in paper for the new Governour and deliver them downe upon the table before the Court and so to passe forth at another doore. Those that are absent send their votes by proxies. All being delivered in the votes are counted, and according to the major part the old Governour pronounceth that such a one is chosen Governour for the yeare ensuing. Then the *Freemen* in like manner bring in their votes for the Deputy Governour who being chosen, the

In Plymouth the general court of election was held "in his Majesties name of England."[1] The election appears to have been by ballot. The votes of all the freemen present were first read, and then the deputies presented the proxies of their towns. The roll of the freemen seems to have been called, for the deputies were bidden to take a list of those whose votes they carried in order that they might answer for them when they were called.[2] At the county courts of election where associates were chosen, a similar course of procedure was followed.[3]

At the meeting which organized the Rhode Island colonial government in 1647, it was agreed that the election of officers should be "by papers,"[4] although I am inclined to believe that the ballot was used before that date.[5] The proceedings at the general court of election were as follows: On the day before, a meeting of the general assembly was held, and at this the deputies presented their credentials and

Governour propoundeth the Assistants one after the other. New Assistants are, of late, put in nomination by an order of general Court, beforehand to be considered of. If a *Freeman* gives in a blanck that rejects the man named; if the *Freeman* makes any mark with a pen upon the paper which he brings, that elects the man named; then the blancks and marked papers are numbered, and according to the major part of either, the man in nomination stands elected or rejected. And so for all the Assistants. And after every new election, which is by their Patent to be upon the last Wednesday of Easter Terme, the new Governour and Officers are all newly sworn. The Governour and Assistants choose the Secretary. And all the Court, consisting of Governour, Deputy, Associates and Deputies of towns, give their votes as well as the rest; And the *Ministers* and *Elders* and all *Church-officers* have their *votes* also in all these elections of chief magistrates. Constables and all other inferiour Officers are sworn in the generall quarter or other courts or before any Assistant." Also, 3 *Massachusetts Historical Collections*, iii, 82; 1 *Memorial History of Boston*, 504.

[1] *Laws*, 1636, 11 *Plymouth Colony Records*, 10, Brigham, 40.

[2] *Laws*, 1658; *Book of General Laws*, chap. 5, § 4; Brigham, 109, 258.

[3] *Laws*, 1691, Brigham, 237.   [4] 1 *Rhode Island Colonial Records*, 148.

[5] At Portsmouth, in 1638, votes are spoken of as "unsealed," *ibid.*, 64; Newport, in 1639–40, *ibid.*, 98; 1 Arnold, *History of Rhode Island*, 131.

took their "engagements." A moderater and a clerk were chosen, and candidates for the freedom of the colony were proposed and admitted by vote. This done, the assembly adjourned till the following day, which was that prescribed by law for the "general assembly and election."[1] The Earl of Bellmont complained that the preliminary assembly was illegal,[2] and it is difficult to see how it complied with the letter of the charter, which required the newly elected assembly to convene on the first Wednesday, and not on the first Tuesday in May.[3]

On Wednesday, the deputies and magistrates assembled and the charter was read. Then the election proper commenced. No regular course of procedure was followed, but special rules were adopted for each session. At one time the election took place after dinner, and at another it began at eight in the morning.[4] In one case the assembly removed to the lower room for the convenience of the electors.[5] During the successive years from 1672 to 1678, for example, the ballots were received in various ways. In 1672 four men were chosen from each town "to view and observe the votes." The next year all votes brought in were passed through the hands of a deputy and a magistrate, while the proxies were divided into four parts, and "in opening each part" a magistrate and a deputy unfolded the ballots and ",putt in the votes as called for into the hat." In 1674 certain members were appointed to see that there was "an orderly and due course, and that no deceit or fraud be practised." The following year ballots were received by a deputy and an assistant, and if doubts were expressed concerning any, the officers might open them and "soe deliver

---

[1] 2 *Rhode Island Colonial Records*, 516, 529, 541, 565 *etc.*
[2] 3 *Rhode Island Colonial Records*, 385.
[3] 2 *Rhode Island Colonial Records*, 8.   [4] *Ibid.*, 38, 374.
[5] 3 *Rhode Island Colonial Records*, 30.

but one from each person into the hat." The proxies were
opened by four deputies. In 1678, a sort of poll was taken,
and two persons were chosen to write down the names of
the voters.[1] When the charter government was restored
after the fall of Andros, the recorder wrote down the names
of those voting for governor, while two tellers took the
ballots from the hands of the electors and put them in a hat.
Four other tellers then unfolded the ballots and put them in
a second hat.[2] The moderator who presided at the election
was frequently the governor. When the votes had been
added up the persons chosen were proclaimed and sworn
into office. If, as not infrequently happened, a person
refused to serve, the assembly filled his place before proceeding to its regular business of legislation.

Previous to 1715 ballots cast at the general election were
unsigned. In that year a law was passed requiring all
electors to sign their ballots as they had previously signed
their proxies. This measure is said to have been adopted
because "great abuse and clandestine proceedings and irreg-
ular practice, as they are creditably informed, hath been
acted by sundry loose and fractious freemen of said colony
by putting or delivering into the hat sometimes two, three
or more votes for one officer." But in a very short time the
practice of signing ballots was found to cause "great dissatisfaction and uneasiness to good people, who deem it a very
great hardship by exposure to the creating of animosity and
heartburning of their particular friends." Accordingly the
obnoxious law was repealed, and a series of severe penalties
was prescribed, with a view of putting an end to fraudulent
practices.[3] With the exception of this short period, the ballot in Rhode Island retained its secret character, though the

[1] 2 *Rhode Island Colonial Records*, 450, 483, 517, 565; 3 *idem*, 4.

[2] 3 *Rhode Island Colonial Records*, 271.

[3] 4 *Rhode Island Colonial Records*, 195, 207.

law requiring proxies to be signed made freemen voting in that manner do so at the price of secrecy. When the statute abolishing the practice of personal voting at the general court was enacted in 1760,[1] the effect of the custom requiring proxies to be signed was to abolish the secret ballot altogether, so far as Rhode Island elections were concerned.

The writer has not been able to ascertain precisely what was the course followed by the freemen of the New Haven colony in casting their votes. The existence of the proxy system seems to be circumstantial evidence tending to establish the belief that the ballot was used. In the London edition of the laws of this plantation (1656) the following provision is, however, to be found:

"That each Freeman, whether present or absent at the Election, may the better improve his Liberty, It is Ordered that he may give or send his Vote as he finds cause, either in the affirmative, by putting in an Indian Corn, or in the Negative, by putting in a Beane, or in such other manner as the Generall Court shall judge convenient."[2]

The passage just quoted refers to elections for the " Magistracy," which term the present writer is inclined to believe was meant to include the governor, as well as the magistrates proper. Now, as already stated,[3] the records of the New Haven jurisdiction previous to 1653 are lost, and the above statute is not found in the existing records so far as published. It is interesting to note in this connection that the London edition of the laws is supposed to have been compiled in 1648, although revised by Governor Eaton in 1655 after he had examined an edition of the Massachusetts laws.[4] This fact, as well as the silence of the existing New Haven records, would seem to indicate that he introduced the pass-

---

[1] 6 *Rhode Island Colonial Records*, 256.

[2] 2 *New Haven Colonial Records*, 567, 568.

[3] See p. 121, *ante.*   [4] 2 *New Haven Colonial Records*, iv, 154, 186.

age under discussion, after reading the Massachusetts law of 1643; and fearing lest his action might not be approved, he inserted the clause giving the general court power to prescribe the method to be followed in elections. This supposition, as well as the language employed in the New Haven statute, confirms the belief already expressed,[1] that in Massachusetts, as well as in New Haven, the identical corn and beans cast in the town "proxings" were sent to the general court of election.

The Hartford Constitution of 1638 expressly provided that the written ballot should be used in the election of officers. Each elector brought to the teller a single piece of paper with the name of his choice for governor written on it, and the candidate receiving the greatest number of such votes was declared elected.[2] With the exception of the assistants, the other general officers were elected by ballot, and no change appears to have been made in the practice.

For the election of magistrates or assistants a peculiar method was followed both in the general court and in the town "proxings." As has been above explained, all candidates for the office were nominated in advance.[3] When the governor and deputy governor could be chosen only from those in nomination, each freeman could vote for any name on the list. As soon as these two officers had been chosen, the secretary read the names of those in nomination, and then "severally nominated them distinctly." As each name was put up, the freemen handed to the teller pieces of paper. Those papers upon which something had been written (not necessarily the name of the candidate) were votes in favor of the nominee; the blanks were votes against him. All persons having more written papers than blanks were elected, but in case less than six were chosen, then a sufficient num-

---

[1] See p. 143, *ante.*   [2] I *Connecticut Colonial Records*, 21.   [3] See p. 121, *ante.*

ber of those having the most written papers were taken to fill up the quota of six.[1] This was the method laid down by the constitution of 1638 and it was doubtless modelled after the Massachusetts law of 1635.[2]

Under the charter of 14 Charles II, the same plan was followed with some elaborations. The general court seems to have arranged the list of persons in nomination, and this came to be of importance, for it was required that the names should be proposed in the order in which they were placed on the list, and as soon as the number of assistants allowed by the charter had been chosen the election was to cease.[3] In the town "proxings," however, the names of all the nominees were proposed in turn, so that a freeman could always vote for any one he pleased, so long as his name was on the list.[4]

The rule prevailing in the town "proxings" seems to have been extended to the general court in 1692, when it was ordered that the proceedings should be as formerly, "onely all those that stand for nomination shall pass through the election;"[5] and that those having the most votes should be elected.[6] After 1750, when freemen could no longer attend the general court, it was provided that no elector could vote for more than twelve assistants.[7] Before this he could vote on the whole list, and if he were opposed to any particular candidate he could signify his dislike by putting a blank ballot into the hat. Under the new system, however, he could still vote against the nominee, but at the price of forfeiting a vote in favor of some one else, for all his ballots both affirmative and negative must not exceed twelve in number. The effect of this method of choosing assistants appears to

---

[1] 1 *Connecticut Colonial Records*, 21.   [2] See p. 142, *ante*.

[3] 2 *Connecticut Colonial Records*, 133.

[4] 4 *Connecticut Colonial Records*, 11; "a white piece of paper" to be a blank vote.

[5] *Ibid.*, 81.   [6] *Session Laws*, ed. 1715, 30.   [7] *Ibid.*, ed. 1750, 45.

have been to make few changes among the incumbents of these offices. The names of those already in office were generally placed at the head of the list of the nominees, and for that reason they were nearly always elected. A contemporary writer[1] says that many electors usually retired before the close of the voting, but that the expectation of reëlection was not strong enough to remove all fear of popular restraint from the court of assistants. Accordingly, the power of the legislature to arrange the order of the names of the eight nominees not in office, had a considerable influence which could be exerted in the direction of maintaining the court of assistants on a footing representing the conservatism of twenty years back, as was indeed actually the case.

The two houses of the legislature had separated in 1698, and the lower house always contended that when a vacancy occurred in the office of Governor, the two houses should sit in convention in order to exercise their power as conferred by charter, of choosing a person to serve during the unexpired term. But the houses appear to have sat separately on such occasions, and while in 1707, their votes were combined.[2] in 1724 the candidate having a majority of the votes of each house was declared elected.[3] In order to be elected during the later years of the colonial government, a candidate was required to receive a majority of all the votes cast. If this did not happen, the assembly elected the officer.[4]

The commentator who has already been quoted, gives an account of the proceedings at Hartford on election day, during the latter part of the eighteenth century, when the freemen took no part in the proceedings except to look on and listen. The representatives met in their chamber at

[1] 1 Swift, *System of the Laws of Connecticut*, 84.

[2] 5 *Connecticut Colonial Records*, 38.

[3] *Ibid.*, 484. See also 8 *Connecticut Colonial Records*, 416.

[4] 8 *Connecticut Colonial Records*, 453.

eight o'clock and elected their speaker and clerk. Credentials were then presented, and the members sworn. A message was sent to the outgoing governor and council, who had meanwhile met in the council chamber. Both houses then marched in procession to the meeting-house, where the election sermon was preached. This done, the houses retired to their apartments and appointed committees to count the votes that had been cast in the towns more than a month before. When the canvass was completed, the persons elected were publicly proclaimed and sworn into office.[1]

Coming as it generally did in the spring time after the rigors of winter had departed, we may believe that the day of the general court of election was the New England holiday. In two of the colonies a typical feature of the celebration was the preaching of an election sermon. Governor Winthrop tells us in his Journal that the position of preacher was regarded as one of very great honor, and that the freemen strictly insisted on the privilege of selecting the clergyman who was to deliver the discourse, and claimed it as a part of their liberty. The magistrates do not seem to have dared to openly contest the question with the freemen or with their deputies.[2]

In the colonial records of Connecticut, we find continual references to the subject of election sermons, and they were preached down to the very close of the colonial period.[3] This custom was found to be so effectual for the promotion of honesty in elections, that in 1708 the general court resolved to send a letter to all ministers of the gospel resident in the colony, asking them to preach on election day before

---

[1] I Swift, *System of the Laws of Connecticut,* 70.

[2] I Winthrop's *New England,* 31, 218.

[3] 1775, 15 *Connecticut Colonial Records,* 271. An extract from one of them is given in 3 *Connecticut Colonial Records,* 179.

the freemen of each plantation, a sermon " proper for direction in the choice of civil rulers."[1]

Feasting also seems to have formed a part of the pro-
gramme, and, strange as it may seem, in a colony so strictly
governed " according to the word of God," as was New
Haven, we find the following entry in the records under date
of 1653 : " Ordered that a dinner should be provided at yᵉ
ordinary for the court and whom they shall invite, vpon the
election day, at the publique charge of the jurisdiction, but
after euery towne is to pvide for theire owne magistrates and
deputies."[2]

2) *Election of Deputies.* The course of procedure to be
followed at the town courts where deputies were chosen does
not seem to have been regarded as a matter of great importance, because very little general legislation bearing on the
subject is to be found. For instance, it is not entirely
clear whether, in case a town was entitled to more than one
representative, each elector placed the names of all the persons he voted for on a single ticket, or on several. We
shall see that the written ballot was generally used in New
England even under the royal governments. Thus in Massachusetts, after 1635, deputies were elected " by papers as
the Gou'nʳ is chosen,"[3] while the laws of Plymouth and New
Hampshire contain no provisions on this subject. The written ballot was so firmly established in Massachusetts that it
continued to be used under the charter of 1691, by virtue of
a statute which required electors to hand in their votes unfolded.[4]

In Rhode Island it was enacted that the free inhabitants
of the towns should elect committees of six to represent

---

[1] 5 *Connecticut Colonial Records*, 61.   [2] 2 *New Haven Colonial Records*, 52.

[3] 1 *Massachusetts Colonial Records*, 157; *Laws*, ed. 1660, 25; ed. 1814, 97.

[4] *Laws* 1693–4, chap 14, § 7, 1 Ames and Goodell, 147.

them at the general court, and that if the number were incomplete, the men of the town, if freemen of the colony, should fill vacancies by an election to be held at the town where the court sat.[1] But this custom seems to have fallen into disuse, for we find that the Earl of Bellmont complained that deputies were chosen by the town council rather than by the inhabitants.[2]

By the Hartford Constitution of 1638, it was provided that the election of deputies should be by ballot, and voters were required to " bring in written on severall papers " the names of those they desired chosen. The three or four having the greatest number of papers were to be deputies to the next general court.[3] In this case it seems plain that each freeman cast as many ballots as there were deputies to be chosen. After the grant of the charter no particular mode of election seems to have been prescribed.[4] Swift in 1790, wrote that deputies were elected by ballot,[5] while a recent writer states that it became customary after the consolidation with New Haven, to elect them by acclamation.[6]

B. THE ROYAL PROVINCES. For want of a better name we have grouped under the title of the royal provinces all those colonies which followed in substance the course of procedure customary in choosing the members of the House of Commons in England. The title is somewhat misleading, for Maryland will be included in this group, although for the greater part of her history she was under proprietary rule;

---

[1] 1 *Rhode Island Colonial Records*, 236.

[2] 3 *Rhode Island Colonial Records*, 385, *et seq.*

[3] 1 *Connecticut Colonial Records*, 21.

[4] See *Session Laws*, 30; "first they shall choose," *etc.*

[5] 1 *System of the Laws of Connecticut*, 66.

[6] Judge Baldwin, *Early History of the Ballot in Connecticut;* 4 *American Historical Association*, pt. iv, 90, Series of 1890.

while the Carolinas and Massachusetts Bay are excluded notwithstanding the fact that during the eighteenth century they were governed directly by the British crown. In New York, New Jersey (after 1701), Maryland, Virginia and Georgia, the English method was introduced, generally, it is believed, on account of the influence of the home government.

In the royal provinces the ballot was unknown; in fact, it was not used in England until after 1872. Under this system secrecy does not appear to have been sought, and it certainly was not attained. For this reason the written ballot of New England was a far superior method and one better calculated to preserve the purity of elections. Although the records of the Puritan colonies show that fraud was sometimes practiced, it is difficult to understand, from a modern point of view, how a system more open to abuse than the English could be devised. In order to fully understand the manner in which elections were carried on in the group of colonies we are about to consider, it will perhaps be advisable to review briefly the development in England from the first parliamentry election in the reign of Edward the First, down to the declaration of American Independence in 1776.

The procedure at the parliamentary elections of the thirteenth and fourteenth centuries is involved in obscurity. " It would be a waste of ingenuity" says Bishop Stubbs, "to speculate on the different courses that a sheriff unguided by custom, may have adopted."[1] The statute of 7 Henry IV[2] provided that the election should take place at the next county court, to be holden after the delivery of the writ. After proclamation, all persons, as well as " suitors duly summoned for the same cause as other," proceeded " freely and indifferently" to the election. This power of citing

---

[1] 3 Stubbs, *Constitutional History of England*, 417.   [2] Chap. 15.

voters was open to great abuse, and made it possible for the sheriff to do about as he pleased.[1]

The will of the electors was expressed by show of hands, or by a *vivâ voce* vote. The sheriff decided who had been elected " by taking a view," and the legality of such a proceeding was affirmed in 1554 by the courts of law. In a contested case decided that year the plaintiff contended that because no poll had been taken, the sheriff could not determine the exact number of electors in favor of any particular candidate. But the judges decided that this was not necessary.[2]

In the twenty-first year of the reign of James I, the House of Commons established the right to a poll by ordering a new election, and declaring the previous one void, although three successive views had been taken.[3] A debate held in the House in 1625, shows that the method of taking the poll was very crude. At the trial of a disputed election it was shown that the sheriff closed the front entrance to the place of election and stood at the postern gate in order to count the electors as they passed out. While he was thus engaged the front gate was forced open. He thereupon stopped taking the poll, acting on the theory that only those present at the view should be counted. The House of Commons, however, decided that a new election must be held.[4] This decision upholds the position that the poll was continued for some days, so that all who desired might have an opportunity of voting, even though they had been absent from the view.

In the latter part of the seventeenth century the court of

---

[1] 3 Stubbs, *Constitutional History of England,* 419.

[2] Plowden, *Commentaries,* 129.

[3] 1 *Resolutions and Orders of the House of Commons,* 729.

[4] *Ibid.,* 801, 804; Cox, *Antient Parliamentary Elections,* 123.

hustings for the election of members to the House of Commons was held in the open air or in a public building. After proclaiming silence, the returning officer read aloud his writ and announced the penalty imposed by law upon illegal voting.[1] After being proposed in his turn by an elector, each candidate addressed the assembled voters from a raised platform. Then, if the number of candidates did not exceed the number of members to be returned, the election was made by acclamation. If not, a show of hands was called for, in order to assist the sheriff in determining "the choice by the view." Any one who chose to be present could participate in the election and raise his hand or his voice. It may, therefore, be imagined that the proceeding was far from orderly.

Any candidate had the right to contest the decision of the sheriff by demanding a poll, which was taken by that officer or by his deputy, assisted by a suitable number of clerks. Only those qualified according to law could be entered in the poll list, which contained the name of each freeholder, the place of his freehold and the name of the person for whom he voted.[2] A statute passed in 1711, required the place of abode to be set down and the word *jurat* in case the freeholder was sworn. In Yorkshire and Cheshire the sheriff was compelled to provide seven "convenient tables or places" to be "made at the costs and charges of the candidates, and to be placed within the shire hall[3] in the following manner: Two each side, two at the upper and one at the lower end." This provision was probably intended for

---

[1] See *Statute* 2 Geo. II, chap. 24, § 9; 3 Geo. III, chap. 15, § 7.

[2] *Statute* 7 and 8 Will. III, chap. 25, § 3. This statute was enacted in some form in Virginia, New York, New Jersey and Georgia. 2 De Franqueville, *Le Gouvernement et le Parliament Britannique*, 417.

[3] This applied only to Chester.

the convenience of the voters, and for the same reason it was customary to continue a poll for several days.[3]

By 1745 the number of electors in each county seems to have grown so large that a more elaborate method of taking the poll was necessary. Within three days before the commencement of the poll, the sheriff was required to erect at the expense of the candidates as many booths as he thought proper. These booths were not to exceed fifteen in number, and were conspicuously labeled with the name of the rape, wapentake, tathe, ward or hundred for which the use of which the booth was designed. At each booth were placed a clerk with a poll book, and also an inspector for each candidate. The inspectors were provided with cheque books in which to enter the names of the freeholders voting. Each clerk was given a list of all the towns, villages, parishes and hamlets situated in the division whose name was on his booth. Copies of these lists were furnished to the candidates or their agents at the price of two shillings apiece, and only inhabitants of the places mentioned in the lists could vote at any particular booth, unless the estate of the voter lay in some district not entered on any of the lists. The compensation of the clerks was fixed at not less than a guinea a day and this was paid by the candidates.[2] Except perhaps in Pennsylvania and Delaware the system of booths does not appear to have been introduced into this country, and there is no evidence that the representatives of the colonial candidates were expressly authorized to use cheque books.

In regard to adjourning or closing the poll, the English law was as follows: No adjournment to another town could be had without the consent of the candidates, nor was any unnecessary delay permitted. Unless the candidates consented, the returning officer must proceed from day to day,

---

[1] *Statute* 10 Anne, chap. 23.

[2] *Statutes* 18 Geo. II, chap. 18, §§ 7, 8, 9; 19 Geo. II, chap. 28, § 6.

and from time to time, until all the freeholders present were polled. Elections were held at the next regular county court after the receipt of the writ, unless the court met within six days thereafter. If so, the sheriff gave ten days notice and adjourned to some convenient day, which could not be a Monday, a Friday, or a Saturday. But county courts of election beginning on a day other than those mentioned, could be adjourned to these days, and from day to day until the election was completed.[1]

On the western side of the Atlantic we find that it was customary in early times for the sheriffs of Virginia to go from one plantation to another and collect the votes of the inhabitants.[2] A law passed by the House of Burgesses in 1639 ordered the sheriffs "not to compel any man to go off the plantation where he lives, to choose burgesses."[3] That it was customary for the electors to exercise their franchise, either by signing a paper which the sheriff carried about, or else by sending their votes by proxy, is shown by a statute of 1646 to the following effect:

"Whereas divers inconveniences are likely to ensue by disorderly and illegal election of Burgesses by subscribing of hands contrary to the warrant directed for the sayd election, by which means it also happeneth that few nor none doe appeare personally according to summons, Be it therefore inacted that noe election shall be made of any Burgesse or Burgesses but by a plurality of voices, and that noe handwriting shall be admitted."[4]

In the future personal attendance of all voters was required under penalty.

Less than ten years after the act just quoted we find that the sheriff was required to determine the election by taking the view,[5] but two statutes passed a little later seem to hint

---

[1] *Statutes* 7 and 8 Will. III, chap. 25; 6 Geo. II, chap. 23.   [2] 1 Hening, xix, xx.

[3] 14 Car. I, Act xix; 1 Hening, 227.   [4] 21 Car. I, Act xx; 1 Hening, 333.

[5] 5–6 Commonwealth, Act vii; 1 Hening, 411.

at something resembling the former custom by using the words: "Provided always that they fairly give their votes by subscription, and not in a tumultuous way."[1]

Whether or not there may have been a tendency towards a written form of ballot, the question was effectively put to rest in Virginia by the statute of 11 William III, chap. 2, which, like the law enacted in New York during the course of the same year, was modelled on the English statute of 7 and 8 William III, chap. 25, from which we have already quoted.[2] In case the election of any burgess could not be "determined upon the view by the consent of the freeholders then present, but that a poll shall be required for determination thereof," the sheriff was empowered to take one with the assistance of clerks to be appointed for that purpose. The name of each freeholder and that of the person for whom he voted were entered in writing.[3] It will be noticed that the language of this statute[4] gives any candidate or freeholder power to demand a poll.

Later enactments elaborated in several particulars the method of taking the poll. Books were to be provided for the purpose, and first of all the name of each candidate was written on a separate page or in a particular column. Then, as each freeholder voted, his name was fairly written in the proper pages or columns under the names of the persons for whom he voted. No freeholder who had once voted for two persons, could afterward poll for any more. The poll could not be concluded until all present had voted, or until after proclamation had been made three times from the court house door, and no more freeholders appeared.[5]

Toward the close of the colonial period we find that

[1] 6 Commonwealth, Act xvi; 1 Hening, 403; 9 Commonwealth, Act xciii; *ibid*, 473.   [2] See p. 158, *ante.*

[3] 3 Hening, 172.   [4] Also 3 Geo. III, chap. 1, § 10; 7 Hening, 519.

[5] 4 Anne, chap. 2, § 4; 3 Hening, 236.

every person having the right to vote for two burgesses must name them both when he first presented himself to be polled, or else forfeit his privilege of voting for a second candidate. As far back as 1705, the English House of Commons had declared that a person having the right to vote for two members could not vote for one and then come back again and vote a second time if he had named but one candidate at first.[1] In case more freeholders appeared on the first day of an election than could be polled before sunset, and if the candidates or their agents so requested, the sheriff could adjourn the poll to the following day. Notice of such an adjournment must be posted on the court house door. After making the three proclamations required, the returning officer must wait at least an hour before closing the poll.[2]

The writer has been unable to ascertain how elections were managed in Dutch times, but when the first legislative assembly was called in the province of New York in 1683, a form of indirect election seems to have been used. Thus in Long Island the freeholders of each town chose a committee of four to meet at the sessions house of each riding and select two representatives for the assembly. A similar course was followed in Esopus, but everywhere else the counties as a whole met and elected assemblymen.[3] Besides this single instance, there is no case of the town being recognized as an election district in New York. Under the first general law, the cities, counties and manors in the province elected representatives, and the procedure was much the same as that existing at the time in Virginia. The language of the statute seems to leave the question whether or not there should be a poll somewhat within the discretion of the sheriff.[4]

[1] 15 *Resolutions and Orders of the House of Commons*, 135, 137.

[2] 3 Geo. III, chap. 1, §§ 9, 10; 7 Hening, 519.

[3] *Introduction to the Journal of the New York Legislative Council*, xi.

[4] 11 Will. III, chap. 74; Van Schaack's *Laws*, 28.

Copies of the polls for the election of the representatives from New York City in 1761, 1768 and 1769 were reprinted in 1880 from the original manuscript. The poll of 1769 was printed soon after the election, and a copy of it is preserved in the library of the New York Historical Society. The poll list of the first of these years contains the names of the electors arranged under the various letters of the alphabet, though not in exact alphabetical order. There are six columns on every page, and each of these is headed with the name of a different candidate. Each elector could name four persons, and a check mark was placed in the column, answering for the candidate for whom he voted. It is worthy of notice that a man did not always cast as many votes as he was entitled to, and we find some instances where but one candidate was named. The pages are not very large in size, and the total number of votes cast for each candidate is given at the end of the book.

In 1768 there were seven candidates, and two additional columns were provided, the one headed *Freeholders* and the other *Freemen.* The abbreviation *do* is placed in the columns in order to designate in which capacity an elector voted. Sometimes we find that the same individual possessed both qualifications. An extra column contains the initials $N R^1$ or S^2 opposite the names of one or two electors. In this poll book there is no summary of the total number of votes cast.

The poll of 1769 differs in some particulars from those already described. The columns headed *Freeholders* and *Freemen* are placed before those containing the names of the candidates instead of after, and a check mark is used instead of the abbreviation *do.* There were eight candidates, and their names are given in full on the first page, the

---

[1] *Non-resident.*   [2] *Sworn.*

columns being headed merely by the initial letters of their surnames. The electors are arranged according to the days on which the poll was taken. Mr. Richard Mercer is stated to have been the first voter, while James Jauncey, Esq., is declared to have been the last. On the final page there is an analysis of the number of votes cast on each day for each candidate, while the total number of electors is 1515. In a few cases the occupations of the voters are stated, and the whole list is further explained by the following series of symbols:

q. Signifies the Person qualified (sworn) with Respect to his Freehold.

§ *Voted in his Right in the Seceder's Meeting.*

* *Stands for Scrutiny.*

N. R., For Non Resident.

The general election law of New Jersey was chiefly noteworthy for its provision that the sheriff should not declare the choice upon the view without the consent of the candidates. The proceedings were begun by the reading of the writ and the poll was taken from day to day until the names of all the electors had been entered. The residences of the electors, as well as their names and those of the candidates for whom they voted, were placed on the list.[1]

In Maryland no particular method of conducting an election was prescribed. "The safest and best rule for the provinces to follow in electing such delegates and representatives," was declared to be " the presidents of the Proceedings in Parliament in England as neare as the Constitution of this Province will admitt." [2] Accordingly, the sheriffs were merely directed to hold the elections " in such manner and forme as ye laws of England and this province doe direct and provide." [3]

[1] 12 Geo. I, chap. 40; Nevill's *Laws*, 142; Allinson's *Laws*, 66.
[2] Act 1678, *Maryland Archives*, 3 *Proceedings and Acts of Assembly*, 60.
[3] 8 Geo. I, chap. 42; 2 Charles Lord Baltimore, chap. 11, Bacon's *Laws*.

When we come to Georgia we find no authorization of the determination of an election either by show of hands or by acclamation. The returning officer was simply commanded to attend the place of election, and enter the names of every person presented or presenting himself as a candidate, in a book or roll, leaving a fair column under each for the names of the voters. As each elector came up to be polled, the returning officer repeated distinctly the name of the candidate voted for, before recording it in the proper column of his book. No elector was allowed to alter his vote after it had once been entered, or to vote twice at one and the same election. Upon adjourning the poll at convenient times during the days of election, the returning officer first added up the votes cast and declared the total to the candidates present. Upon reopening the poll he again announced the number of votes received by each candidate. The limit of an election was fixed at two days unless a scrutiny were demanded. Upon waiting two hours after the last vote had been given, or at any time if the candidates present consented, the poll could be closed.[1]

C. THE PROPRIETARY GOVERNMENTS. The six colonial governments whose method of taking the vote remains to be considered were all proprietary in their origin and the procedure followed at elections appears to have combined the best features of the Puritan ballot and the English poll. From this combination a general system was evolved which ought to have been less liable to abuse than those prevailing in the other colonies. Under the proprietary governments, whenever an elector was entitled to vote for more than one candidate, it was customary to place on the same ticket the names of all officers having similar functions. In this and other respects the ballot in this group of colonies bore a

---

[1] Act June 9th, 1761. Published in Appendix B to this work.

strong resemblance to those in common use in the United States just before the introduction of the Australian ballot.

The earliest mention of the ballot in this group of colonial governments appears in 1676 in the Concessions and Agreements granted by the proprietors of West Jersey. It should be remembered in this connection that the word *ballot* did not occur in New England; the term *papers* being always used instead. The writer is therefore inclined to believe that this is the first appearance in America of the ballot under its later and specific name.

The language of the West Jersey constitution with reference to the subject was as follows:

"And the said elections shall be made and distinguished by ballating Trunks, to avoid noise and confusion and not by holding up of the hands or otherwise howsoever." [1] "And also that all such elections as aforesaid be not determined by the common and confused way of crys and voices, but by putting Balls into Balloting Boxes to be provided for that purpose for the Prevention of all Partiality and whereby every Man may freely choose according to his own Judgement and honest Intention." [2]

These two passages are also noteworthy for their distinct repudiation of the system then in vogue in England of elections by acclamation or by show of hands. The Concessions and Agreements went into operation, but the writer has not been able to discover anything which throws light upon the *modus operandi* of these balls and boxes.

In East Jersey the paper constitution of 1683 went no further than to provide in general terms that all elections should be by ballot. [3] Whatever may have been the manner of voting under the Jersey proprietary governments, their

---

[1] Chap. 3, Leaming and Spicer, 385.

[2] Chap. 32, Leaming and Spicer, 405.

[3] Fundamental Constitutions, chaps. 2, 3, 5, *etc.*; Leaming and Spicer, 153; 1 *New Jersey Archives*, 397.

surrender to the crown in 1701 caused the introduction of the English poll.[1]

It is believed that the ballot as it appeared in the Jerseys and in Pennsylvania under its earlier frames of government was derived from Harrington.[2] In his description of the ideal commonwealth of Oceana, the English philosopher made provision for an elaborate and complicated system of balls and boxes,[3] modelled upon what he had seen in Venice. A recent writer seems to derive the written ballot in New England as well as Pennsylvania from the town of Emden in Friesland, where Penn had resided for a short time.[4] In support of both views it may, however, be stated that the Dutch system and that of the *Oceana* were in essence somewhat similar, and both may, therefore, have had an influence on the institutions of the American colonies. But in the Jersey and Pennsylvania plans all of the cumbersome details that characterized the European systems were omitted, so that nothing more than the germ appears to have been transplanted to America.

When we come to Pennsylvania we find something more substantial than the vague language of paper constitutions. By his first frame of government, as well as by the act of settlement, William Penn provided that all elections should be by ballot.[5] How this provision was construed is shown by a debate which took place in April, 1689, in the Provinvincial Council. The matter under discussion was a disputed election. One of the members stated that the election was attended by great disorder and that many persons came over from Jersey and voted in Chester County. As the " Poll

---

[1] See p. 164, *ante.*   [2] See Chalmers, *Political Annals,* 642.

[3] See Harrington's works, ed. Toland. 1771, 80, 83, 103 *et seq.*

[4] 2 Campbell, *Puritan in Holland, England and America,* 431 *et seq.*

[5] § 20 of Frame, I *Pennsylvania Colonial Records,* 33: § 18 of Act of Settlement or Charter of 1682-3, I *Pennsylvania Colonial Records,* 42.

and Ballot" had not been used, he argued that it could not
be known whether these persons were really residents or
not. The return made by the sheriff was exhibited, and it
stated on its face that the electors were not willing to vote
by ballot. Some of the councillors seemed to think that a
balloting box was used in only one county and that unless
there was doubt as to who had been elected, the delegates
should be chosen by "votes," meaning we suppose a *vivâ
voce* election. Another member of the council declared that
the ballot was used at Upland and in all the lower counties,
"by black and white beanes put into a hatt, wch is balloting
in his sence and cannot be denyed by the charter, when it
is demanded."[1]

This debate is of the utmost importance as throwing
light upon the course of procedure prevailing in Pennsylvania during the earlier years of her history. The phrase
"Poll and Ballot," as here used, aptly characterizes the system of elections in the proprietary governments during the
eighteenth century. The bean ballot may possibly have
been borrowed from Massachusetts, although we should
imagine that her influence among the Quakers of Pennsylvania would be very slight. The fact that the beans were
put into hats, added to what has already been stated in regard to some of the New England colonies,[2] shows that articles of head gear were used as balloting boxes in America
as well as in ancient Greece. The doubt as to the proper
course of procedure which seems to have prevailed in the
minds of the councillors, indicates that in the earlier times
the returning officer was free to act as he pleased in regard
to matters of detail. If there is any general principle to be
gathered from the debate in the Pennsylvania Council, it is
that the ballot took the place of the poll in the English sys-

---

[1] 1 *Pennsylvania Colonial Records*, 279.   [2] See pp. 142, 147, 148 *ante.*

tem of elections. Unless, therefore, the ballot was demanded, or the returning officer was in doubt, elections were decided by show of hands or by acclamation.

No further action, whether by legislation or otherwise, appears to have been taken on the subject of elections until 1706, when the poll and ballot was introduced by a statute which prescribed in detail every step in the process of voting. On the day of election the clerks were first sworn "Truly and indifferently to take the said Poll, and set down the names of each Freeholder and Elector and the Place of his Freehold or Estate, and to poll no Elector who is not attested, if so required by the Inspectors of such Clerks." This oath explains the entries in the poll books, for the pages of these books were divided into as many " distinct columns on fair Paper as there shall be candidates voted for."

As each elector came to the polls he delivered to the sheriff or judge of election a piece of paper on which were written the names of the persons for whom he voted.[1] If the elector was illiterate, the judge was required to open the paper and read aloud the names of the persons written therein, and ask the elector if those were the candidates for whom he voted. Upon receiving an affirmative answer, the judge put the paper, as well as all other ballots handed to him, into a box which the sheriff was required to provide. In case, however, a voter brought no tickets, or an illiterate elector did not wish to vote for the persons whose names were written on his paper, he could give verbally the names of the candidates he "mostly desired should be chosen," and the clerks were required to make entry accordingly.[2] The element of secrecy in Pennsylvania elections depended, therefore, upon the option of the individual voter, who could use the simple English poll if he saw fit. This recognition of

[1] Each county, it will be remembered, returned eight members.
[2] 4 Anne, chap. 129, Franklin ed., 1742, 67.

the illiterate voter is not found outside of the proprietary dominions of Penn, and it would seem to have been necessary
wherever it was not desired to confine the suffrage to persons
who could read and write.   In New England, for example,
except in the election of assistants which an unlearned man
could easily understand, it would seem that the written ballot rendered it extremely difficult for an illiterate freeman to
vote as he desired.   A friend or a neighbor might prepare his
ballot, but then he could not be sure whether it contained
the names of those for whom he wished to vote.   The Pennsylvania statute met this difficulty and electors could be rea-
sonably certain that they voted as they desired.   Of course
the honesty of the election officers was an important factor
in bringing about this result.

After 1718 each elector handed a second ticket to the
judges and on this were written the names of six persons for
assessors of the county taxes.[1] Seven years later the additional
ballots also contained the name of a candidate for the office
of county commissioner.[2]   In this province the poll could be
closed as soon as the electors who appeared had cast their
votes.   It could not, however, be delayed in any way or adjourned from place to place.[3]   The official report of a riot
which took place at the regular election of 1742 in Philadelphia gives us a picture, although an imperfect one, of the
manner in which the voting was conducted under the law of
4 Anne.   The poll was taken in a public street or square
and the freeholders were twice attacked by a mob of sailors
and roughs.   In the first instance the electors were engaged
in chosing inspectors, and in the second the voting proper
was in progress.[4]

[1] 4 Geo. I, chap. 213, Franklin ed., 1742, 156.
[2] 11 Geo. I, chap. 2, Hall and Sellers ed., 1775, 131.
[3] 4 Anne, chap. 129, Franklin ed., 1742, 67.
[4] 4 *Pennsylvania Colonial Records*, 620.

In the latter part of the colonial period another general
election law was enacted which further elaborated the course
of procedure. Before nine o'clock on the morning of the
regular day for choosing representatives, the judges of
election met and "with all expedition," allotted to each
township, ward or district a separate door, window or other
convenient place of the house where the election was to be
held. At each of the places so designated was written or
printed " in large Characters or Letters the Names of each
Township, Ward or District whose Inspectors shall attend to
receive the Tickets of that Place." An inspector was allowed to receive only the votes from the district which he
represented. As an elector came up, his name and residence
were called out in a voice loud enough to be heard by the
inspectors and clerks of the other divisions. The inspector
checked off the name of the voter by writing the word *voted*,
or, if qualified, by adding the word *sworn* or *affirmed* on the
margin of the list of taxables of the township from which he
came. Meanwhile, two clerks took down in writing the
names and residences of the electors and the number of votes
received by each candidate as they were called out by the
inspectors. The ballots were placed in a box which the
inspector bound and sealed with tape and gave to the sheriff
as soon as the voting was over.[1]

Elections were conducted in Delaware in substantially the
same way as in Pennsylvania. The statute of 4 Anne in the
latter government was reënacted with a few changes in the
former.[2] So also was that of 6 George III, with the addition
of a provision requiring the sheriff to purchase at the expense
of the county a ballot box for each hundred. These boxes
had the name of the hundred printed on the cover and were

[1] 6 Geo. III, chap. 8, §§ 3, 5, 8, 10; 13 Geo. III, chap. 13; Hall and Sellers ed.,
1775, 323.

[2] 7 Geo. II, chap. 61a, Franklin and Hall ed., 1752, 118; Adams ed., 1797, 147.

delivered to the inspectors who could put only the ballots received from their own hundred into the proper box.[1]

The Pennsylvania method of dividing each county into districts and providing a separate polling place for the electors of each division was doubtless necessary on account of the great size of the counties, and it was also due to the system of inspectors chosen, as has already been shown,[2] from the various divisions of the county. It is, moreover, highly probable that the English statute of 18 George II, chap. 18, which provided separate booths for each district,[3] had some influence on the Pennsylvania statute of 6 George III.

Although by the act of settlement of 1682–3,[4] the inhabitants of Penn's dominions were given the privilege of electing a double number of sheriffs and coroners who were to be presented to the governor for confirmation, it was not until 1706 that a statute explained how the franchise was to be exercised in Pennsylvania. This law provided that after the election of the members of the assembly had been completed, the coroner or the judge of election should cause a double number of sheriffs to be chosen in each county. The persons selected were ordered to present themselves before the governor within two days after their election, and if he refused to commission either of them, the candidate first named in the return was to hold the office for one year.[5] After the sheriffs had been chosen, the sheriff or judges proceeded in a similar manner to choose a double number of coroners. Some years afterward, however, the procedure was greatly simplified by requiring electors to hand in with their ballots for assemblymen and assessors a third ticket

---

[1] 12 Geo. III, chap. 207, Adams ed., 1797, 500.   [2] See pp. 116 *et seq., ante.*

[3] See p. 159 *ante.*   [4] § 16, 1 *Pennsylvania Colonial Records*, 16.

[5] 4 Anne, chap. 153, Franklin ed., 1742, 105.

containing the names of two persons for sheriff and two for coroner.[1]

Delaware had anticipated her neighbor by enacting in 1700 a law similar to that of 4 Anne, except that the governor was allowed six days within which to commission a a sheriff.[2] A later act provided that the under-sheriff must never be the person chosen but not commissioned, and that a sheriff could not have another term until he had been three years out of office.[3]

Locke's Constitution contained no provision in regard to the method of voting in the Carolinas and, on account of his inability to obtain copies of the earlier election laws, the writer has no positive information about the condition of affairs there in the seventeenth century. The revised statute of 1715 in North Carolina merely required that all persons offering to vote for members of the assembly should bring to the marshall or deputy a list containing the names of the persons he voted for. That this law was not framed with a view to secrecy is shown by the subsequent clause requiring the voter to subscribe his own name or cause the same to be done.[4]

In 1744, however, North Carolina adopted the secret ballot. The election was commenced at or before ten o'clock on the morning of the appointed day by the sheriff making three proclamations. Each voter handed to the sheriff in the presence of the inspectors " a Scroll of Paper rolled up with the Name or Names of the Person or Persons he votes for written therein." The sheriff put all scrolls so received into " a small Box with a Lid or Cover having a Hole in it

[1] 11 Geo. I, chap. 269, Franklin ed., 1742, 293.

[2] 12 Will. III, chap. 21a, Franklin and Hall ed., 1752, 29; Adams ed., 1797, 63.

[3] 13 Geo. III, chap. 65, Franklin and Hall ed., 1752, 133; Adams ed., 1797, 164.

[4] 2 *North Carolina Colonial Records*, 213.

not exceeding Half an Inch in diameter; which said cover shall be sealed and secured on the Box in the Presence of the Inspectors." A list of all the persons who voted was taken in writing by the sheriff and by each of the inspectors. The hole in the box was first sealed when the poll was adjourned from one till "Half an Hour after Two of the Clock."[1] The law just quoted continued in force for about sixteen years. In 1760 a statute was enacted which, after declaring that there was no election law then in operation, substituted for the secret ballot the English method according to which the sheriff took the poll in the presence of the inspectors. The provision requiring all the votes to be given openly and leaving to the sheriff the duty of recording them,[2] seems from a modern point of view, to indicate a backward tendency. Possibly the ballot was too far ahead of the times to be practicable in North Carolina.

In South Carolina the complaint of the lords proprietors in reference to the practice of allowing one elector to bring in the vote of another seems to indicate that some form of written ballot existed as far back as 1683.[3] The election law of 1704 seems to recognize the ballot as well as the *vivâ voce* method of voting. According to it the returning officer was to open the election by reading aloud his precept. All voices or votes given before the reading of the writ were void, and the electors might afterwards alter their votes, if they saw fit, or make a new election. Whenever the poll was adjourned the returning officer was required " to seal up in a paper bag or box all the votes given in that day in the presence of, and with the seals of two or more of each contending party." At the commencement of each session proclamation was made, and the sheriff broke the seals " in the

[1] 17 Geo. II, chap. 1, §§ 1, 2, 11; Davis and Swann ed., 1752, 177, 233, 312.

[2] 33 Geo. II, chap. 1, §§ 1, 2; Davis ed., 1773, 247.

[3] Rivers, *South Carolina*, Appendix, 406.

presence of the parties with whose seales they were sealed up, if they will and do attend to see it done."[1]

After the parish became the election district, the names of all the voters were " fairly entered in a book or roll, to prevent voting twice." The electors brought to the church wardens scrolls containing in writing the names of the persons they voted for. These scrolls were rolled up, and when the poll was closed they were placed in " some box, glass or paper, sealed up with the seals of any two or more" of the electors present. When the poll was re-opened the box was unsealed.[2] After 1719, however, it seems to have been the duty of the elector to place " in a box, glass, or sheet of paper prepared for that purpose a piece of paper rolled up, whereon is written the name of the Representatives he votes for."[3] It is important to note that in South Carolina the secrecy of the ballot seems to have depended upon the option of each individual voter, for the statutes of both 1716 and 1719 expressly declared that electors should *not be obliged* to subscribe their names to the papers they handed in.

§ 8. *Count of the Votes.* It is scarcely necessary to state that when an election was made by show of hands, no particular method of counting the vote was needed. Whenever a poll was taken the mere addition of the names or marks in the particular column or page assigned to each candidate would suffice. In North Carolina we find that the number of votes given for each candidate must be cast up by the sheriff in the presence of the inspectors,[4] while in Georgia[5] a simple addition and declaration was required.[6]

---

[1] Act 1704, no. 227, §§ 8, 10, 2 Cooper, 249.

[2] Act 1716, no. 365, §§ 2, 3, 2 Cooper, 683.

[3] Act 1719, no. 394, § 5, 3 Cooper, 50.

[4] 33 Geo. II, chap. 1, § 1, Davis ed., 1773, 247.

[5] Act June 9th, 1761. [6] Virginia, "Examination," 3 Hening, 236.

In New England where the general use of the ballot would seem to have required some special method of counting the votes, there was very little legislation on the subject. During the later years of the first Massachusetts government the ballots cast at the general election were counted by tellers, and these officers as well as all the other persons present at canvass were under oath.[1] The Hartford Constitution provided that the " papers should be received and told by one or more chosen by the court."[2]

Three of the proprietary governments prescribed a detailed course of procedure which was to be followed in counting ballots. In Pennsylvania the ballot box was opened as soon as the poll had been closed and the papers were taken out in the presence of the inspectors. The ballots were then delivered one by one to the clerks who entered the names " therein expressed, in Columns or otherwise, so that they shall cast up how many times each person's name is repeated in the same and set it down, and shall then pronounce publicly to the people, him whose name is oftenest mentioned in said Papers to be first elected," and so on until the regular number of eight had been chosen.[3] When there were separate ballot boxes for each division of the county, it was provided that the judges should proceed to " read, count and cast up " the votes, contained in the boxes which the inspectors had delivered to them " bound with tape and sealed up." The clerks and inspectors were liable to a penalty of £10 for not delivering their lists and tallies to the sheriff.[4]

The method of counting the votes in Delaware under the district system was more complicated. The boxes were

---

[1] 5 *Massachusetts Colonial Records*, 262, 292.   See pp. 132, 141, *ante*.

[2] 1 *Connecticut Colonial Records*, 21.

[3] 4 Anne, chap. 129. Franklin ed., 1742, 67.   Similarly, Delaware: 7 Geo. II, chap. 61a, Franklin and Hall ed., 1752, 118.

[4] 6 Geo. III, chap. 8, § 10, Hall and Sellers ed., 1775, 323.

opened in succession, and the tickets contained in each one were counted separately. When the ballots had been compared with one another, and the names of the persons voting in each hundred had also been ascertained, all the ballots were placed in one large box antl thoroughly mixed; "after which no more tickets or votes shall be received on any pretence whatever." Then the sheriff or coroner took the tickets out of the larger box, and after reading them aloud handed them one by one to the clerks. The inspectors and clerks were required to deliver to the sheriff their tax lists and tallies undefaced "with the number of persons voting ascertained in words at length in a certificate thereof on the said lists signed by them respectively." The lists of the clerks were required to be "cast up and the number of votes for each candidate mentioned in words at length," and signed by the clerks and two or more inspectors.[1] The thoroughness of the Delaware method of counting the votes ought to have reduced to the lowest limit any possibility of fraud or collusion on the part of the election officers.

As long as North Carolina used the ballot she also prescribed a regular method for conducting the canvass. At sunset the ballot box was opened by the sheriff in the presence of the candidates and the inspectors. The scrolls were then taken out one by one and the names written on them were read aloud, while each inspector kept a tally of the number of votes received by each candidate.[2]

In most of the proprietary governments there were provisions in regard to defective ballots. Thus, in Pennsylvania,[3] Delaware,[4] North Carolina,[5] and South Carolina,[6] ballots con-

[1] 12 Geo. III, chap. 207, §§ 5, 7, Adams ed., 1797, 500.
[2] 17 Geo. II, chap. 1, § 2, Davis and Swann ed., 1752, 177.
[3] 4 Anne, chap. 129, Franklin ed., 1742, 67.
[4] 7 Geo. II, chap. 61a, Franklin and Hall ed., 1752, 118; Adams ed., 1797, 147.
[5] 17 Geo. II, chap. 1, § 2, Davis and Swann ed., 1752, 177.
[6] Act 1716, no. 365, § 3, 2 Cooper, 683.

taining more than the proper number of names were declared
void.   Delaware also rejected those containing less than the
required number.[1]   In Pennsylvania ballots found "deceit-
fully folded together," so as to contain the names of more
candidates than a single elector was entitled to vote for, were
thrown out.[2]   The laws of both the Carolinas provided that
if two or more scrolls were rolled together and put in the box
as one, they must "be cast away as useless and void.[3]

In a few instances we find that official notices of their election were given to the successful candidates.   Thus in South
Carolina the wardens were required to notify them in writing
at the church door or at some other public place, and that
within seven days after the ballots had been counted.[4]   In
Maryland the sheriffs were merely required to notify the persons chosen in case they should have been absent from the
court of election.[5]

The laws did not definitely fix the proportion of votes cast
which should be required to elect a candidate.   A clear distinction was not in all cases drawn between the meaning of
the words *majority* and *plurality*, and this is shown by at
least one statute which uses the two words synonymously.[6]
In the middle of the eighteenth century Connecticut declared
that all officers must receive a majority of the votes cast in
order to be elected.   If this did not occur the election must
be decided by the assembly.[7]   In Massachusetts,[8] New

---

[1] 7 Geo. II, chap. 61a, § 4, Franklin and Hall ed., 1752, 118; Adams ed., 1797, 147.

[2] 4 Anne, chap. 129, Franklin ed., 1742, 67; Delaware: 7 Geo. II, chap. 61a,
Franklin and Hall ed., 1752, 118; Adams ed., 1797, 147.

[3] North Carolina: 17 Geo. II, chap. 1, § 2, Davis and Swann ed., 1752, 177;
South Carolina: Act 1716, no. 365, § 3, 2 Cooper, 683, "invalid and of no effect."

[4] Act 1716, no. 365, 2 Cooper, 683.

[5] 8 Geo. I, chap. 42; 2 Charles Lord Baltimore, chap. 11, Bacon's *Laws*.

[6] See 4 Geo. II, chap. 3, Nevill's *Laws*, 200.

[7] 8 *Connecticut Colonial Records*, 453.   This is the law in Connecticut at the
present day.   [8] Charter 1691, 1 Ames and Goodell, 11.

York,[1] New Jersey,[2] South Carolina[3] and Georgia,[4] a majority seems to have been required. In the other colonies as a rule a simple plurality was sufficient. Thus Rhode Island enacted that inasmuch as there might "happen a division in the votes soe as the greater half may not pitch directly on one certaine person, yett the person which hath the most votes shall be declared elected."[5] There can be no doubt that the passages just quoted from the Connecticut and Rhode Island colonial records place those colonies squarely in opposition to one another on this point, but as to other provinces the writer does not feel so sure of his position.

§ 9. *Return of the Writ.* In order to fully understand the subject of the return of the writ, it is necessary to consider the history of England with reference to this question, for it was there that the custom originated, and the American colonies merely adopted with a few modifications the practice of the mother country.

In the earliest times the return was effected by the sheriff simply appending to the writ the names of the persons chosen and those of the sureties for their attendance at the parliament.[6] This method rendered false returns so easy that a statute was passed in 1405, requiring the names of those chosen to be written in an indenture "under the seals of all them that did choose them and tacked to the same writ of the parliament, which indenture so sealed and tacked shall be holden for the sheriff's return of the said writ touching the knights of the shire."[7] But long before this time returns

---

[1] 3 William and Mary, Bradford ed., 1710, 17.   [2] Act 1704.

[3] Act 1716, no. 365, § 3, 2 Cooper, 683.   [4] Act 1761.

[5] 2 *Rhode Island Colonial Records*, 83. See also Pennsylvania, 4 Anne, chap. 129, Franklin ed., 1742, 67; "fair majority," *ibid.*, 346; 4 *Connecticut Colonial Records*, 8; Virginia: 4 Anne, chap. 2, 3 Hening, 236; North Carolina: 17 Geo. II, chap. 1, Davis and Swann ed., 1752, 177.

[6] Cox, *Antient Parliamentary Elections*, 125.

[7] *Statutes* 7 Hen. IV, chap. 15, § 5; 6 Hen. VI, chap. 4, § 4.

were occasionally made by indenture. Prynne refers to such a document as early as the twelfth year of Edward the First.[1] In 1444 a statute was enacted which required the sheriff to issue precepts to the mayor or bailiff of every city or borough within his county, and ordered them to return the precepts by indenture to the sheriff, so that the latter might make return of the writ.[2] Although the statute of 7 Henry IV seems to require the indenture to be signed by all the voters participating in the election, the custom soon arose of having a few of the electors sign in behalf of the rest.[3] This practice has been continued almost down to the present day, although in recent years the original method of return by endorsement of the sheriff on the back of the writ has been revived.[4]

In the general elections of the Puritan colonies there was no necessity for any form of return, unless the sending of the proxies to the capital town may be regarded in that light. Still in Massachusetts, although no writs were issued for the election of deputies, we find that the constables of the towns were required to make return under their own hand.[5] As a natural consequence of the writ and precept system of the provincial government, the selectmen of the towns made their returns to the sheriffs of the counties, and the latter in turn notified the secretary at least one day before the sitting of the general court.[6]

Unlike her northern neighbors, Hartford provided for the

---

[1] Prynne, *Brevia Parliamentaria*, 190.   [2] 23 Hen. VI, chap. 14.

[3] See Cox, *Antient Parliamentary Elections*, 131, and preceding pages, where the subject is thoroughly discussed and the above view supported.

[4] 2 De Franqueville, *Le Gouvernment et Le Parlement Brittaniques*, 446.

[5] 4 *Massachusetts Colonial Records*, pt. i, 326; 3 *Massachusetts Colonial Records*, 356; *Laws*, ed. 1660, 25, ed. 1814, 97. Also 1 *New Hampshire Provincial Papers*, 408.

[6] *Laws*, 1692–3, chap. 38, 1 Ames and Goodell, 89. For forms, see Appendix A of this work.

issue of writs, and under the Constitution of 1638 returns were made by the constable endorsing on the back of his warrant, under his own hand, the names of those elected.[1]

Among the colonies which followed the English method of elections, the earliest statutory provision in regard to returns is found in Virginia. By this the sheriff was simply directed to make a return before the sitting of the assembly by subscription and "the major part of the hands of the electors."[2] Subsequent laws required the return to be made by endorsement on the back of the writ, according to a specified form.[3] The law in Georgia was similar, except that an election officer was forbidden to return himself.[4] In Maryland the earlier returns were signed by all the freemen participating in the election.[5] The general election law of 1678 provided that the four persons elected in each county should be returned by four separate indentures made between the sheriff on the one hand and the freemen electing on the other. It was required that these indentures should bear the date of the day of election, and mention the time and place of the same.[6] After 1715 two indentures were provided for each candidate, each instrument bearing the hands and seals of both the sheriff and the electors.[7] The writer has found no legislation on this subject in New York beyond that contained in the law of 11 Will. III, which provided that the

---

[1] 1 *Connecticut Colonial Records*, 21.

[2] 5–6 Commonwealth, Act vii, 1 Hening, 411. See also 14 Car. II, Act i, 2 Hening, 82.

[3] 11 Will. III, chap. 2, 3 Hening, 172; 4 Anne, chap. 2, § 7, 3 Hening, 241.

[4] Act 1761.

[5] See *Maryland Archives*, 1 *Proceedings and Acts of Assembly*, where a number of these are given.

[6] Act 1678, *Maryland Archives*, 3 *Proceedings and Acts of Assembly*, 60. Also 4 William and Mary, chap. 76; 4 Anne, chap. 35; Appendix A of this work.

[7] 8 Geo. I, chap. 42, Baskett ed., 1723, 121; 2 Charles Lord Baltimore, chap. 11, Bacon's *Laws*.

persons elected should be returned "by Indentures sealed betwixt the said sheriffs and the said Chuser so to be made."[1] Returns were made in Pennsylvania by a pair of indentures sealed between the sheriff or the judges and six or more of the electors."[2] Such was the rule for assemblymen, commissioners and assessors, as well as in regard to the double number of persons chosen for the offices of sheriff and coroner.[3] This, as we have seen, was substantially the practice in England at that time. Toward the close of the colonial period a law was enacted requiring that as soon as all the votes had been counted, the sheriff should call in four reputable freeholders as assistant judges. Indentures were then sealed between the assistant judges and the sheriff as one party, and at least six inspectors as the other.[4] Six years after this law, a Delaware statute provided that indentures should be sealed between the sheriff or coroner and at least two inspectors together with four of the electors.[5]

In a few of the colonies the laws required that returns should be addressed to a particular office or officer. Thus, in Maryland, sheriffs were directed to certify one part of each indenture "and transmit it to the Chancellor, close sealed up under his hand and seal, and directed to the Lord Proprietary of this Province and alsoe the said Chancellor."[6] A subsequent statute ordered that the return should be addressed to the governor or to the keeper of the great seal of the province.[7] The other part of the indenture was always

---

[1] Chap. 74, Van Schaack's *Laws*, 28.

[2] 4 Anne, chap. 129, Franklin ed., 1742, 67.

[3] *Ibid.*, chap. 153, Franklin ed., 1742, 105; 2 Geo. I, chap. 269, Franklin ed., 1742, 293.

[4] 6 Geo. III, chap. 8, § 11, Hall and Sellers ed., 1775, 323.

[5] 12 Geo. III, chap. 207, Adams ed., 1797, 500.

[6] Act 1678, *Maryland Archives*, 3 *Proceedings and Acts of Assembly*, 60.

[7] 2 Charles Lord Baltimore, chap. 11, Bacon's *Laws*.

kept by the sheriff for his justification. In Virginia, however, returns were made to the secretary's office at James City,[1] at least one day before the date mentioned in the writ.[2] In South Carolina returns were made to the master in chancery within ten days after an election."[3]

In Pennsylvania the practice in this matter was slightly different. One of the two indentures used in certifying the return of assemblymen was delivered to the governor and the other to the assembly,[4] while the returns of the double number of coroners and sheriffs were sent to the governor, who had the power of appointing these officers.[5] But in the case of the commissioners and assessors the returns were addressed to the justices at the general sessions of the peace,[6] and entered on the records in the sessions' minute book by the clerk of the justices. The reason why the indentures of assemblymen were thus addressed seems to be that they served a twofold purpose, *viz.*, as a certificate of election, and as a power of attorney enabling the newly chosen members to act for their constituents.

It may be inferred that the provisions just enumerated in regard to the transmission of returns were derived from statutes in force at that time in the mother country. Doubtless many of the details not covered by the colonial statutes were regulated according to the English custom. Some time before the date set for the assembling of the newly chosen parliament, and with all convenient expedition within a period of fourteen days after an election, the sheriff was required to make return, either in person or by deputy, to the clerk of the crown in the high court of chancery. For the entry of

[1] 14 Car. II, Act l, 2 Hening, 82.　　[2] 4 Anne, chap. 2, § 9, 3 Hening, 236.
[3] 23 Geo. II, no. 885, § 6, 4 Cooper, 98.
[4] 4 Anne, chap. 129, Franklin ed., 1742, 67.
[5] 4 Anne, chap. 153, Franklin ed., 1742, 105.
[6] 11 Geo. I, chap. 269, Franklin ed., 1742, 293; Hall and Sellers ed., 1775, 131.

the return the sheriff was to pay the ancient and lawful fees of four shillings for every knight of the shire, and two shillings for every citizen, burgess or baron of the Cinque Ports whom he returned.   The charges were paid by the king out of his account in the exchequer.[1]   The clerk of the crown was required to enter every return and amendment within six days after receiving the same, in a large book to which all persons had free access at reasonable times.[2]

It might sometimes happen that two or more candidates received exactly the same number of votes, and the question would then arise as to which one should be returned.   In England the solution of this problem caused considerable difficulty to the returning officers.   In 1625, for example, the mayor of New Lymington made return that two candidates had received the same number of voices, and he would therefore leave the decision to the House of Commons.   This seems to have been usually done, but at the present day the question is settled so far as the United Kingdom is concerned by the act of 1872.   It gives the sheriff, who is generally disqualified in other cases, a casting vote if there is a tie between two or more opposing candidates.[3]

This question seems to have arisen in but two of the American colonies, and in both of them it was decided that the sheriff could return whichever one of the candidates he thought fit.   In Virginia his casting vote was at first made conditional on the fact of his being a freeholder,[4] but after 1763 this was not necessary.[5]   If it appeared on a scrutiny before the House of Burgesses that the petitioner and the sitting member had an equal number of votes, and if the officer who took the poll declared on oath that if the votes had been found equal at the time of the election he would

---

[1] *Statute* 10 and 11 Will. III, chap. 7.   [2] *Statute* 7 and 8 Will. III, chap. 7.

[3] 2 De Franqueville, *Le Gouvernment et Le Parlement Brittaniques*, 444.

[4] 4 Anne, chap. 2, § 4, 3 Hening, 236.   [5] 3 Geo. III, chap. 1, 7 Hening, 519.

have returned the petitioner, then the petitioner was declared to have been chosen.[1] The privilege of a casting vote was also granted in North Carolina, but it was expressly provided that in no other case could the sheriff have a voice in the election of a burgess.[2]

§ 10. *Provisions against Fraud.* Many of the provisions that were framed for the express purpose of preventing fraud have been enumerated in other parts of this work. Some of the special provisions which did not conveniently fall under any of the preceding subdivisions will be considered in the present section. For example, in New York the court of election was required to be held in the most public and usual place in the county. The poll could be taken only at the place of election, and could be neither delayed nor protracted until all the electors had voted.[3] Returning officers were forbidden to take any reward or fee for their services.[4]

A case which occurred in New Jersey in 1725 affords a good example of the abuses which the law requiring the consent of the candidates to an adjournment of the poll[5] was aimed to prevent. It appears that the sheriff of Burlington in his desire to favor a particular candidate kept a poll open for a fortnight and adjourned it to the very edge of the county without the consent of the other candidate, who was a Quaker. So gross was the partiality of this action that both parties united in passing a law against similar occurrences in the future.[6]

In none of the American colonies has the writer found a trace of the English custom of allowing the justices of the assize to take inquest against a sheriff in order to test the

---

[1] 3 Geo. III, chap. 1, § 12, 7 Hening, 519.

[2] 17 Geo. II, chap. 1, § 11, Davis and Swann ed., 1752, 177.

[3] 11 Will. III, chap. 74, §§ 4, 7, Van Schaack's *Laws*, 28.   [4] *Ibid.*, § 3.

[5] For example, New Jersey; 12 Geo. I, chap. 4c, Nevill's *Laws*, 142.

[6] Governor Burnet to the Lords of Trade; 5 *New York Colonial Documents*, 767.

truth of his return and permitting the latter to traverse an office found.[1]

As a further means of preventing fraud a few of the colonies followed the English precedent,[2] by requiring that copies of the poll must be delivered on demand to persons who were willing to pay a reasonable charge for the labor of writing them. This was the rule in Rhode Island,[3] New York,[4] and New Jersey.[5] Attested copies of the poll could be obtained on demand of the candidates in both Virginia[6] and North Carolina.[7]

Subsequent legislation, in Virginia at any rate, seems to have done away with the practice of requiring copies of the poll to be delivered to the candidates. Instead, the sheriff was required within twenty days after the election to faithfully deliver upon oath "unto the clerks of the same county court attested copies of the original poll of such election, without any embezzlement or alteration, to be recorded among the records of such county court."[8] A similar plan had been adopted in England some years previously, except that in the mother country the poll books were to be preserved among the records of the sessions of the peace.[9] In 1763 and thereafter the sheriff was ordered to deliver to the

[1] See *Statutes* 11 Hen. IV, chap. 1; 6 Hen. VI, chap. 4.

[2] See *Statute* 7 and 8 Will. III, chap. 25, § 6.

[3] Hall's *Code*, 1767, Title *Elections*, 78.

[4] 11 Will. III, chap. 74, § 8, Van Schaack's *Laws*, 28.

[5] 12 Geo. I, chap. 40, Nevill's *Laws*, 142.

[6] 11 Will. III, chap. 2, 3 Hening, 172; 4 Anne, chap. 2, § 7, 3 Hening, 236. "The sheriff shall, as soon as may be, cause a true and perfect copy" to be made, and shall deliver it with his own hand "to the candidate or other person applying for it on his behalf."

[7] 17 Geo. II, chap. 1, § 9, Davis and Swann ed. 1752, 177; 33 Geo. II, chap. 1, § 9, Davis ed., 1773, 247. By this act the attested copy must be delivered within ten days to the candidates or to persons applying for it in their behalf.

[8] 10 Geo. II, chap. 2, § 8, 4 Hening, 475.   [9] *Statute* 10 Anne, chap. 23, § 5.

county clerk, on oath, an attested copy of the poll, and a list
of those not sworn, with the names of the persons for whom
they had voted.[1]

In Pennsylvania just before the Revolution, sheriffs were
ordered to return on demand to the House of Assembly the
list of the taxables and the lists and tallies of the clerks.[2]   A
similar rule had been introduced in South Carolina a few
years before the date of the Pennsylvania statute.   The
church wardens were required to attend the assembly with
the master in chancery, who was to carry the return and
leave with the clerk of the house a list of the persons that
had voted.[3]   In the former of these colonies there were express statutory provisions to the effect that the votes and
tickets of all such as refused to take the oath should be
openly rejected.   The ballots of every person swearing or
affirming were to be put in a box, and a ticket so received
could not be suppressed.[4]

§ 11. *Contested Elections.*   At the meeting of His Majesty's
Privy Council in 1684, when the New York Charter of Liberties was under discussion, the clause of that instrument which
gave to the assembly with the consent of the governor power
to judge of undue elections and the qualifications of members, was objected to on the ground that " It may be inconvenient and is not practised in some other Plantations."[5]
Notwithstanding the opinion of the Privy Council, the present
writer believes that he has found sufficient evidence to justify
him in stating as a general rule that contested elections in the
American colonies were everywhere decided by the body to

---

[1] 3 Geo. III, chap. 1, § 15, 7 Hening, 519.   This seems to supersede the act of
10 Geo. II.

[2] 6 Geo. III, chap. 8, § 9, Hall and Sellers ed., 1775, 323.

[3] 23 Geo. II, no. 885, 4 Cooper, 98.

[4] 13 Geo. I, chap. 284, Franklin ed., 1742, 356.

[5] 3 *New York Colonial Documents*, 359.

whose membership the candidate aspired. Thus Massachusetts by the very law which authorized the sending of deputies to the general court, gave them power to hear and determine among themselves any differences that might arise as to the election of any of their number.[1]

The general court of Plymouth reserved to itself the power, of rejecting unfit deputies and of directing the towns to make a new choice.[2] New Hampshire nearly a century afterwards gave to the town officers the power of settling disputes in regard to elections, and in case of their failure to agree the decision was left to the house of representatives.[3] The Hartford constitution conferred upon the deputies the power of judging of their own elections,[4] and it may be conjectured that when the general management of elections was delegated to a grand committee of both houses in Rhode Island, the decision of contests was included as well as control over other matters.[5]

The various provisions we have enumerated refer, it will be noticed, only to the elections of members of the lower houses of the New England legislatures. The writer has found nothing which would tend to show how contests concerning the election of governors and other general officers were decided. The rule in regard to contested elections in the Puritan colonies was equally true in both the royal[6] and the proprietary governments. The laws of 1682 recognized the right of both houses of the Pennsylvania legislature to judge of the elections of their own members,[7] although when the up-

---

[1] 1634–5; 3 *Massachusetts Colonial Records*, 119.   [2] Brigham, 109.

[3] 1 Geo. II, chap. 107; Fowle ed., 1771, 142; ed. 1771, 166.

[4] 1638; 1 *Connecticut Colonial Records*, 24.

[5] Hall's *Code*, 1767, Title *Elections*, 78.

[6] See in particular the Georgia law of June 9th, 1761, published in Appendix B, *post*.

[7] *Laws agreed on in England*, chap. 3, 1 *Pennsylvania Colonial Records*, 37.

per house ceased to be an elective body its power in this respect was necessarily abolished. The method of trying a contested election case was by a scrutiny or examination of the votes cast, for the purpose of correcting any errors that might exist in the poll. In 1737 the New York legislature spent a month in making a scrutiny.[1] Virginia recognized the English method of contest by petition of the defeated candidate as well as the scrutiny,[2] before the house of burgesses.

In the three most southern colonies there were more specific provisions in regard to contested elections. Thus in North Carolina, sheriffs were required to attend the assembly for the first three days of its sitting (unless previously dismissed), for the purpose of giving information in case of contested elections, and also of showing the assembly a list of the votes cast for every person.[3] The sheriffs, and afterwards the church wardens, were ordered to attend the assembly of South Carolina during the first two days of the session, for the same purpose as in the northern province, although the wardens were accompanied by the master in chancery.[4]

In Georgia a scrutiny must be made if it were demanded, while returning officers were compelled upon summons from the commons house of assembly to attend and give information to the best of their knowledge of any matters or disputes that arose about the election of members returned by them. They were also required to show the poll, and were liable to a fine of fifty pounds sterling for refusal to do so.[5]

---

[1] 6 *New York Colonial Documents*, 56. The proceedings are given in full in the first volume of the journal of assembly, *circa* page 700. Also South Carolina, Act 1716, no. 365, §§ 1, 4, 2 Cooper, 683.

[2] 3 Geo. III, chap. 1, §§ 12, 14, 7 Hening, 519.

[3] *Laws* 1715, 2 *North Carolina Colonial Records*, 213.

[4] Act 1704, no. 227, § 4; Act 1716, no. 365, § 22, 2 Cooper, 227, 683; 23 Geo II, no. 885, § 6, 4 Cooper, 98.   [5] Act 1761.

§ 12. *Privileges of Voters.* In three of the southern colonies electors were granted certain privileges, in order, it may be supposed, that they might be the more willing to exercise their franchise. The writer has been unable to find any provisions of this, sort among the statutes regulating elections in England during the colonial period.

In Virginia, for example, no arrests were permitted on election days except for felony and breach of the peace, and processes executed at the election of burgesses were void.[1] In South Carolina an elector was exempt from the serving of writs or processes *eundo, manendo, redeundo,* that is to say, during his journey to and from the polls, or during his stay there for the purpose of voting, or for forty-eight hours after the scrutiny was finished. The penalty for breach of this law was a fine of twenty pounds paid to the aggrieved party by the officer offending, and the nullity of the writs.[2] The rule in Georgia was similar to that in South Carolina, and civil officers were forbidden to execute writs or other processes upon the body of the elector, provided he did not consume more than forty-eight hours upon his journey.[3]

§ 13. *Compulsory Voting.* Probably the earliest law enacted in the American colonies on the subject of compulsory voting was that passed by the general court of Plymouth in 1636. It provided that " for default in case of appearance at the election before mentioned without due excuse, each delinquent to be amerced in 3ˢ ster."[4] Compulsory voting in this colony was required as late as 1671, if not later. In the revision of the laws published in that year it was provided that " whosoever of the Freemen do not appear at Election in Person or by Proxy, he shall be for such neglect

---

[1] 14 Car. II, Act lvii, 2 Hening, 86; 4 Anne, chap. 3, § 6, 3 Hening, 248.

[2] Act 1716, no. 365, § 24, 2 Cooper, 683.   [3] Act 1761

[4] 11 *Plymouth Colony Records,* 10; Brigham, 37.

amerced to the Treasury Ten Shillings."[1] Virginia was the only other colony which insisted upon compulsory voting throughout her history. The earliest statute bearing on the subject was passed in 1646, and it speaks of the small number of persons who attended the elections. In order to remedy the evil it was then enacted that all freemen absent without lawful cause should be fined one hundred pounds of tobacco.[2] After 1662 the amount of the penalty was increased to two hundred pounds of the same staple.[3] The law as to compulsory voting was reënacted in 1705,[4] and again in 1763.[5]

In a previous chapter it has been explained that from the earliest times in Maryland attendance in person or participation in the election of a representative to the assembly was required of all freemen.[6] Later on the rule in this colony as to compulsory voting seems to have fallen into disuse until 1715, when it was revived, and all electors were compelled to attend the court of election under penalty of one hundred pounds of tobacco,[7] unless they could show sufficient cause for their absence. Whether this provision remained in force until the Declaration of Independence, or whether it fell into disuse, the writer is not prepared to state. Nothing that would prove the repeal of the law has been found.

In Delaware, by a statute of 7 George II, it was enacted that every elector convicted at the next quarter sessions on the oath of one credible witness of having absented himself from

[1] *Book of General Laws*, chap. v. § 4, Dilgham 258.

[2] 21 Car. I, Act xix, 1 Hening, 333.

[3] 14 Car. II, Act l, 2 Hening, 82.   [4] 4 Anne, chap. 2, § 3, 3 Hening, 236.

[5] 3 Geo. III, chap. 1, § 9, 7 Hening, 519.   [6] See p. 34, *ante*.

[7] 8 Geo. I, chap. 42, Baskett ed., 1723, 121; also 2 Charles Lord Baltimore, chap. 11, § 6, Bacon's *Laws*.

an election should be fined twenty shillings, unless he had been detained by sickness or unavoidable accident.[1]

Outside of the four colonies already mentioned, compulsory voting at general elections does not appear to have existed. North Carolina, we shall see, introduced the prin ciple in parish elections.[2] In a Massachusetts statute the following permissive clause has been found which might possibly have reference to compulsory voting at the election of assistants, the principle being applied when the names of the candidates were in turn balloted upon. " In all cases where any freeman is to give his vote, be it in court of election . . . . or the like, if he cannot see light or reason to give it positively one way or the other, he shall have liberty to be silent and not pressed to a determinate vote, which yet shall be interpreted and accounted as if he voted for the negative."[3]

Under the head of compulsory voting it is perhaps well to include a few laws which were in force in several of the northern settlements during the earlier years of their history. Thus in Providence, under the date of 1636, we find a provision that any one not appearing at the town meeting within fifteen minutes after the time mentioned by the person who gave warning, should be fined one shilling sixpence.[4] In a similar way Portsmouth fined freemen who were more than a half hour late,[5] and New Haven imposed a mulct of one shilling upon all the planters who came in after their names had been called.[6]

§ 14. *Bribery and Other Means of Influencing Voters.* It is a remarkable fact that with one exception, and that of comparatively late date, there are absolutely no statutes in

---

[1] 7 Geo. II, chap. 61a, Franklin and Hall ed., 1752, 118; Adams ed., 1797, 147.

[2] 5 Geo. III, chap. 2, Davis ed., 1773, 305.

[3] *Laws*, ed. 1660, 78; ed. 1814, 200. [4] 1 *Rhode Island Colonial Records*, 13, 15.

[5] *Ibid.*, 81. [6] 1 *New Haven Colonial Records*, 80.

any of the New England colonies on the subject of bribery. Whether the reason of this was that elections were really purer in that part of the continent, or because the Puritans considered it beneath their dignity to speak of the sale or purchase of votes, the writer does not venture to decide. The absence of such laws should speak for itself.

The single exception referred to was in Rhode Island, where a general act against bribery and corruption was passed in 1737. Judging from the provisions of the statute, this evil must have been prevalent to an alarming extent in that colony. Persons offering bribes were declared liable to forfeit double the sum offered and persons accepting them were to be similarly punished besides being incapitated for voting for any officer during the space of three years. When there was insufficient proof the accused could purge himself by oath, but in default of this he was adjudged guilty.[1] Ten years later a more stringent law was passed. By this all persons were required to take an oath that they had not been bribed, while the officers and justices were ordered to swear that they "justly and truly abhorred the most detestable crime of Bribery," and that they would do their best to expose all persons guilty of such practices. Upon proof to the assembly that a single vote had been unlawfully obtained by the " procurement, knowledge and consent " of any successful candidate, his election was to be declared null and void. The oath of a person giving a bribe was to stand against that of a person receiving one, and upon conviction a freeman who had been bribed was forever excluded from voting, acting as a freeman, holding office, or giving evidence in a court of justice.[2] It is difficult to imagine how bribery could exist under laws as stringent as these.

---

[1] 10 Geo. II, Franklin ed, 1744, 193.   [2] 20 Geo. II, Franklin ed., 1752, 13.

Passing beyond New England, we find that the laws of New York and Maryland were silent on the subject of bribery, but that those of all the remaining colonies had something to say on the subject. Thus, in East Jersey, notwithstanding the careful methods provided by the constitution of 1683, it was thought well to order that all elections should be free and voluntary, and that whenever any bribe or indirect means could be proved both the giver and the receiver were to forfeit forever their privilege of voting or being voted for.[1] West Jersey was almost as severe, and no person could be elected if he gave, bestowed or promised " directly or indirectly to the said parties electing; any Meat, Drink, Money or Moneys worth for procurement of their Choice and Consent." Persons receiving bribes could neither elect nor be elected for seven years, nor could they execute any office of trust during that period.[2] New Jersey merely prohibited bribery in any form, and disfranchised all offenders.[3]

The aim of one of the earliest of the Pennsylvania laws was to prevent the crime of bribery, and its provisions were similar to those of the West Jersey constitution, except that the person bribed was also deprived of his right to vote.[4] In the Delaware government candidates bribing or treating electors were let off with a fine of ten pounds, while a voter accepting a bribe was fined half that amount. A bribe was defined to include a " Gratuity, Gift, Bribe, strong Drink, Treats, Entertainments or other Reward."[5] Virginia[6] and

[1] Leaming and Spicer, 153.

[2] West Jersey Concession and Agreement, chap. 33, Leaming and Spicer, 405.

[3] 12 Geo. I, chap. 40, §§ 3, 4, Nevill's *Laws*, 142; Allinson's *Laws*, 69.

[4] *Laws agreed upon in England*, 1682; also chap. 58; chap. 36, *Petition of Right*, 1693; Markham's *Frame of Government*, 1696; *Laws*, ed. Harrisburg, 1879, 99, 122, 203, 249; 4 Anne, chap. 129, Franklin ed., 1742, 67.

[5] 13 Geo. II, chap. 65, Franklin and Hall ed., 1752, 133; Adams ed., 1797, 164.

[6] 11 Will. III, chap. 2, 3 Hening, 172; 4 Anne, chap. 2, §§ 10, 11, 3 Hening, 236; 3 Geo. III, chap. 1, § 19, 7 Hening, 519.

North Carolina[1] merely declared that the elections of persons who offered bribes should be null and void.[2]

The two southernmost colonies had laws framed with the idea of putting a stop to all forms of influencing voters. Thus in South Carolina, persons coercing or bribing voters, or abusing or menacing them afterward because they had voted in a particular way, were taken before a justice of the peace and bound over in the sum of fifty pounds, with two sureties of twenty-five pounds. If convicted at general sessions, such offenders were fined fifty pounds.[3] The provisions of the Georgia statute were more stringent than those of the South Carolina law. Any person violating the freedom of the day of election by arresting, menacing or threatening, or attempting to overawe, affright or force any person, properly qualified, to vote against his inclination or

---

[1] 17 Geo. II, chap. I, § 8, Davis and Swann ed., 1752, 177.

[2] The language of the law respecting bribery in the former colony is so carefully framed with a view of covering the entire field that it has seemed proper to publish it in full.

"And be it further enacted by the authority aforesaid, and it is hereby enacted, That no person or persons hereafter to be elected as a burgess shall directly or indirectly, by any ways or means at his or their proper charge, before his or their election, give, present or allow to any person or persons haveing voice or vote in such election any money, meat, drink or provision, or make any present, gift, reward or entertainment, or any promise, ingagement or obligation to give or allow any money, meat, drink or provision, present, reward, or entertainment in order to procure the vote or votes of such person or persons for his or their election to be a burgess or burgeses, and every person or persons soe giveing, presenting or allowing, makeing, promiseing or engageing any money, meat, drink or provision in order to procure such election being elected shall be disabled and incapable to sit and act as a burgess in that assembly, but that such election shall be void to all intents and purposes as if the said returne or election had never been made." 11 Will. III, chap. 2, 3 Hening, 172.

As though the above provisions were not sufficient, the act of 4 Anne added a clause forbidding the bribery of persons in particular, or "any such county, town or corporation in general, or to or for the use, advantage, benefit, imploiment, profit or preferment" thereof.

[3] Act 1716, no. 365, § 23, 2 Cooper, 683.

conscience, or obtaining any vote by bribery, or who should, after the election was over, menace, "despightfully use" or abuse any person for voting as he desired, such persons, upon sufficient proof presented before two justices of the peace, should be bound over to the next general sessions. If convicted at his trial, the offender was to forfeit not more than twenty pounds. Returning officers were forbidden to influence, or even attempt to influence or persuade, any elector so as to prevent him from voting as he had first intended.[1]

In addition to the provisions already enumerated concerning attempts to influence voters by means other than bribery, we find that in New Jersey a fine of ten pounds was imposed on persons who "Either by Assertions or False Reports of any of the Candidates, either in Words or Message or Writing, or in any other Manner, and endeavour to frighten or by indirect Means persuade any Elector to give or dissuade any Elector from giving his Vote."[2]

In Pennsylvania persons were forbidden to disturb the freedom of an election day by menacing voters or by threatening them with force of arms. Candidates offering to serve for nothing or for less than the law allowed in order to influence voters, were liable to a fine of five pounds.[3] In this province the elections of sheriffs and coroners furnished an excellent opportunity for influencing voters. We learn from a law passed with a view of preventing bribery and corruption on these occasions that it was a common practice to make electors vote in a particular manner " by giving them strong Drink and using other Means inconsistent with the Design of voting freely at Elections by Means whereof many unguarded Persons are unwarily drawn in to engage their Votes and rendered altogether incapable of discharging their Duty

---

[1] Act June 9th, 1761.   [2] 12 Geo. I, chap. 40, § 5, Nevill's *Laws*, 142.

[3] 4 Anne, chap. 129, Franklin ed., 1742, 67.

in that sober and weighty manner the Occasion requires, but become more particularly disorderly at these Times whereby great Confusions and Mischiefs arise." With a view of putting a stop to these abuses a fine of five pounds was imposed on persons bribing or bribed. Candidates guilty of such practices could not be elected to office for a year, and were also subject to a fine of ten pounds.[1]

In England the laws against bribery were almost as stringent as those in the colonies. A resolution of the House of Commons in 1677 touched upon the subject with special reference to excessive treating of voters. It was forbidden that after the test of a writ any meat or drink exceeding " the true value " of ten pounds should be given to electors in any place except at the dwelling place or habitation of a candidate. That was defined to be the place where he had lived for six months previous to the election. The election of a person offering bribes in this or any other way was declared void.[2] In 1700–1 the lending of money to a corporation without interest with intent to influence the election of such corporation was declared to be an unlawful and dangerous practice.[3] General statutes on the subject of bribery were enacted some years afterward.[4] Both the electors and the returning officers were required to take an oath that they had not been bribed; if they had been, they were declared guilty of perjury, and were rendered forever afterward incapable of voting or holding office or franchise, and forfeited the sum of five hundred pounds as well. Offenders were indemnified if within a year after the election they turned king's evidence against a person who had taken a bribe. Under

---

[1] 25 Geo. II, chap. 6, Hall and Sellers ed., 1775, 237.

[2] 9 *Resolutions and Orders of the House of Commons*, 411.

[3] 13 *Resolutions and Orders of the House of Commons*, 400.

[4] *Statutes* 2 Geo. II, chap. 24; 9 Geo. II, chap. 38.

this law an attempt to make an elector promise that he would refrain from voting was just as much an act of bribery as was an attempt to influence him to vote in any particular way.

§ 15. *Sanction of the Election Laws.* Without exception the American colonies enforced their election laws by means of a series of penal sanctions. The crimes punished by these provisions were numerous and included any neglect, omission, or failure of duty upon the part of the persons or officers intrusted with the execution of the election laws. The admission of the vote of an unqualified person, the making of a false return, or the failure to make any return at all, were some of the offenses which rendered a sheriff liable to a penalty. On the part of an elector, illegal voting, fraud, repeating, the putting of more than one vote into a ballot box and voting for a candidate known to be unqualified,[1] were among the crimes reached by the punitive sanctions of these laws.[2]

The penalties were almost always of a pecuniary nature, and it seems unnecessary to go into the subject at any great length. Suffice it to say that the fines ranged in amount from a few shillings[3] to three hundred pounds or more.[4] Usually sterling was meant, but in some instances, in the more southern colonies, "current money"[5] or "proclamation money"[6]

---

[1] Massachusetts, *Laws*, ed. 1660, 25.

[2] North Carolina, 17 Geo. II, chap. 1, Davis and Swann ed., 1752, 177. It is not possible to give references to all provisions relating to this subject, as they are contained in almost every statute which has been mentioned in this work. In the laws the subject was treated in much the same way as in England. The index to Troward, *Elections*, gives a list of the various offenses which were punishable in the mother country.

[3] Plymouth, *Laws*, 1636, 11 *Plymouth Colony Records*, 10. It is worthy of note that the fines in New England were much smaller than in the other colonies.

[4] New Jersey, 12 Geo. I, chap. 40, Nevill's *Laws*, 69.

[5] Virginia, 4 Anne, chap. 2, § 2, 3 Hening, 236.

[6] North Carolina, 17 Geo. II, chap. 1, § 6, Davis and Swann ed., 1752, 177.

were specified as the rates at which the payments of fines should be made.   In Virginia, and also in Maryland, the fines were usually payable in kind, ranging in quantity from one hundred[1] to thirty thousand pounds of tobacco.[2]   This last penalty was imposed by the Bacon Assembly upon sheriffs making false returns.   Although thirty thousand pounds was an extraordinarily large amount, there seems to have been some need of it, for more than twenty years before, in 1676, an assembly had found it necessary to inflict a fine of ten thousand pounds of tobacco upon sheriffs neglecting their duty.[3]

The proceeds of these fines were applied to a great variety of uses.   As a general rule one-half went to the sovereign for the support of the government,[4] or in the proprietary colonies to the lords proprietors[5] or to the governor.[6]   In many cases the other moiety went to the person informing and suing for it.[7]   New Jersey divided one particular fine into thirds, giving one portion to the king, another to the aggrieved party, and the remaining third to the poor,[8] while Massachusetts assigned one moiety to the poor and the other to the informer.[9]   In cases of bribery in South Carolina the fines went to the benefit of the poor of the parish.[10]

In Georgia the proceeds of fines were used to defray the expense incurred by the sessions of the general assembly,[11]

---

[1] 21 Car. I, Act xx, 1 Hening, 333.   [2] *Bacon's Laws*, Act vii, 2 Hening, 356.

[3] 5–6 Commonwealth, Act vii. 1 Hening, 411.

[4] Virginia, 4 Anne, chap. 2, 3 Hening, 236.

[5] South Carolina, Act 1704, no. 227, § 4, 2 Cooper, 249.

[6] Pennsylvania, 4 Anne, chap. 129, Franklin ed., 1742, 67.

[7] Virginia, 4 Anne, chap. 2, 3 Hening, 236.   An earlier statute gave the aggrieved party the first claim on the second moiety.   11 Will. III, chap. 2, 3 Hening, 172.

[8] 12 Geo. I, chap, 40, § 2, Nevill's *Laws*, 142.

[9] *Laws*, 1738–9, chap. 26, 2 Ames and Goodell, 980.

[10] Act 1716, no. 365, § 23, 2 Cooper, 683.   [11] Act 1761.

while the neighboring colony of South Carolina punished a sheriff guilty of an untrue return by making him forfeit ten pounds to the lords proprietors for each false vote and a hundred pounds to the persons who should have been returned.[1] North Carolina applied the proceeds of penalties for false returns towards the building of any court house, church or chapel which the governor should designate. If however, no such building was needed, then the lords proprietors and the aggrieved parties were the beneficiaries.[2]

The method to be employed in recovering a fine was not always specifically described. When an informer sued, the form of action was stated to be a *qui tam* action, in which the plaintiff described himself as suing for the commonwealth as well as for himself.[3] Virginia prescribed the means of recovery to be " with full costs of suit by action of debt, byll, plaint, or information in any court of record in his majesties collony and dominion wherein noe essoigne, protection or wager of law, privilege or imparlance shall soe be admitted or allowed."[4] This provision was modelled upon the phrase which appears in a similar connection in almost all the Eng-

---

[1] Act 1704, no. 227, § 3, 2 Cooper, 249.

[2] *Laws*, 1715, 2 *North Carolina Colonial Records*, 213.

[3] 1 Salkeld, ‡ 29, n; 1 Viner, *Abridgement*, 197. South Carolina, 23 Geo. II, no. 885, 4 Cooper, 98.

[4] 11 Will. III, chap. 2, 3 Hening, 172. This statute contains the following comprehensive definition of a violation of duty on the part of an election officer : •

" If any sheriff or his officer, before the returne be endorsed on the writt, shall deny and refuse to take the poll in writeing as aforesaid if it be demanded by any candidate or ffreeholder, or shall refuse to give copyes of the poll to such candidate or candidates, if by them required, or shall neglect to give legall notice of the election time and place of election, or shall make a false or double returne of those who are not duly elected burgesses as aforesaid, or who shall not make any return, or shall make returne in any forme then is herein expressed, he or they so offending in any one of the premises, and being thereof lawfully convicted, shall for every such offense forfeit and pay the sum of fforty pounds sterling money."

lish statutes passed during the colonial period. The only difference was that in the mother country the courts of record were limited to those at Westminster Hall, and one imparlance was sometimes permitted.[1] In nearly all the colonies the method of recovery was by " bill, plaint or information."[2]

In actions for recovery of penalties for illegal voting, two colonies placed the *onus probandi* on the defendant.[3] Rhode Island enacted that certain fines incurred by towns were to be recovered by an action on the case brought by the treasurer and the proceeds devoted to the use of the colony.[4] Other fines were levied by warrant of distress.[5] Delaware enforced judgments against persons incurring fines of twenty shillings for making a second attempt to vote, by seizing their goods, or in case they had none, by putting them in gaol until the judgment was satisfied.[6]

Besides the punishments inflicted on persons convicted of bribery, which have been enumerated in the preceding section[7] there were several instances where the penal sanctions of the election laws amounted to more than a fine, and involved physical punishment of some sort. These sanctions, however, applied to delinquent electors rather than to offending officials.

Rhode Island with her usual severity did not spare voters guilty of fraud. They were at first liable to a fine of five pounds or twenty-one stripes upon their naked backs, or im-

---

[1] See, for example, *Statutes* 1 Geo. I, Stat. 2, chap. 56: 6 Anne, chap. 7; 7 and 8 Will. III, chap. 25; 12 and 13 Will. III, chap. 10.

[2] For example, Massachusetts Bay: 1 Ames and Goodell, 88; Pennsylvania: 25 Geo. II, chap. 6, Hall and Sellers ed., 1775, 237; Delaware: Adams ed., 1797, 429; Maryland: 8 Geo. I, Baskett ed, 1723, 121; North Carolina: *Laws,* 1715, 2 *North Carolina Colonial Records,* 213; Georgia: Act 1761.

[3] Virginia: 3 Geo. III, chap. 1, § 7, 7 Hening, 519; North Carolina: 17 Geo. II, chap. 1, § 7, Davis and Swann ed., 1752, 177.

[4] 6 *Rhode Island Colonial Records,* 323.   [5] 12 Geo. II, Franklin ed., 1744, 217.

[6] 12 Geo. III, chap. 207, § 6, Adams ed., 1797, 500.   [7] See p. 192 *et seq., ante.*

prisonment for a month.[1]   The penalty was soon increased
to forty stripes or imprisonment in the stocks, and conviction
was secured upon confession or upon the testimony of two
witnesses that the voter had put more than one paper in the
hat.   The governor and council could inflict these punishments at the general court of election, but the assistant
justices and wardens had jurisdiction at town or quarter
meetings.   The latter officers could not subject an offender
to a fine of more than forty shillings or to more than twenty-
one stripes.   They could, however, set him in the stocks.[2]
In 1739 the penalty for putting in more than one ballot was
a fine of forty shillings with disfranchisement for three years.[3]
South Carolina punished persons voting illegally by six
months' imprisonment without bail.[4]   In default of payment
of a fine imposed on conviction for an attempt to illegally
influence a voter, Georgia provided for imprisonment without bail or mainprize.[5]

[1] 4 *Rhode Island Colonial Records*, 195.   [2] *Ibid.*, 207.
[3] 12 Geo. II, Franklin ed., 1744, 217.   [4] Act 1704, no. 227, § 6, 2 Cooper, 249.
[5] Act 1761.

PART II.—LOCAL ELECTIONS.

CHAPTER I. HISTORY OF LOCAL ELECTIONS.

Under the subject of general elections it has been found expedient to touch upon the manner of choosing some of those colonial officers whose functions were local rather than general in character. Such for example were the associates in Plymouth, and the sheriffs, coroners, commissioners and assessors in Pennsylvania, whose duties were confined to the county in which they were elected. The reason for treating these officers in that connection was that they were chosen by persons possessing the county franchise rather than the town franchise, and also because in the latter colony they were voted for at the same time and place as the members of the legislature. In Pennsylvania and Delaware the inspectors were essentially local officials chosen by the hundreds of each county; but their duties were so intimately connected with the management of general elections that it was deemed advisable to consider them in that connection.

It is not my intention to give the subject of local elections a treatment so exhaustive as has been bestowed on those at which the general officers of the colonies were chosen. The reason for this is that although the various town, vestry, manor, city and borough elections were to some extent governed by statutes general in their nature, it is none the less reasonable to suppose that each locality followed its own judgment in regard to matters of detail. To engage in a thorough investigation of the subject would, therefore, necessitate greater labor and more extended research than is at present within the power of the writer. Accordingly, in the following pages no attempt will be made to give more than a rough sketch of the methods of conducting local elections, as laid down by statutes of general import. This will be done in the hope of furnishing a basis of comparison with the system of choosing general officers, rather than with a view of exhausting the subject. Neither has it been thought necessary to consider in detail the subject of military elections, in which the citizens at large had sometimes a voice. For example, in Massachusetts an order of the general court gave all the freemen of the colony a vote in the election of the officers of the trainbands.[1] This proves that the suffrage for military officers was not always restricted to enlisted men.[2] Outside of the Puritan colonies the officers of the militia were generally appointed, and when they were elected it was probably by the soldiers themselves.

§ 1. *Town Elections.* It may perhaps be stated as a general proposition, that so far as the election of local officers is concerned, the New England town of to-day does not differ very much from its predecessor of the seventeenth and eighteenth centuries. From the earliest times the more important town officers have been elective, and that by a popular suffrage.

Thus, for example, an early enactment of the general court of Plymouth required " constables for each part and other inferiour officers " to be chosen annually by the freemen.[3] A law passed in 1658 would seem to indicate that

---

[1] 1647, 2 *Massachusetts Colonial Records*, 191.

[2] See also Plymouth *Laws*, 1667, Brigham, 151; 1 *Rhode Island Colonial Records*, 98, 121; 2 *Rhode Island Colonial Records*, 110; 1 *Connecticut Colonial Records*, 409; 3 *New York Colonial Documents*, 655.

[3] *Laws*, 1636, 11 *Plymouth Colony Records*, 7; Brigham, 37.

the town officials had to be confirmed by the general court.[1] An order of 1652 commanded that "in every town three or five Celectmen be chosen by the Townsmen out of the free-men such as shalbee approved by the court for the better."[2] In Massachusetts by an order of 1635–6 the towns were given power to elect their own officers, such as selectmen, surveyors for the highways, constables, *etc.*[3] Under the charter of 1691 the inhabitants of the towns were called to-gether annually for the purpose of electing a town clerk and three, five, seven or nine selectmen.[4] After 1700 a treasurer was also chosen by each town,[5] though before that time a treasurer was elected for each county by the votes of those possessing the town suffrage.[6] The first provincial legisla-ture of New Hampshire passed a law providing that an an-nual meeting should be held in each town for the election of constables, selectmen, jurors and other officers.[7]

The towns of Rhode Island elected a large number of local officers, including among others a town council.[8] In the four towns of that colony which had first been settled, the chief judicial officer was one of the assistants, and as such

---

[1] "Other inferiour officers, as constables, grandjurymen and surveyors for the highwaies, bee then also confeirmed, if approved by the Court." *Laws*, 1658, Brigham, 109.

[2] *Laws*, 1662, Brigham, 138. See *Book of General Laws*, 1671, Brigham 260, 264, for provisions concerning the annual elections of selectmen and constables.

[3] 1 *Massachusetts Colonial Records*, 172; Coffin, *History of Newbury*, 19. The maximum number of selectmen appears to have been nine. *Laws*, ed. 1660, 76; ed. 1814, 195.

[4] *Laws*, 1692–3, chap. 28, 1 Ames and Goodell, 65.

[5] *Laws*, 1699–1700, chap. 2, 1 Ames and Goodell, 385.

[6] *Laws*, 1692–3, chap. 27, § 1, 1 Ames and Goodell, 63.

[7] 1680, 1 *New Hampshire Provincial Papers*, 396, 403. This statute was re-pealed, but later re-enacted in substance. 5 Geo. I, chap. 88, Fowle ed. 1761, 34, 201, 213; ed. 1771, 137. Ministers were also elected; ed. 1771, 155.

[8] 18 Car. II, Franklin ed., 1744, 9.

was, of course, chosen at the general court of election.[1] The act under which Block Island was incorporated, in 1672, gave the freemen of that corporation power to elect wardens and a " sargent."[2] The charter of Providence, in 1649, gave full power to the inhabitants to rule themselves and elect officers of justice on the first second day of June in each year.[3]

In the New Haven colony we find that the Fundamental Orders of 1643 provided for the election of as many magistrates as were necessary for each plantation.[4] As early as 1636 constables were sworn in Newton to act till " newe be chosen," so that it seems reasonable to assume that even at that early date local officers were elected in the Hartford colony.[5] Under the Connecticut charter each town chose annually not more than " seven selectmen, one town clerk, constables, surveyors of highways, fence viewers, listers, collectors of rates, leather sealers, haywards, inspectors, chimney viewers, and other ordinary town officers."[6] Among the latter were packers of beef, pork and other goods, clerks of trainbands, gagers, sealers of measures, branders, appraisers and so forth.[7]

The New England colonies were included with New York in the " Dominion " ruled by Andros from 1687 until his imprisonment in 1689.[8] Under this government the only officers elected by the people were local in character. Each town was permitted to meet but once a year for the purpose

---

[1] 1 *Rhode Island Colonial Records*, 148, 401.

[2] 2 *Rhode Island Colonial Records*, 466.

[3] 1 *Rhode Island Colonial Records*, 214.   [4] 1 *New Haven Colonial Records*, 113.

[5] 1 *Connecticut Colonial Records*, 1.   [6] Connecticut, *Session Laws*, ed. 1715, 113.

[7] *Ibid*, 90, 91, ed. 1750, 54, 69, 240. The reader will find in 1 Howard, *Local Constitutional History of the United States*, 78–99, a list of the town officers that were elected in Massachusetts.

[8] For his commission, see 3 *New York Colonial Documents*, 544.

of choosing its own officers, and among them were a commissioner, constable and four selectmen. The latter held office for two years, half of the number going out of office each year.[1] That the custom of annually electing their town officers was regarded by New Englanders as essential to their welfare is shown by the fact that a little colony of Puritans on the coast of Georgia elected their selectmen and other officers regularly each year.[2]

In the Dutch towns of New Netherland there existed a system of local elections similar to those which had long flourished in Holland. A petition from the Eight to the Nineteen of the Amsterdam Chamber, in 1644, stated that it would be impossible for the rural districts to be cultivated unless the people were permitted to "elect from among themselves a Bailiff or Schout and Shepens, who will be empowered to send their deputies and give their votes in public affairs with the Director and Council."[3] The charter of Flushing, issued the following year, granted that town the right to "Nominate, Elect and Choose a certain officer over them, who may bear the name or Title of Scout or Constable of fflushing."[4] Gravesend, by a charter granted at about the same time, was allowed to elect three magistrates and a schout subject, however, to confirmation by the governor.[5] Other towns followed the custom, already referred to, of electing a double or triple number of magistrates, from which the Director appointed one.[6] The reply of Governor Stuyvesant to the convention of 1653 justifies the inference that the English towns on Long Island elected their magistrates without presenting them to him for confirmation.[7] During

---

[1] *Ordinance of Council,* 3 *Connecticut Colonial Records,* 427.

[2] 1 Stevens, *History of Georgia,* 380.   [3] 1 *New York Colonial Documents,* 213.

[4] O'Callaghan, *Laws and Ordinances of New Netherland,* 49.   [5] *Ibid.,* 55.

[6] 1 O'Callaghan, *History of New Netherland,* 393.

[7] See 2 O'Callaghan, *History of New Netherland,* 250.

the second Dutch occupation, in 1673, we find that the council of war sent orders to a number of towns, both in New York and New Jersey, requiring them to elect and return a double number of schouts and schepens, from whom the council should appoint the magistrates.[1]

The Duke's Laws, under which for a time New York and parts of New Jersey and Pennsylvania were administered, provided that " all votes in the private affairs of particular towns should be given and Determined by the Inhabitants, Freeholders, 'Householders."[2] Under this code eighteen overseers were chosen by a majority of the freeholders of each town. The terms of four of these expired each year, their places being filled by popular vote. From the outgoing overseers the freeholders elected a constable and returned him to the justices for confirmation.[3] In 1666 the number of overseers in each town was reduced to four, and the freeholders were ordered to meet in their towns, and dismiss by vote two of the new overseers chosen that year, as well as two of the overseers that had held office during the previous year.[4]

The Monmouth patent, issued by Governor Nicolls in 1665, empowered the inhabitants of that town to elect their local officers.[5] In the more southern portion of the Duke's dominions we find that in 1672 Newcastle was incorporated as a " Balywick." The first officers were appointed, but thereafter a high sheriff and bailiff were to be elected annually. The method of selection was the double nomination, two candidates being chosen by the people, and from these the governor appointed one. Four assistants might also be

[1] 2 *New York Colonial Documents*, 574, 577, 579, 580, 586; 1 *New Jersey Archives*, 125 *et seq.*

[2] Title, *Votes*, page 22. The code is published in the *Charters and Laws*, reprinted by the State of Pennsylvania, Harrisburg, 1879.

[3] Title, *Overseers, ibid.*, 44.   [4] *Ibid.*, 68.

[5] 1 *New Jersey Archives*, 45.

chosen annually.[1] During the proprietorship of the Duke, as well as afterward, many towns received charters or patents giving them the power of electing officers.

The Duke's Laws gradually went out of use, but it was not until after 1690 that they became a dead letter in New York. The writer is unable to say how far, during the period they were in force, the towns availed themselves of the privilege of electing their own officers. We shall see that in Pennsylvania and Delaware, except in the incorporated settlements, no general system of local elections was introduced until just before the Revolution. New Jersey began to develop local elections much earlier than her southern neighbors, but outside of New England the honor of developing them into a permanent system belongs to the province of New York.

In 1691 the New York assembly passed a law commanding the freeholders of every town to meet annually at the times expressed in their patents. At such meetings they were to choose three persons to be surveyors and " Ordrers of the Work for laying out and the amendment of the Highways and Fences," according to the rules to be prescribed by the freeholders.[2] But the indefinite language of the preceding act was the cause of numerous mistakes, and in 1703 another statute required each town to elect annually a person to " compute, ascertain, examine, oversee and allow the contingent, publick and necessary Charge of each County." This officer was called a supervisor, and in electing him each inhabitant of a manor, liberty, jurisdiction, precinct and plantation was given power to join his vote with those of the next adjacent town. The " Mannor of Ranslaerswick" was excluded from this last provision, and was permitted to choose a separate supervisor. In addition each town, manor, or precinct was authorized to choose two assessors and one

[1] 12 *New York Colonial Documents*, 496.
[2] 3 Will. and Mary, Van Schaack's *Laws*, 3.

collector. Vacancies were filled at special elections, and in case of failure or refusal to elect, power of appointment was vested in the justices of the peace.[1] This was generally the rule with the middle colonies. A later act authorized the choice of special officers for the collection of quit-rents.[2] Subsequent changes in these statutes affected only the number of officers to be chosen, and the dates when elections were to be held.[3]

The manor of Rensselaerwyck was from the beginning treated as if it were a town. It was permitted to choose officers with the same names and duties as those of the towns, and in addition overseers of ovens and chimneys.[4] In the course of time similar privileges were extended to the manors of Livingston[5] and Cortlandt.[6] In early times the duties of an overseer of the poor were performed by the church wardens. It was not until 1773 that a law was enacted providing that overseers of the poor might be chosen in every town, manor or precinct where there was no established vestry.[7]

In New Jersey, by a statute of 7 Anne, town or precinct meetings were authorized to be held for the purpose of choosing overseers and assessors of the poor.[8] In 1730 it was ordered that an assessor and a collector should be chosen annually by the voters of every town, division, precinct and district.[9] In default of an election, the justices of the peace could appoint to these offices. Just before the Revolution it was provided that not more than four overseers of the poor

---

[1] 2 Anne, Van Schaack's *Laws*, 541.   [2] Van Schaack's *Laws*, 404.

[3] See 13 Geo. III, chap. 1621, Van Schaack's *Laws*.

[4] 4 Anne, chap. 151, Van Schaack's *Laws*, 67; also 70, 545, 568, 689, *etc.*

[5] 3 Geo. I, chap. 323, Van Schaack's *Laws*, 106.

[6] 11 Geo. II, chap. 651, Van Schaack's *Laws*, 192.

[7] 13 Geo. III, Van Schaack's *Laws*, 756.

[8] 7 Anne, chap. 6, Nevill's *Laws*, 9.   [9] 3 Geo. I, chap. 22. Nevill's *Laws*, 44.

should be chosen at the annual town meetings throughout the colony, and that vacancies might be filled by special elections.[1]   In 1730 the election of four persons from among whom the justices of the peace should select two to be surveyors of highways, was authorized.[2]   In addition to the officials just mentioned, every New Jersey town elected two " chosen freeholders." It seems to have been the duty of these persons to aid the justices of the peace in deciding about the building of goals and court houses, and in certain other administrative matters.[3]

Besides these elections we find in New Jersey two instances in which a locality voted upon a formal proposition in a manner resembling somewhat the Rhode Island *referendum*.[4]   In two counties the court houses had been burned, and in order to decide where new ones should be erected, special elections were held.   The justices of the peace were ordered with the aid of the chosen freeholders to draw up advertisements and have them posted in the most public place in every township.   The purpose of these was to summon all persons who were properly qualified to vote for representatives, to meet on the site of the old court house.   The meeting must take place within forty days after the advertisements were posted, provided twenty days' notice was given.   On the day appointed the justices took the votes and the chosen freeholders acted as judges.   The poll could be adjourned from day to day for three days, until all those attending had voted.   Then the justices added up the totals and the new court house was erected in the place in favor of which the majority of votes had been cast.[5]

---

[1] 14 Geo. III, Allinson's *Laws*, 408.   [2] 3 Geo. I, chap. 23, Nevill's *Laws*, 48.

[3] 12 and 13 Anne, chap. 17, Nevill's *Laws*, 32.   For other functions see 7 Geo. II, chap. 108, Nevill's *Laws*, 216.   [4] See p. 10, *ante*.

[5] Monmouth County, 4 Geo. II, chap. 54; Somerset County, 12 Geo. III, chap. 62; Nevill's *Laws*, 200, 247.

In 1725 it was enacted in Pennsylvania that three commissioners should be chosen for each county. One of these went out of office each year and his successor was chosen at the regular elections for the assembly. After 1718 six assessors were chosen at the same election.[1] For a long period in the history of that province the only local officers chosen by popular vote besides the inspectors, were the pound keepers.[2] All the other town officers appear to have been appointed, and it was not until 1772 that the voters of every town in the province were authorized to choose two supervisors of highways.[3] In 1771 provision had been made for the annual election in each town of a board of three freeholders whose duty it was to " settle" the books of the overseers.[4] After the following year a board of four auditors was chosen to examine the accounts of the supervisors.[5]

In Delaware almost all the local officers were appointed, and with the exception of sherfffs, coroners and inpectors, the only elected officers were the assessors. At first these were chosen at the county elections for assemblymen,[6] but after 1766 on the day appointed for choosing inspectors,[7] an assessor was elected in each hundred. In the southern colonies the only local officers subject to election by popular suffrage were, if we except the vestrymen and wardens, the constables provided for by Locke's Constitution.[8]

§ 2. *Parish Elections.* The parish was primarily an English institution, and existed only in those colonies where there

---

[1] 4 Geo I, chap. 213, Franklin ed., 1742, 156; 11 Geo. I, chap. 3, Hall and Sellers ed., 1775, 131. See p. 170, *ante.*

[2] 2 Geo. II, chap. 2, Hall and Sellers ed., 1775, 149.

[3] 12 Geo. III, chap. 15, Hall and Sellers ed., 1775, 444.

[4] 11 Geo. III, chap. 18, Hall and Sellers ed., 1775, 404.

[5] 12 Geo. III, chap. 15, § 15, Hall and Sellers ed., 1775, 444.

[6] 16 Geo. II, Franklin and Hall ed., 1752, 231.

[7] Adams ed., 1797, 429.   [8] Art. 91, 1 *North Carolina Colonial Records*, 199.

was an established church. On both sides of the Atlantic
the parish had its secular as well as religious side, and as the
smallest governmental division its affairs were administered
by a vestry whose functions were somewhat analogous to
those of the New England selectmen.[1] The writer has
found no trace of a vestry outside of New York, Maryland,
Virginia and the two Carolinas. It may be stated as a general rule that in each parish ministers were chosen by the
vestry and that they became *ex-officio* members of that
board. Sometimes the wardens were elected by popular
vote, but usually this was done by the vestry.

By the statute of 4 William and Mary, the Church of England was established in the city of New York and in the
counties of Richmond, Westchester and Queens. Two
churchwardens and ten vestrymen were elected every year
by the freeholders of these districts.[2] After 1746 each
of the seven wards in New York city chose two vestrymen,
and the membership of the board was thus increased to fourteen.[3]

Maryland received her establishment in the same year as
New York.[4] A subsequent statute fixed the number of the
vestry at six and made the minister, if he was worth forty
pounds, a member of the board. Two wardens were chosen
annually by the vestry and the freeholders. Two members of
the vestry went out of office each year, their successors being chosen at the annual meeting of the parish. The vestry
could remove a member after giving him personal notice, or,
if he was out of reach, by affixing a public notice to the
great door of the church for three successive Sundays. All
vacancies were, however, filled at special meetings of the

---

[1] See on the general subject, 1 Howard, *Local Constitutional History of the
United States,* 117 *et seq.*

[2] Van Schaack's *Laws,* 19.   [3] 19 Geo. II, Van Schaack's *Laws,* 267.

[4] 4 Will. and Mary, chap. 2, Bacon's *Laws.*

freeholders called for the purpose.[1] In no province was there wider popular control over the vestry than in Maryland.

Continuing in geographical order, we find that a statute enacted by Virginia in 1643, indicates that church wardens were annually elected and the vestrymen were appointed.[2] In the following year, however, it was definitely stated that the vestry should be elected by the voices of the majority of the parishioners who attended the annual meeting.[3] In 1661 the number of vestrymen was limited to twelve,[4] but in the following year the minister and vestrymen were given the power of choosing wardens and of filling vacancies in their own number.[5] The vestry thus became self-renewing and, to all intents and purposes, a close corporation. That this change was not favorably received is shown by the action of Bacon's legislature in 1676. This body complained of the evils that arose from the long continuance of vestries, and with a view of reforming the abuse, passed a law providing that once every three years twelve vestrymen should be elected by the votes of the freeholders and freemen of each parish.[6]

The course of development in North Carolina was precisely the reverse of that in Virginia. At first the vestry was a close corporation,[7] but after 1741 twelve vestrymen were elected for terms of two years by the freeholders of each parish.[8] After 1765 vestry elections were held at intervals of three years.[9] The wardens were, however, chosen

---

[1] 1 Anne, chap. 1, Bacon's *Laws*; Act no. 5, Baskett ed., 1723, 13.

[2] 18 Car. I, Act i, 1 Hening, 240.   [3] 19 Car. I, Act. v, 1 Hening, 290.

[4] 13 Car. II., Act xxi, 2 Hening, 25.   [5] 14 Car. II, Act ii, 2 Hening, 44.

[6] *Bacon's Laws*, Act. vi, 2 Hening, 356.

[7] *Laws*, 1715, 2 *North Carolina Colonial Records*, 206.

[8] 14 Geo. II, chap. 23, Davis and Swann ed., 1752, 157.

[9] 5 Geo. III, chap. 2, Davis ed., 1773, 305.

by the vestrymen, who also had power to fill vacancies until the next election.

The English church was established in South Carolina in 1704. The first elections were held the following year, two wardens and nine vestrymen, being chosen in each parish. Vacancies were filled at special elections called with all convenient speed.[1] A subsequent act reduced the membership of the vestry to seven and gave the rector a seat in the board.[2] The rector of a parish was chosen by a majority vote of its inhabitants, and commissioners were given power to hear and settle disputed elections.[3] After 1712 vacancies among the wardens were filled by the vestry.[4]

In Connecticut a system of parish or church society elections flourished. In these a clerk and committee were annually chosen by the settled inhabitants of each parish.[5] Ministers were also chosen at these meetings.[6] Moreover, a method was provided by statute for the organization of new societies after other societies had been drawn off from them.[7]

§ 3. *Municipal Elections.* So far as the writer has been able to ascertain, the only cities which elected their own officers were New York and Albany. Philadelphia was a close corporation. In its charter the first set of aldermen and councilmen were named and it empowered them to appoint the mayor and select their own successors.[8] The coroner

---

[1] Acts 1704, no. 225, §§ 21, 22, 27; no. 241, 2 Cooper, 242, 259.

[2] Act 1706, no. 256, § 29, 2 Cooper, 287.

[3] Acts 1704, no. 225, § 14; 1706, no. 256, § 21; 1712, no. 307; 2 Cooper, 236, 287, 366.

[4] Act 1712, no. 307, § 7, 2 Cooper, 366.

[5] 4 Geo. I, 6 *Connecticut Colonial Records*, 33; *Session Laws*, 231.

[6] 2 Geo. II, chap. 33, 7 *Connecticut Colonial Records*, 211; *Session Laws*, 362.

[7] 13 Geo. I, 7 *Connecticut Colonial Records*, 74, *Session Laws*, 335; 2 Geo. II, chap, 41, *Session Laws*, 366; 9 *Connecticut Colonial Records*, 218.

[8] Pennsylvania *Laws*, Miller ed., 1762, 10, 11.

and the sheriff were the only officers elected by the people, but this was done by virtue of their capacity as a county, and in this particular their action differed in no respect from that of the inhabitants of the other counties.[1] After 1771 the freeholders of Philadelphia annually elected two wardens.[2]

As has been already seen,[3] the smaller Dutch towns possessed the privilege of electing their officers, though their choice was subject to the approval of the Director General. New Amsterdam had not been granted this privilege, although it had been demanded in 1642 and again in 1649.[4] At last, in 1652, Director Stuyvesant was instructed to have a schout, two burgomasters and five schepens " elected according to the custom of the metropolis of Fatherland." He, however, continued for a long time to appoint municipal officers, and when a protest was made he replied that he had done so " for momentous reasons." " For, if," he said, "this rule was to become a cynosure, if the nomination and election of magistrates were to be left to the populace who were the most interested, then each would vote for some one of his own stamp, the thief for a thief, the rogue, the tippler, the smuggler, for a brother in iniquity, that he might enjoy greater latitude in his vices and frauds." The magistrates had not been appointed contrary to the will of the people, because they were " proposed to the commonalty in front of the City Hall by their names and surnames, each in his quality, before they were admitted or sworn to office. The question is then put, does any one object?"[5] Finally, in 1658 Stuyvesant allowed the burgomasters and schepens

---

. [1] See Penn's Charter of Privileges; 1 Proud, *History of Pennsylvania*, 444.

[2] 11 Geo. III, chap. 19, § 17, Hall and Sellers ed., 1775, 417.   [3] See p. 207, *ante*.

[4] 1 O'Callaghan, *History of New Netherland*, 193; 1 Brodhead, *History State of New York*, 540.

[5] 2 O'Callaghan, *History of New Netherland*, 192, 213, 250, 311, 312; 1 Brodhead, *History of the State of New York*, 540, 548.

to nominate their successors, but the city did not have a schout of its own till 1660.[1]

By the terms of the treaty of peace in 1664, the inferior civil officers and magistrates in New York were to hold until their successors were elected or appointed.[2] In 1665 Governor Nicolls appointed the first mayor.[3] During the second Dutch occupation, when the city was called New Orange, a double number of magistrates were elected by the people and presented to the governor for appointment.[4] In 1686 the Dongan charter gave the lieutenant governor the power of appointing the mayor and sheriff of New York city, but an alderman, an assistant and a constable were to be chosen for each ward by a majority of the inhabitants of that ward.[5] During his short lease of power Leisler issued warrants for the election of the mayor and sheriff by "all Protestant freeholders." The resulting election was a farce, as only seventy of the inhabitants voted. The illegality of this action in defiance of the provisions of the Dongan charter was one of the chief causes of complaint against Leisler.[6] The Montgomery charter, granted to New York in 1730,[7] authorized the election of one alderman, an assistant, two assessors, one collector and two constables in each ward.[8]

The charter of Albany was granted by Governor Dongan in 1686, and it resembled in many respects the instrument

[1] 2 O'Callaghan, *History of New Netherland,* 370.

[2] Art. 16, 2 O'Callaghan, *History of New Netherland,* 534.

[3] 2 Brodhead, *History of the State of New York,* 212.

[4] See the Provisional Instructions for the Schout, Burgomasters and Schepens of New Orange, 2 *New York Colonial Documents,* 680.

[5] *Manual of the Common Council of New York, 1868,* 7, 9.

[6] 3 *New York Colonial Documents,* 645, 655, 675; 2 Brodhead, *History of the State of New York,* 578, 9.   [7] 4 Geo. II.

[8] *Manual of the Common Council of New York, 1868,* 26; Explanatory Act: 11 Geo. III, chap. 1492, Van Schaack's *Laws,* 620.

under which the city of New York was first organized. It provided that six aldermen, six assistant aldermen, constables and other magistrates, should be chosen annually. The mayor as well as the sheriff was appointed by the governor.[1]

In the province of Pennsylvania several boroughs were created by charter. Chester, Bristol, and Lancaster, erected in 1701, 1720, and 1742, respectively, were empowered by their charters to elect annually "fit and able men" to be burgesses. The burgess first chosen was to be high constable.[2] In 1773 Lancaster was granted the privilege of electing annually two supervisers and two assessors.[3] In North Carolina the electors who were qualified to vote for the representative from Wilmington, were authorized to meet annually and elect five men, from whom the governor was to appoint three commissioners.[4]

[1] Weise, *History of Albany*, 200.

[2] For the charters of these boroughs see Pennsylvania *Laws*, Miller ed. 1762, 14, 16, 18.

[3] 13 Geo. III, chap. 1, §§ 7, 8, Hall and Sellers ed., 1775, 495.

[4] *Laws*, 1740, Davis and Swann ed., 1752, 114.

CHAPTER II. THE SUFFRAGE.

§ 1. *Town Elections.* It is believed that all persons qualified to vote at a general election could vote in town meetings.
In New England, for instance, freemen of the colony seem to
have been permitted to vote for their town officers as well as
for their deputies. In the present work the deputies to the
general court have been treated as general officers, following
thus the analogy of those colonies which elected only representatives or delegates to the assembly. But the deputy of
the Puritan colony was, perhaps, a local officer in that he
represented the freemen of the town from which he came.
Though little authority has come within the notice of the
writer,[1] he believes that deputies were elected by the freemen
of the colony residing in the towns rather than by those voting in the town meetings or in the election of local officers.
The reason of this is that the deputy was a substitute for
each freeman of his town, and was chosen for the purpose of
exercising the functions which were the inherent right of the
freemen of the colony but which it was impossible for them
to exercise directly. The present section, therefore, treats
only of the qualifications of those voters who were not freemen of the colony, the latter being always qualified to vote
for local officers.[2] It is a general truth that local suffrage
was wider, more inclusive, than colonial suffrage, *i. e.*, than
that by which the election of deputies to the general court
was regulated.

[1] See New Hampshire, Act 1770, Fowle ed., 1771, *Temporary Laws*, 40.

[2] Plymouth : *Laws*, 1669, Brigham, 156. Massachusetts : *Laws*, ed. 1660, 76; ed.
1814, 195. Connecticut : *Session Laws*, 113, 269.

In the Plymouth colony freeholders of twenty pounds ratable estate and of good conversation who were not Quakers, and who had taken the oath of fidelity, could vote for town officers.[1] Since many who had not taken the oath of fidelity tried to vote and this was found to " much obstruct the carrying on of religion in the publicke weale" it was enacted later that a record of those who had taken the oath must be kept by the clerk of each town.[2] Some years later voters in towns were required to be orthodox in the fundamentals of religion.[3]

In 1635 Massachusetts enacted that only freemen could vote in towns " in actions of authoritie or necessity, or that which belongs to them by virtue of their freedom as receiving inhabitants and laying out town lots, &c." This law extended to towns, the law permitting only church members to vote, but it is a question whether this restriction applied to the electing of officers.[4] On account of the " ability" of those who were not church members it was at a later time found advisable to permit them to vote, provided that they were at least twenty-four years old.[5] A subsequent enactment gave a vote in the choice of selectmen and other town officers to all "Englishmen, settled inhabitants and householders, of the age of twenty-four, of honest and good conversation, being rated at eighty pounds estate in a single country rate, and that had taken the oath of fidelity to this government."[6]

Under the provincial government of Massachusetts Bay, all persons coming to live in a town except " freeholders, proprietors of land in the town, those born or having served an apprenticeship or removed elsewhere," must obtain the consent of the selectmen of the town before they could

[1] *Laws,* 1658, Brigham, 114; *Laws,* 1669, *ibid.,* 156.

[2] *Laws,* 1678, Brigham, 188.   [3] *Book of General Laws,* 1671, Brigham, 258.

[4] 1 *Massachusetts Colonial Records,* 161.

[5] 2 *Massachusetts Colonial Records,* 109.   [6] *Laws,* ed., 1660, 76; 1814, 195.

vote."[1] Officers were elected by freeholders and other inhabitants rated at twenty pounds beside the poll, " real estate to be set at so much only as the rent or income thereof for the space of six years would amount to were it let at a reasonable rate, and personal estate and faculty to be estimated according to the rule of valuation" prescribed for assessing taxes. Disputes on this point were settled by the moderator.[2] Quakers and Anabaptists were exempt from taxes for religious purposes, and on that account not permitted to vote on questions concerning ministers and meeting houses.[3]

The qualifications for electors of town officers in New Hampshire were the same as those in the province of Massachusetts Bay.[4] This is true, though one of the earliest New Hampshire laws declared the suffrage in town elections to be no wider than that existing in the elections held for the choice of assemblymen.[5] A temporary law passed just before the Revolution restricted the suffrage in town elections to persons ratable according to the tax laws, for thirty shillings, *including* their polls.[6]

In each of the Narragansett towns before the charter of 19 Charles I, freemen were admitted and disfranchised or suspended by vote of the entire body assembled in town meeting.[7] Under the charter, towns were a long time permitted to exercise their option in admitting such inhabitants as they pleased.[8] Ultimately the distinction between the free-

---

[1] *Laws,* 1700–1, chap. 23, 1 Ames and Goodell, 452.

[2] *Laws,* 1692–3, chap. 28, § 4, 1 Ames and Goodell, 65; 1735–6, chap. 8, § 1, 2 Ames and Goodell, 761.

[3] 1731, 2 Ames and Goodell, 620, 715, 877, 1022.

[4] 4 Geo. I, chap. 82, § 3, Fowle ed., 1761, 230; ed., 1771, 124; 5 Geo. I, chap. 87, Fowle ed., 1761, 34, 201, 213; ed., 1771, 137.

[5] 1 *New Hampshire Provincial Papers,* 396, 403.

[6] Fowle ed., 1771, *Temporary Laws,* 40.

[7] 1 *Rhode Island Colonial Records,* 53, 85, 119.

[8] 18 Car. II, Franklin ed., 1744, 9.

dom of a town and the freedom of the colony seems to have been obliterated, and the qualifications for electors came to be the same in both cases.[1]

In New Haven the writer has found no distinction between a free burgess of the colony, and a free burgess of a town.[2] Hartford, on the other hand, permitted persons with certain qualifications to vote in town meetings, although they could not be freemen of the colony.[3] No one could reside in a town unless he was formally admitted by a vote of the townsmen.[4] It seems at first to have been the rule that any admitted inhabitant could vote for town officers, but ultimately it was enacted that besides freemen, only an " admitted inhabitant, Householder and a man of sober conversation with a Freehold estate, Rated at fifty shillings in the common list beside his person," should be allowed to vote in town elections, under a penalty of twenty shillings.[5] This act seems to have been passed with the intention of shutting out all who had only a transient interest in a town. Under a later statute the owner of a personal estate of fifty pounds, as well as he who possessed a fifty-shilling freehold was allowed to vote, provided that he was twenty-one years old.[6]

Outside of New England the qualifications of persons voting for town officers do not appear to have been very definitely fixed. In New York the term " freeholder and inhabitant" is common.[7] By this phrase we are probably to understand a person residing in the town and possessing a freehold within its limits. It does not seem reasonable to suppose that the word *inhabitant* was of wider meaning than the word *freeholder*. The two terms were intended to qualify each other, in order to limit the suffrage to those possessing

---

[1] 16 Geo. II, Franklin ed., 1744, 252.   [2] 1 *New Haven Colonial Records*, 113.

[3] *Session Laws*, 113.   [4] 1643, 1 *Connecticut Colonial Records*, 96.

[5] *Session Laws*, 113.   [6] *Ibid.*, eds. 1750, 1754, 1769, 240.

[7] Van Schaack's *Laws*, 3.

more than a transitory interest in the town. The same remark applies to the suffrage at parish elections in New York and in the South.

The town suffrage in New Jersey was definitely fixed in 1766, when a statute was enacted which provided that, except in towns corporate, no person should vote unless he was a freeholder, or a tenant for years, or a householder, and a resident in the township or precinct where he voted.[1] In Pennsylvania the pound-keeper of each township was elected by the inhabitants who were owners or possessors of land,[2] but the suffrage for supervisor elections was the same as that for members of the assembly, though all freeholders seem to have been allowed to vote.[3]

§ 2. *Parish Elections.* In general it may be stated that the possession of property and residence within a parish was sufficient to qualify persons to vote for wardens and vestrymen.

In a few cases the suffrage was more explicitly defined. Thus, in New York City, vestrymen were chosen by persons qualified to vote in municipal elections.[4] In Maryland only those inhabitants who were freeholders within the parish and who contributed to the public taxes and charges thereof, could vote.[5] The parish suffrage in North Carolina was restricted to a "freeholder in actual possession of estate, real for his life or that of another or greater estate, either fifty acres or a lot in town saved according to law within the parish."[6]

---

[1] 6 Geo. III, chap. 450, Allinson's *Laws*, 287. The earlier statutes used the words "freeholders and inhabitants, householders;" 3 Geo. I, chap. 22, Nevill's *Laws*, 44.　　　　[2] 2 Geo. II, chap. 2, Hall and Sellers ed., 1775, 149.

[3] Hall and Sellers ed., 1775, 444.

[4] 11 Geo. III, chap. 1492, Van Schaack's *Laws*, 624.

[5] 1 Anne, chap. 1, § 8, Bacon's *Laws*, Baskett ed., 1723, 13.

[6] 5 Geo. III. chap. 2, Davis ed., 1773, 305. See also 14 Geo. II, chap. 23, Davis and Swann ed., 1752, 157.

South Carolina was not so liberal as her northern sister, for she required membership in and conformity to the religion of the Church of England. In addition voters were required to be freeholders and residents contributing to the public charges of the parish.[1]

In the Connecticut society meetings an elector was required either to be in full communion with the church or else to possess the same amount of property as a voter in a town election.[2]   Dissenters who were on that account exempt from paying taxes were not permitted to vote.[3]

§ 3. *Municipal Elections.*   The Dongan charter gave the inhabitants of each ward in New York City power to elect aldermen.[4]   We have already seen that Leisler had the mayor and sheriff elected by the Protestant freeholders.[5]   The Montgomery charter seems to have gone no further than that óf Dongan in defining the qualifications of a voter.[6]   It was not until 1771 that the assembly passed an explanatory act,[7] in which it was stated that the aldermen were to be chosen by the freemen and freeholders of each ward.   The freemen must have held their freedom for at least three months,[8] and have actually resided in the ward for one month before the election day.   The qualification of a person voting in right of a freehold was similar to that required in general elections.   This was a freehold of forty pounds not held in trust for any body corporate or politic or for any pious or religious use;

---

[1] Act 1704, no. 225, § 21, 2 Cooper, 242.

[2] Fifty shillings in freehold, or forty pounds in the common list.   12 Geo. II, chap. 33, *Session Laws*, 362; 7 *Connecticut Colonial Records*, 211.

[3] 9 *Connecticut Colonial Records*, 218.

[4] *Manual of the Common Council of New York, 1868*, 9.

[5] 3 *New York Colonial Documents*, 675.

[6] *Manual of the Common Council of New York, 1868*, 26.

[7] 11 Geo. III, chap. 1492, Van Schaack's *Laws*, 620.

[8] In the city of London, liverymen and freemen must have been such for twelve calendar months.   *Statute* 11 Geo. I, chap. 18.

and it must have been in the possession of the voter for one month before the day of election unless it was acquired within that time by descent or devise. A mortgagor could vote if he was in possession and in receipt of the profits. If not, the franchise belonged to the mortgagee. The estate of a voter must be situated within the ward in which he voted.

The qualifications of municipal electors in Albany were not clearly defined until 1773, when a contested election case was decided by the common council. A set of regulations, founded, it was said, upon the custom of the board, was adopted, and these show that the suffrage was very wide. Every person twenty-one years of age, and born within British dominions, could vote in the ward where he resided, provided he had been a resident of the city for six weeks. This was the general rule, and to it there were a few exceptions: a bond servant could not vote during the time of his servitude; the votes of persons who were influenced by bribes were declared null and void; aliens were prohibited from voting, whatever might have been the length of their residence; persons not naturalized, or who had not taken the oaths of supremacy or allegiance, were debarred; and no one could vote in a ward to which he had removed just before the day of election. The rule in regard to residence was much more strictly enforced than it would be to-day, and a man who occasionally went out of town to visit his family was declared a sojourner, and on that account debarred from voting.[1]

Lancaster is the only one of the Pennsylvania boroughs whose charter clearly expressed the qualifications of an elector. The suffrage was restricted to inhabitants, householders within the borough, who had resided there for a year preceding the date of the election, and who had hired a house and ground of the yearly value of five pounds sterling.[2]

[1] 1 *Collections on the History of Albany*, 250, *et seq.*   [2] Miller ed., 1762, 18.

CHAPTER III. THE MANAGEMENT OF LOCAL ELECTIONS.

The statute books of the American colonies contain very few provisions which show in what manner local elections were conducted.   There is greater dearth of material on this subject than on that of local suffrage which, in New England at least, was defined with some degree of precision.   The manner in which local elections were to be called, and the date on which they were held, were usually prescribed, but beyond this no general regulation appears to have been attempted.   The absence of statutory provisions concerning the management of town elections would, therefore, seem to show that the matter was largely governed by local custom and usage, that was to a great extent moulded by the influence of the practices then current at general elections.

§ 1. *Town Elections.* In Massachusetts, under the second charter, town elections were held during the month of March,[1] while in Connecticut[2] they took place in December.   In the former colony the exact date was fixed, and notice was given by the constable,[1] while in the latter this duty devolved upon the selectmen.[2]

In Rhode Island the freemen of each town appear to have appointed a date for their local elections,[3] and a fine was imposed on all towns which failed to elect the required number of officers.[4]   This latter provision would seem to have been

---

[1] *Laws*, 1692–3, chap. 28, 1 Ames and Goodell, 65,   Additional acts on the subject of town elections are: *Laws*, 1735–6, chap. 8, § 1, 2 Ames and Goodell, 761; *Laws*, 1738–9, chap. 26, *ibid.*, 980; *Laws*, 1742-3, chap. 28, § 1, 3 Ames and Goodell, 47.   [2] *Session Laws*, 113.

[3] Franklin ed., 1744, 9.   [4] Hall's *Code*, 1767, 87.

necessary in the other New England colonies as well, in view of the fact that the election of the prescribed number of officers proved a burden from which the towns would have been glad to have escaped. The charter granted to Providence in 1649 gave to the inhabitants of that town power to choose their officers of justice on the first second day of June of each year.[1] During the governorship of Andros the towns embraced in his "dominion" elected their officers annually on the third Monday in May.[2] The writer is inclined to believe that the written ballot was generally used in New England town elections. In the Plymouth colony we find a statute providing that selectmen should be chosen "by papers,"[3] and as far back as 1637 such appears to have been the practice in at least one Massachasetts town.[4]

In the middle colonies town elections were usually held in the spring. The Duke's Laws appointed the first of April as the date for choosing constables.[5] Thus, in New York they took place on the first Tuesday in April, or on the days expressed in the charters and patents of the several towns.[6] In New Jersey the various local officers were chosen on the second Tuesday in March,[7] while in Pennsylvania supervisors and boards of audit were elected on the third Saturday of the same month.[8] In the latter province the election of a pound-keeper took place in each town on the twentieth of May, or on the following day if that should happen to be First Day.[9] The county officials were chosen in the autumn

[1] 1 *Rhode Island Colonial Records*, 214.   [2] 3 *Connecticut Colonial Records*, 247.

[3] *Book of General Laws*, 1671, chap. 5, Brigham, 260.

[4] Coffin, *History of Newbury*, 23.   [5] Page 70, ed., Harrisburg, 1879.

[6] 3 Will. and Mary; 2 Anne; Van Schaack's *Laws*, 3, 54, 756. In Albany and Tyron counties, as well as in the Manor of Rensselaerwyck, they were held on the corresponding day of May, Van Schaack's *Laws*, 689.

[7] Nevill's *Laws*, 32, 44, 48.   [8] Hall and Sellers ed., 1775, 404, 444.

[9] 2 Geo. II, chap. 2, Hall and Sellers ed., 1775, 149.

at the time of the selection of assemblymen,[1] while in Delaware the various hundreds voted for assessors on September 15th.[2]

For the purpose of electing poor officers in New Jersey, meetings were called at a convenient time and place on the warrant of any one justice of the peace.[3] After 1744, however, these officials were chosen at the regular town meetings, and vacancies were filled at special elections called "on a short day," by means of a precept from a justice.[4] In Pennsylvania there were provisions requiring a notice of five days of all town elections. Advertisements were posted in the most conspicuous places of the several towns and boroughs.[5] These elections were generally held in the afternoon between the hours of three and six,[6] though in the borough of Lancaster the hours were from ten until four.[7] Ten days' notice was required for the elections of assessors in Delaware, and they must take place before six o'clock in the afternoon.[8] In New Jersey the chosen freeholders were elected in the most public place of each town.[9] This was also true of pound-keepers in Pennsylvania,[10] although supervisors were chosen at a point as near to the centre of the township as was possible.[11]

In the laws of the middle colonies very little is said in regard to the procedure at town elections. In Pennsylvania it was provided that the voting should be by means of "tickets in writing."[12] There was nearly always some provision in regard to the choice by a majority or a plurality of voices, but a precise meaning does not always attach to these terms.

---

[1] October 1st.   [2] 6 Geo. III, Adams ed., 1797, 429.

[3] 7 Anne, chap. 6, Nevill's *Laws*.   · [4] 14 Geo. III, Allinson's *Laws*, 408.

[5] Hall and Sellers ed., 1775, 404, 444, 495.

[6] *Ibid.*, 444.   [7] *Ibid.*, 495.   [8] Adams ed., 1797, 429.

[9] 12 and 13 Anne, chap. 18, Nevill's *Laws*, 32.

[10] Hall and Sellers ed., 1775, 149.   [11] *Ibid.*, 444.   [12] *Ibid.*, 404, 444.

For example, the writer has found one statute in which the words *majority* and *plurality* occur in the same connection, and are apparently used interchangeably.[1] In Pennsylvania the persons chosen as supervisors were returned in writing before March 25th to the office of the clerk of the quarter sessions. Their certificates were under the hands of the supervisors of the public roads.[2]

§ 2. *Parish Elections.* Wherever the Church of England was established it would seem proper to have parish elections take place on Easter Monday. Such was indeed the rule in Maryland[3] and in both North[4] and South[5] Carolina. In New York, however, vestry elections were held on the second Tuesday in January,[6] although after 1770 the city vestry was chosen at the city hall on the feast of St. Michael, which was also the day appointed for municipal elections.[7] Before this two vestrymen had been chosen in each ward. In this province the electors were called together by warrants issued by the justices of the peace to the various constables.[8]

In Virginia no particular date was fixed for parish elections. The earlier statutes required that warning should be given,[9] while the law passed by Bacon's assembly commanded the wardens to publish an election on two successive Sundays.[10] In South Carolina notice of vestry elections

---

[1] New Jersey: 4 Geo. II, chap. 4, Nevill's *Laws*, 200.

[2] Hall and Sellers ed., 1775, 444.

[3] 1 Anne, chap. 1, § 8, Bacon's *Laws;* Baskett ed., 1723, 13.

[4] 14 Geo. II, chap. 23, Davis and Swann ed., 1752, 157; 5 Geo. III, chap. 2, Davis ed., 1773, 305.

[5] Act 1704, no. 225, §§ 21, 22, 2 Cooper, 242.

[6] 4 Will. and Mary, Van Schaack's *Laws*, 19. The date for Richmond County was afterwards changed to the third Tuesday in March. Van Schaack's *Laws,* 250.

[7] 10 Geo. III, chap. 1492, Van Schaack's *Laws*, 624.

[8] Van Schaack's *Laws*, 19, 566.   [9] 16 Car. I, Act v, 1 Hening, 290.

[10] *Bacon's Laws*, Act vi, 2 Hening, 356.

was given by public summons.[1] In North Carolina, on some Sunday at least forty days in advance, the sheriff posted notices on every church and chapel and also publicly read the election law at the door of the court house between the hours of twelve and one on the second day of the court preceding the election. Such thorough publication was doubtless necessary because in this province elections took place but once in three years, and the attendance of all except Quakers was required. The only valid excuse for absence was " bodily infirmity or legal disability," and the penalty for non-attendance was twenty shillings proclamation money, which could be recovered within ten days by a warrant from a justice of the peace.[2] In case of " badness of weather or any other unavoidable hindrance" and " unforeseen accidents" in both the last named provinces, vestrymen could be elected on days other than those appointed by law. In such a contingency a sheriff in North Carolina appointed a day not less than ten nor more than twenty days in the future, and personally summoned the freeholders; while in South Carolina public notice on two Sundays was sufficient. The old vestrymen held over until their successors were elected, and, if the conditions precedent were strictly complied with, the election though postponed was as valid as if it had taken place on Easter Monday.[3] In general it may be stated that vestry elections took place in the parish church, or if there was none at some convenient place.[4]

A peculiar feature of the Maryland parish meeting was the preliminary voting in order to determine which of the

[1] Act 1704, no. 225, §§ 21, 22, 2 Cooper, 242.

[2] 5 Geo. III, chap. 2, Davis ed., 1773, 305.

[3] North Carolina: 5 Geo. III, chap. 2, Davis ed., 1773, 305. South Carolina: Act 1712, no. 307, § 6, 2 Cooper, 366.

[4] South Carolina: Act 1704, no. 225. § 21, 2 Cooper, 242. Maryland: 1 Anne, chap. 1, § 8, Bacon's *Laws*.

vestrymen in office should be discharged. The law required that two vestrymen should go out of office each year, but gave to the parishioners the power of deciding who should be put out.[1] In South Carolina an election for the choice of a minister was called by commissioners, and returns were made to them within two months. If this last step was omitted the commissioners could declare an election void.[2]

The statutes governing parish elections contain the usual vague provisions in regard to plurality or majority of voices, one term being used about as often as the other. The writer thinks that parish officers were chosen by *vivâ voce* vote, though he is aware that in the only two instances where detailed regulations were given, provision is made for a poll.

At first in New York City vestrymen were chosen in every ward,[3] but after 1770 they were elected at the City Hall at eleven o'clock on the morning of the festival of St. Michael the Archangel. The Mayor, Deputy and Recorder presided, and if no poll were demanded it became their duty at the expiration of two hours, to declare who was elected. If a poll were required they appointed and swore in a clerk, who was to take it down in writing. If in two days all the votes could not be recorded, the presiding officer had authority to adjourn the poll. The election could not be closed so long as there were any voters awaiting to be polled or until proclamation had been made and an interval of fifteen minutes had elapsed.[4]

In North Carolina the course of procedure was similar. At ten o'clock on the morning of the election, which was held "at the usual place," the sheriff or his deputy made procla-mation and began to take the poll. The name of each elec-

[1] 1 Anne, chap. 1, § 8, Bacon's *Laws.*
[2] Act 1712, no. 307, 2 Cooper, 366.   [3] Van Schaack's *Laws,* 267.
[4] 11 Geo. III, chap. 1492, § 12, Van Schaack's *Laws,* 624. See also *ibid.,* 566.

tor was entered in a book, but in all cases the full number of twelve vestrymen must be voted for. All votes were given openly, and at sunset the sheriff cast up the votes and announced the election of the twelve candidates having the highest number of suffrages. In case of a tie the sheriff was given a casting vote. For illegal voting there was a fine of £5, half of which went to the informer and half to the poor. In such cases the *onus probandi* was placed on the defendant.[1]

There were few provisions in regard to parish elections in Connecticut, and these disclose no vital differences from the methods followed in town meetings. The settled inhabitants of parishes met annually in the month of December for the purpose of choosing a new clerk and committee. Five days' notice of such meetings were given by the persons in office.[2] After new societies had been drawn off, organization was effected at a meeting called by a warrant issued by an assistant and a justice on the demand of three inhabitants.[3] Town and society elections do not seem to have been very peacefully managed in this colony, for a law was passed imposing a fine of five shillings upon all persons participating in disturbances at such meetings.[4]

§ 3. *Municipal Elections.* We have seen that the freeholders and freemen of New York were authorized by the Dongan and Montgomery charters to elect certain officers on the feast of St. Michael the Archangel. The earlier instrument prescribed a majority of votes as necessary to constitute an election, while the second declared a plurality sufficient. Each ward was constituted an election district, and no

---

[1] 5 Geo. III, chap. 2, Davis ed., 1773, 305.

[2] 6 *Connecticut Colonial Records*, 33; 4 Geo. I, *Session Laws*, 231.

[3] 7 *Connecticut Colonial Records*, 74; 13 Geo. I, *Session Laws*, 335.

[4] 2 Geo. II, chap. 41, *Session Laws*, 366.

further provision was made beyond empowering the aldermen of each ward to appoint the place of election. In consequence many abuses arose, but it was not until 1771 that a statute was enacted explaining the manner in which New York City officers were to be chosen.[1]

By virtue of this law, the Mayor, Aldermen and Commonalty were authorized to appoint returning officers and fix the places of election eight days in advance. The returning officer was always a resident of the ward in which he acted, and clerks were also appointed to take the poll, at a compensation of twenty shillings, lawful money of New York. Every elector was required to declare publicly whether he voted by virtue of his freedom or of his freehold. For refusal to so declare, his vote was null and void. Persons having freeholds fronting on the East side of Broadway could vote only in the West ward.[2]

In the Dongan charter of Albany the provisions in regard to the manner of conducting elections were as vague as those in the New York charter.[3] From the evidence submitted at the trial of a contested election case in 1773, we are able to gather some information bearing on this subject. The day of election, as fixed by charter, was the festival of St. Michael the Archangel, and the aldermen appear to have taken the poll on the stoops of their several residences. The elections began at nine o'clock in the morning, and the polls were open until between four and five o'clock in the afternoon. One of the electors testified that on going to the stoop where he had heard that the poll for his ward was being taken, he

---

[1] Both charters were published in the *Manual of the Common Council, 1868.*

[2] 11 Geo. III, chap. 1492, §§ 3, 6, 9, Van Schaack's *Laws*, 620. Some of the provisions of this act were probably taken from the English statute of 11 Geo. I, chap. 18, which regulated the elections of aldermen and other municipal officers within the city of London.

[3] Weise, *History of Albany*, 200.

found it closed.   He complained that he received no notice
of the time of closing, but as it appeared that he did not
offer to vote until after five o'clock, and had failed to call on
the magistrate afterwards, the common council held that he
had forfeited his vote, because the poll had not in fact been
closed until after four o'clock, and then only because no
more electors had offered to vote.

The testimony of several of the witnesses shows that
bribery prevailed to an alarming extent at this election.
From five to ten pounds appears to have been the usual
price for a vote.   In two cases it appears that forty pounds
were paid, and it was proved that one of the persons who
had sold themselves at this price told a bystander that he
was going to buy cattle with his money, and that " he would
be d—d if he would vote before he had been paid."[1]

The nearest approach to a municipal election in Philadelphia is found after 1771.   In that year the freeholders of the
city were first permitted to vote for two wardens, at the same
time that they elected burgesses for the assembly.   The
names of the candidates were ordered to be written on a
separate piece of paper, and delivered to the tellers.   The
persons elected were returned by certificate " to the Mayor,
Recorder and Aldermen at their general sessions of the
peace," and entry was made in the minute book by the clerk
of the court.[2]

The laws contain no specific provisions concerning the
manner of holding elections in the Pennsylvania boroughs.
The day on which officers must be chosen was usually fixed
by the terms of the charter.   In Chester the burgesses and
the high constable were elected by ballot.[3]   In Lancaster the

[1] I Collections on the History of Albany, 250, et seq.

[2] 11 Geo. III, chap. 19, § 2, Hall and Sellers ed., 1775, 417.

[3] Miller ed., 1762, 14.   All the Pennsylvania city and borough charters are also
given in full by Hall and Sellers.

names of the persons chosen as borough officers were certified under seal to the governor within ten days after the election.[1] In the election of a supervisor and assessor Lancaster was treated precisely like an ordinary town, except that the voting took place at the court house between the hours of ten and four. Returns were made by one of the burgesses.[2]

[1] Miller ed., 1762, 15.

[2] 13 Geo. III, chap. 2, §§ 7, 8, Hall and Sellers ed., 1775, 495.

APPENDICES

APPENDIX A.

WRITS, RETURNS AND OATHS.

In the following pages are collected a number of the writs and returns which were in use at various times in the American colonies. Some of the forms were prescribed by statute, and the writer has added copies of the writs used in calling the first elections in New Jersey, Pennsylvania and Maryland, as well as the instrument used by Governor Dongan of New York, in summoning his second assembly. In Massachusetts Bay a statute prescribed the form of the precepts which were addressed by the sheriffs to the selectmen of the several towns and of the returns made by the latter. The early returns in Maryland are crude examples of a return by indenture.

In regard to oaths, it should be noted that a statute did not in all cases lay down the precise form to be followed. In the case of an election officer, as a rule, it was simply enacted that he should swear to do certain things in a proper manner. On the other hand, the oaths to be taken by electors were usually given in full, and it is these that form the second portion of this appendix. The oath of a freeman in a New England colony was taken at the time of his admission, and it was therefore in one sense an elector's oath, because the suffrage was limited to freemen. In other cases the oaths were usually administered upon demand of the candidates or upon challenge. The occasions on which an oath was required are mentioned in the following pages, and whenever a particular oath resembles one of those used in England the proper reference is given.

I. WRITS AND RETURNS.

MASSACHUSETTS.[1]

Writ for calling a great and general court or assembly.

William and Mary, by the grace of God, of England, Scotland, France and Ireland, king and queen, defenders of the faith, &c.

To our sheriff or marshal of our county of   Greeting: WEE command that upon receipt hereof you forthwith make out your precepts, directed unto the selectmen of each respective town within your precinct requiring them to cause the freeholders and other inhabitants of their several towns, duly qualified as in and by our royal charter is direct, to assemble at such time and place as they shall appoint, to elect or depute one or more persons (being freeholders within our said province), according to the number set and limited by an act of our general assembly within the same, to serve for and represent them respectively, in a great and general court or assembly by us appointed to be convened held & kept for our service at the town house in Boston upon the   day of   next ensuing the date of these presents. And to cause the person or persons so elected and deputed by the major part of the electors present at such elections, to be timely notified and summoned by the constable or constables of such town to attend our service in the said great and general court or assembly on the day above prefixed by nine in the morning: and so de die in diem during their session and sessions, and to return the said precepts with the names of the persons so elected and deputed unto yourself. Whereof you are to make return together with this writ and of your doings therein under your hand, unto our secretary's office at Boston, one day at

---

[1]*Laws*, 1692–3, chap. 36; 1 Ames and Goodell, 80. Other forms may be found in this volume of the *Acts and Resolves*.

least before said court's sitting. Hereof you may not fail at your peril. Witness Sir W. P., Knight, our captain general and governor in chief and over our province of the Massachusetts Bay in New England. Given at Boston under the publick seal of our province aforesaid, the   day of 169 in the   year of our reign.

By his excellencie's command.

Precept to the selectmen for the choice of representatives.
Suffolk : ss.

In observance of their majesties' writ to me directed.

THESE are in their majesties' names to will and require you forthwith to cause the freeholders and other inhabitants of your town, that have an estate of freehold within this province or territory of forty shillings per annum at the least, or other estate to the value of forty pounds sterling, to assemble and meet at such time and place as you shall appoint, then and there to elect and depute one or more persons (being freeholders within the province), according to the number set and limited by an act of the general assembly to serve for and represent them in a great and general court or assembly appointed to be convened, held and kept for their majesties service at the town house in Boston upon   the   day of   next ensuing the date hereof; and to cause the person or persons so elected and deputed by the major part of the electors present at such election to be timely notified and summoned by one or more of the constables of the town to attend their majesties' service in the said great and general court or assembly, on the day above prefixed by nine in the morning, and so de die in diem during their session and sessions. Hereof fail not, and make return of this precept with the name of the person or persons so elected and deputed, with their being summoned, unto myself on or before the   day of   abovesaid.

Given under my hand and seal at the   day of
169 in the   year of their majesties' reign.
AB   of the county of
To the selectmen of the town of   greeting.

Return to be endorsed on back of precept.

Pursuant to the precept within written, the freeholders and
other inhabitants of this town qualified as is therein directed,
upon due warning given, assembled and met together the
    day of   and then did elect and depute AB and CD
to serve for and represent them in the session and sessions
of the great and general court or assembly appointed to be
begun and held at Boston on the   day of   , the said
persons being chosen by the major part of the electors present at said meeting.

Dated in   the   day of

....   ⎫
⎬ Selectmen.
....   ⎭

The persons chosen are notified thereof and summoned to
attend accordingly.

By me : AB, constable of C.

NEW YORK.

Writ calling the second Assembly.[1]

James the Second by the Grace of God, King of England,
Scotland, France and Ireland, Defender of the Faith, &c.,
Supreme Lord and Proprietor of the Colony and Province
of New York and its dependencies in America.

To   Esq., Sheriff of   County Greeting.

Wee Require Cōmand and strictly Enjoyne you that forthwith you cause all the Freeholders of your County to meett
together in some convenient Place there to chuse one per-

[1] *Introduction to Journal of Legislative Council, iv.*

son to be theire Representative for   County in a General
Assembly to be holden at the Citty of New Yorke on the
twentieth day of October next ensueing the date hereof in
order to consult with our Gouernor and Council of New
Yorke and its dependencyes what Lawes are fitt and necessary to be made and established for the good weale and
Gouernment of the said colony. and you are in 5 weekes after
the election to have the name of the Person so Elected Returned unto the Secretaryes Office.

In testimony whereof I haue caused the seale of the
Province to be hereunto afixed this 17th day of Augst, 1685.
Passed the office   Test, THO. DONGAN.
JOHN SCRAGGE, Secry.

NEW JERSEY.[1]

Proclamation of Gov'r Carteret calling the first Assembly.

Whereas by the Infinite Goodness Providence and bless-
ing of Almighty God this Province of New Jersey is in a
probable way of being populated there being a Considerable
number of families already settled in severall parts of the
same and many more that in a short tyme will come and
place themselves vnd^r this Gouernment, for the better prop-
agating and Incouragement thereof I have thought fit with
the advice of my Councill to appoint a Generall Assembly
to begin the XXVth day of May next Ensuing the date hereof
for the making and Constituting such wholsome Laws as
shall be most needfull and Necessary for the good government of the said Province & the maintayning of a religious
Communion & ciuil society one wth the other as becometh
Christians without which it Vmpossible for any body
Politicq to prosper or subsist. Wherefore These are in the
Lords Proprietors Names to Will and Require all the free-

[1] 1 *New Jersey Archives*, 56.

holders belonging to   To make choice and appoint
two able men that are freeholders and dwellers W^th in the
said Limits to be your Burgesses and Representatives for
you, And they being Impowered by you are to make their personall appearance at Elizabethtowne the 25th day of May
next as aforesaid & there to join wth me your Gouernour &
my Councill to advise in the Management of the affaires that
are needfull and Necessary for the Orderly & Well Gouern-
ing of the said Province hereof you may not faile as You and
Every of you Will answere your contempt to the contrary.
GIVEN vnd^r the seale of Prouince the seauenth day of Aprill
1668 and in the XX yeare of the Reign of Ou^r Souereign
Lord Charles the Second of England, Scotland, France &
Ireland, King Defend^r of the Faith &c.

PH CARTERET.

PENNSYLVANIA.

Writ calling the first assembly, 1682.[1]

(L. S.) WILLIAM PENN, Proprietary and Governor of the
province of Pennsylvania and the territories thereunto belonging:

I do hereby in the King's name, empower and require
thee to summon all the freeholders in thy bailiwick to meet
on the 20th day of the next month, at the polls upon the
Delaware River; and that they then and there elect and
chuse out of themselves, twelve persons of most note for
wisdom and integrity, to serve as their delegates in the provincial Council to be held at Philadelphia, the 10th day of
the first month next; and that thou there declare to the said
freemen, that they may all personally appear at an Assembly,
at the place aforesaid according to the contents of my

---

[1] 1 Proud *History of Pennsylvania*, 234.

charter of liberties; of which thou art to make me a true and faithful return.

Given at Philadelphia, the   day of the   month 1682,   WILLIAM PENN.

To Richard Noble, High Sheriff of the county of Bucks; and the other five Sheriffs likewise for their several counties.

MARYLAND.

Writ calling the first assembly.[1]

       Warr^t to Capt Evelin
       Touching the Generall Assembly.

After my hearty Commendãons &^{c} whereas my dear brother the Lord Propriet^r of this Province, hath by his Commission to me directed in that behalfe bearing date at London in the Realme of England, the 15th day of Aprill 1637 appointed a grãll assembly of all the freemen of this Province to be held at his town of S^t maries on the five and twentieth day of January next   These are therefore in his Lo^{ps} name to will and require you (all excuses sett apart) to make your psonall repaire to the ffort of S^t maries on the said five and twentieth day of January, then and there to consult and advise of the affaires of this Province. And further to will and require you at some convenient time when you shall thinke fitt within 6 daies after the receipt hereof at the furthest, to assemble all the freemen inhabiting within any part of yor iurisdiction: and then and there to publish and proclaim the said generall assembly; and to endeavour to perswade such and so many of the said freemen as you shall thinke fitt to repair psonally to the said assembly at the time & place prefixed; and to give free power & liberty to all the rest of the said freemen either to be pñt at the said assembly if they so please: or otherwise to elect and

---

[1] *Maryland State Archives,* I *Proceedings and Acts of Assembly,* I.

nominate such and so many persons as they or the main part of them so assembled shall agree vpon to be the deputies or burgesses for the said freemen, in their name and steed to advise and consult of such things as shalbe brought into deliberation in the said assembly; and to enter all the severall votes or suffrages vpon record; and the record thereof, and of whatsoever you shall doe in any the premises to bring along with you; and exhibite it at the day and place prefixed to the Secretary of the Province for the time being, And for so doing this shalbe yᵒʳ warrᵗ Given at St. maries this 30ᵗʰ day of January 1637.

Second Assembly, Feby 15 1638–9 [1]

After my hearty commendation &c Whereas I have appointed to hold a General Assembly at Sᵗ Maries on the twelfe day of ffebruary next there to advise and Consult upon the enacting of Laws and other Serious affairs of the Province, These are therefore to will and require you at Some Convenient time where you Shall think fit after the receipt of these Letters to assemble at Kent ffort, all the Freemen inhabiting within the Isle of Kent and then and there to propound to the Said ffreemen to chuse from amongst themselves two or more discreet honest men to be their deputies or Burgesses during the next assembly according to the form of an Instrument which I herewith Send unto you, to which Instrument, which I herein Send you, to wᶜʰ Instrument all the Said ffreemen are to set their hands, And if they agree not in the election, then you are to return upon the Instrument the names of Such two or more persons upon whome the Major part of the ffreemen Soe assembled Shall consent, And you Shall require the ffreemen So assembled to agree upon a Certain Contribution for the defraying of the Charges wᶜʰ Such Burgesses Shall Sustain

---

[1] *Maryland State Archives,* 1 *Proceedings and Acts of Assembly,* 27, 28.

by the repairing to the assembly and together with them you Shall return hither the Instrument of their Election Signed as is appointed afore, and for Soe doeing this Shall be your warrant, Given at St Marie's this 21th Decem^b 1638

To my Loveing Kinsman Will: Braithwait
Commander of the

Cæcillius Lord Proprietary &c^a to our dear Friend & Councillor Thomas Cornwaleys Esqr Greeting whereas we have appointed to hold a General Assembly of the Freemen of our Province at our Fort of St Marys on the five and twentieth day of February next we do therefore hereby will and require you that all excuses and delays sett apart you repair in Person to said Assembly at the time and Place prefixed there to advise and counsult with us touching the important affairs of our Province

Given at St. Marys the 18th January, 1638.
(These were sent to four others.)

Cæcilius Lord Proprietory &c^a to our trusty Ric^d Garnett Senior Richard Lusthead Anum Benum Henry Bishop Joseph Edlo Lewis Freeman and any other the Freemen inhabiting at Mattapanient Greeting whereas we have appointed to hold a General Assembly of the Freemen of our Province at our Fort of St Marys On the five and twentieth day of this instant month of February these are therefore to will and require you that to-morrow or on thursday next at the furthest between one and two of the clock in the afternoon you & every one of you be at Our Secretarys house at St Johns there to make such nomination and Election of your Burgesses for that mannor or division of Mattapanient for this next Assembly as you shall think fitt hereof fail not you Perill given at St Maries this 11th of February 1638.

(The like were sent to the freemen of three other hundreds.)

Returns were made in this form:—

14th February 1638

Memd that this day came before me Richard Garnett Senior, Richard Lusthead, Annum Benum Henry Bishop, Joseph Edlo Lewis Freeman & Robt Wiseman and chose for the Burgess of the hundred of Mattapanient Henry Bishop and have Given unto him full and free Power for them and for every of them to be present in their names at the next Assembly as their Burgess or deputy and in witness thereof have hereunto set their hands.

The mark of RICHARD + GARNETT

The mark of RICHARD + LUSTHEAD

The mark of JOSEPH + EDLO

ROBERT WISEMAN

The mark of ANUM + BENUM

The mark of LEWIS + FREEMAN

(Similarly for other hundreds.)

Writs for election of Burgesses for Oct. 12th, 1640.[1]

Writ.

Caecilius &ca to all the freemen of our hundred of St Marys Greeting we do hereby summon you to be before our Secretary at Saint Johns on tuesday next at One of the clock after dinner to make election of one or two Burgesses for that hundred for the next Assembly. Given at Saint Marys 12th Septr 1640.

Return.[2]

15th September 1640.

The freemen of Saint Marys hundred chose for their Burgesses the next Assembly Mr Secretary & Mr Greene.

coram me JOHN LEWGER Secretary.

(Similar writs and returns for other hundreds.)[3]

---

[1] *Maryland State Archives,* I *Proceedings and Acts of Assembly,* 87.   [2] *Ibid.,* 88.

[3] Other Warrants: *ibid.* 114, 115, 121, 369, 381, 382.

1659[1]

January 12th

Caecilius absolute Lord and Proprietary of the Province of Maryland and Avalon Lord Barron of Baltimore &c. To the Sheriffe of Saint Maryes County Greeting Whereas by the advice and consent of our Councell We haue determined to hould an Assembly of the ffreemen of our Province at M[r] Thomas Gerrards on the last Tuesday in ffebruary next ensuing there to consider of certaine things concerning the State and welfare of this our Province of Maryland Wee command you Nicholas Guyther Sheriffe of St Maryes County that makeing Proclamation as soone as conveniently may be after the receipt of this writt you cause fower discreete Burgesses to be elected to serve the said Assembly there to doe and consent to such things as by comon consent shall happen to be ordained and enacted in the buisness aforesaid so that through want of sufficient power or inconsiderat election of the aforesaid Burgessses the buisnesses aforesaid may not remaine vndon or neglected, and make your retourn of this Writt into the Secretaries Office by the Seventeenth of ffebruary next Given at Saint Maryes vnder our Greate Seale of our said Province of Maryland the twelfth day of January in the Eight & twentieth yeare of our Dominion over the said Province Annoque Domini One thousand Six hundred ffifty Nyne.[2]

C:—Absolute Lord and Proprietor of the Provinces of Maryland & Avalon Lord Baron of Baltimore to the Sheriffe of A: Greeting these are to authorize and require you imediately upon receipt hereof to call together four or more of the comissioners of your County with the Clerke who are hereby required to sitt as a Court and dureing their sitting

---

[1] *Maryland State Archives,* 1 *Proceedings and Acts of Assembly,* 381.

[2] Other Returns: *ibid,* 28, 29, 88, 89, 104, 105, 128, 129, 260, 382, 396.

by virtue of your office to make or cause to be made Publick
Proclamation thereby giveing notice to all the freeman of
your said County who have within your said County a freehold of fifty acres of land or a visible personall estate of forty
pounds starling att least Requireing them to appeare at the
next County Court to be holden for your County att a certaine day within a reasonable time after such Proclamation
made for the electing & chuseing of Deputyes and Delegates
to serve for your County in a Generall Assembly to be
holden att the citty of St Marye's the   day of   at
which time of Proclamation aforesaid the said freemen so required to appeare or the major part of such of them as shall
then appeare shall and may and are hereby authorized and
required to Elect and Chuse four severall & sufficient freemen
of your County each of them having a freehold of 'fifty acres
of land or a visible personall estate of forty pounds starling
att least within your County and you shall give authority to
each of them severally and respectively by four severall and
respective indentures under their hands and seales to be
Deputyes and Delegates for your County and to appeare and
serve as Deputyes and Delegates for your County att the
said next Generall Assembly to doe and consent to those
things which then by the favour of God shall there happen
to be ordained by the Lord Proprietary by the advice and
consent of the great Councell of this Province concerning
such occasions and affaires as shall relate to the government
state & defence of this Province but wee will not in any case
that you or any other sheriffe in our said Province be elected
which said indentures shall be between you the Sheriffe of
the one part and the said freemen Electing on the other part
and shall beare date the same day upon which the said election shall be made and shall mention the time and place of
such election and the persons soe elected and shall be signed
and sealed each part of them as well by you the sheriffe as

by the said freemen by whom the said election shall be made and that upon such election you the Sheriffe shall soe soon as conveniently may be certifie and transmitt to the Chancellor of this Province for the time being one part of the said severall and respective Indentures close sealed up under your hand & seale and directed to the Lord Proprietary of this Province and alsoe to the said Chancellor & the other part of the said Indentures you are to keepe for your Justification wittness our selfe at our Citty of St. Marye's &ca[1].

ANNE by the grace of God of England Scotland France and Ireland Queen Defender of the faith &c. To the Sheriff of A County Greeting These are to authorize and empower you immediately upon receipt hereof to call together four or more Commissioners of your County with the Clerk who are hereby required to sitt as a Court and during the sitting by virtue of your office to make or cause to be made publicq proclamation thereby giving notice to all the freemen of your said County who have within your said County a freehold of fifty acres of land or a visible estate of forty pounds sterl. at the least requiring them to appear at the next County Court to be holden for your County at a certain day within a reasonable time after such proclamation made for electing and choosing of Deputys and Delegates to serve for your County in a Generall Assembly to be holden at the port of Annapolis the   day of   at which time of proclamation aforesaid the said freemen so required to appear or the major part of such of them as shall then appear shall and may and are hereby authorized and required to elect and choose four severall and sufficient freemen of your County each of them having a freehold of fifty acres of land or visible estate of forty pound sterl. at the least within your County and you shall give to each of them

[1] Act of 1678, *Maryland Archives*, 3 *Proceedings and Acts of Assembly*, 60. The writ given in the act of 4 Will. and Mary, chap. 76, is similar, *mutatis mutandis*.

severally and respectively by four severall and respective
Indentures under their hands and seals to be Deputys and
Delegates for your County at the said next Generall Assembly to do and consent to those things which then by the
favour of God shall happen to be ordained by the advice
and consent of the great Councill of this province concerning such occasions and affaires as shall relate to the Government State and defence of this province   But we will
not in any case that you or any other sheriff in our said
province be elected.   Which said Indentures shall be between you the said sheriff of the one part and the said
freemen electing of the other part and shall bear date the
same day upon which the said election shall be made and
that upon such election you the said Sheriff shall so soon as
conveniently may be certify and transmitt to the Chancelour
of this province for the time being one part of the said
severall and respective Indentures close sealed up under
your hand and seale and directed to the Governour of this
province and also to the Chancellour and the other part of
the said Indentures you are to keep for your justification.
Witness our trusty and well beloved John Seymour Esq.
our Capt and Chief Governour of this our province at
Annapolis &c.[1]

GEORGE by the grace of God of Great Brittain, France and
Ireland King Defender of the faith &c. &c. To the sher'f
of   County Greeting.   These are to command authorize
and empower you imediately upon receipt hereof to call
together three or more Justices of your County whereof one
to be of the Quorum with the Clerk of the County Court
who are hereby required to sit as a Court and dureing their
sitting by vertue of your office to make or cause to be made
Publick Proclamation thereby giveing notice to all the free-

---

[1] 4 Anne, chap. 35; Baskett ed., 1723, 121.

men of your said County who have within the said County a
freehold of fifty acres of land who shall be residents and have
a vissiable Estate of forty pounds sterling at the least therein
requireing them to appear at your County Court house at a
certaine time not less than ten days after such proclamation
made for electing and chooseing dep^{tys} and delegates to
serve for your said County in a Generall Assembly to be
holden at the   day of   to which time you shall adjourn your
said Court and dureing the Courts sitting the said freemen
so required to appear or the major part of such of them as
shall then appear shall and may and are hereby authorized
and required to elect and choose four severall and sufficient
freemen of your County each of them having a freehold of
fifty acres of Land or who shall be a resident and have a
vissiable estate of forty pounds sterling at the least within
your County whether the partys so elected be present or
absent, the said election to be made in such manner and
forme as ye laws of England and this province doe direct and provide and you are to insert the names of the
said persons elected in certain Indentures to be then made
between you the said Sheriff and the Electors (that is to
say) two Indentures for each Delegate each Indenture haveing thereto your hand and seale and the hands and seales of
the severall Electors by them subscribed that the said Dep^{ts}
and delegates for themselves and the County afd may have
severally full and suff^t power to do and consent to those
things which then and there by the favour of God shall
happen to be ordained by the advice and consent of the
Great Councill of this Province concerning such occasion
and affairs as shall relate to the Government state and defence thereof.   But we will not in anywise that you or any
other Sherr' in our said Province be elected and that upon
election you the said sherr' so soon as conveniently may be
give notice to the parties elected if absent and certifie and

transmit to the Chancellor of this province for the time being one of the two severall and respective Indentures affixed to these presents close sealed up and Directed to the Chancellor of this province for the time being and the other part of the said Indentures you are to keep for your Justification WITNESS &c.[1]

VIRGINIA.

No particular form is prescribed for the writs, but each sheriff or his deputy is required to endorse his return upon the back in the following form:

"BY vertue of this writt I have caused to be legally summoned the freeholders of my county to meet this day being the   day of   at the court house of this county being the usuall place for election of burgesses and have given them in charge to make election of two of the most able and discreet persons of the said county for theire burgesses, who accordingly have elected and chosen A B and C D burgesses for the said county for the next generall assembly to be held at the   day of   "[2]

A later act required the return to be made as follows:

Upon the writ are to be endorsed the words:

"The execution of this writ appears in a certain schedule hereto annexed."

The schedule is to be in the following form, *mutatis mutandis*, viz.:

"By virtue of this writ to me directed, in my full county held at the court house of my said county, upon the   day of   in the   year of the reign of   by the grace of God of England, Scotland, France and Ireland, Queen: defender of the faith &c., by the assent of my said county I

---

[1] 8 Geo. I, chap. 42. See Appendix B, *post.*

[2] 11 Will. III, chap. 2, 3 Hening 172.

have caused to be chosen (two Burgesses) of my said county, to wit, A B and C D, to act and do as in the said writ is directed and required."

For a town or for the college of William and Mary, the return is to be made in this form:

" By virtue of this writ, to me directed, I did make lawful publication thereof; and afterwards, to wit, upon the day of   in the   year of the reign of   by the grace of God, of England, Scotland, France, and Ireland, Queen, defender of the faith (at the said town of   ) or (at the said college) by the assent of the (freeholders) or (President, and Masters or Professors) thereof, I have caused to be chosen one Burgess for the said (town) or (College) to wit A B of   to act and do as in the said writ is directed and required." [1]

II. OATHS.

§ 1. *Freemen and Electors.*

NEW PLYMOUTH.

Oath of a Freeman. [2]

You shall be truly loyall to [our Sov. Lord King Charles his heirs and successors   (the State and Govern[t] of England as it now stands—] [3] You shall not speake or doe, devise or advise any thing or things act or acts directly or indirectly by land or water, that doth shall or may tend to the destruccon or over throw of this prnt plantacons Colonies or Corporacon of New Plymouth, Neither shall you suffer the same to be spoken or done but shall hinder oppose & discover the same to the Govr & assistants of the said Colony

---

[1] 4 Anne, chap. 2, § 7, 3 Hening, 236.

[2] 11 *Plymouth Colonial Records*, 8; Brigham, 38. A similar oath is given in 11 *Plymouth Colonial Records*, 80.

[3] The passage in brackets is erased in the original document.

for the time being or some one of them. You shall faithfully submit unto such good & wholsome laws & ordinances as either are or shall be made for the ordering & govrnm^t of the same, and shall endeavor to advance the growth & good of the severall plantations wthin the limit of this corporacon by all due meanes & courses. All wch you promise & sweare by the name of the great God of heaven & earth simply truly & faithfully to pforme as you hope for help fro God who is the God of truth & punisher of falsehood.

MASSACHUSETTS.

Oath of Fidelity.[1]

I A B being by God's providence an Inhabitant within the jurisdiction of this Commonwealth do freely and sincerely acknowledge my self to be subject to the Government thereof And do here swear by the great and dreadfull name of the Ever living God, that I will be true and faithfull to the same, and will accordingly yeild assistance thereunto, with my person and estate as in equity I am bound: And will also truely endeavour to Maintain and preserve all the Liberties and Priviledges thereof, submitting my self unto the wholesom Laws made and established by the same.

And farther that I will not plot or practice any evill against it or consent to any that shall so do but will timely discover and reveal the same to lawfull Authority now here established, for the speedy preventing thereof. So help me God in our Lord Jesus Christ.

Oath of a Freeman.[2]

I, A B being by God's Providence an Inhabitant within the jurisdiction of the commonwealth and now to be made free; doe here freely acknowledg my self to be subject to

---

[1] *Laws*, ed. 1660, 84.

[2] *Laws*, ed. 1660, 84; 1 *Massachusetts Colonial Records*, 117.

the Government thereof: and therefore do hear Swear by the great and dreadfull Name of the Everliving God, that I will be true and faithfull to the same, and will accordingly yeild assistance and support thereunto, with my person and estate as in equity I am bound, and will also truely endeavour to maintain and preserve all the Liberties and Priviledges thereof submitting my self unto the wholesome Laws made and established by the same. And farther, that I will not plot or practice any evill against it or consent that any shall so do; but will timely discover and reveal the same to law-full authority now here established for the speedy prevention thereof.

Moreover I do solemnly bind my self in the sight of God, that when I shall be called to give my voice touching any such matter of this State, wherein Free-men are to deal; I will give my vote and suffrage as I shall in mine own con-science judg best to conduce and tend to the publick weal of the Body without respect of persons or favour of any man. So help me God &c

RHODE ISLAND.

During the earlier years of Rhode Island, the newly chosen officers "engaged" themselves by taking an oath. The freemen then took the following "Reciprocal Engage-ment" which falls perhaps under the category of an oath of allegiance or of fidelity rather than of an elector:

"We the Inhabitants of the Province of Providence Plan-tations being here orderly met, and having by free vote chosen you to public office and officers for the due adminis-tration of justice and the execution thereof throughout the whole Colonie do hereby engage ourselves to the utmost of our power to support and uphold you in your faithfull per-formance thereof."[1]

---

[1] 1 *Rhode Island Colonial Records,* 150.

Oath to be taken by electors (*1665*).[1]

YOU AB, sollemly and sincearly engage true and faithfull aleagiance vnto his Majesteye' Charles the Second, King of England, his heirs and successors, to beare and due obediance vnto the lawes established, from time to time in this jurisdiction to yeald vnto the utmost of your power, according to the previlidge by his said Majesty granted, in religious and civill concearnments to this collony in the charter; which said engagment you make under the perrill and penalty of perjury.

Oath required on admission as freemen or at the time of voting.[2]

YOU AB do solemnly swear (or affirm) That you have not, nor will not receive any money or other reward, nor any promise of Money or any other thing, by which you may expect any money or future reward, at the Election of any officer to be chosen in this colony; and that you will not bargain or contract with any person, directly or indirectly, contrary to the true meaning of this Oath (or affirmation); but that you will use your freedom for the Good of the Government only, without any other Motive. And this Declaration you make without any Evasion, Equivocation or Mental Reservation whatsoever.

Oath required of those suspected of receiving or making fraudulent conveyances in order to multiply or create votes:[3]

YOU, AB, do solemnly swear that you are really and truly possessed in your own Right of the estate of which a Conveyance is made you by CD according to the Tenor of the said Conveyance; and that you now hold and improve the same to your Use, Benefit and Behoof, and that you have not given any promise or assurance of any nature or kind

---

[1] 2 *Rhode Island Colonial Records*, 112. [2] 20 Geo. II, Franklin ed., 1752, 13.
[3] Hall's *Code*, 1767, Title *Elections*, 78.

whatsoever, that you will reconvey said estate to the said CD
or any Person in his Behalf. And this Declaration you
make without any Evasion, Equivocation, or Mental Reservation whatsoever.

NEW HAVEN.

Oath of a Freeman[1] (*1639.*)

Yow shall neither plott, practise nor consent to any evill
or hurt against this Jurisdiction, or any pte of it, or against
the civill gouernment here established. And if you shall
know any pson, or psons wch intend, plott or conspire any
thing wch tends to the hurt or prejudice of the same, yow
shall timely discouer the same to lawfull authority here
established, and yow shall assist and bee helpfull in all the
affaires of the Jurisdiction, and by all meanes shall promove
the publique wellfare of the same, according to yor place,
ability, and opptunity, yow shall give due honno^r to the
lawfull magistrats, and shall be obedient and subject to all
the wholesome lawes and orderes, allready made, or w^{ch}
shall be hereafter made, by lawfull authority afforesaid.
And that both in yor pson and estate ; and when yow shall
be duely called to give yor vote or suffrage in any election
or touching any other matter which concerneth this common wealth yow shall give it as in yor conscience yow shall
judg may conduce to the best good of the same.

Oath of fidelity administered to all freemen.[2]

I A B being by the providence of God an inhabitant
within Newhaven jurisdictiõ, doe acknowledge myselfe to be
subject to the governm^t thereof, and doe sweare be the great
and dreadfull name of the everliving God, to be true and
faithfull vnto the same, and doe submitt both my person and
my whole estate therevnto according to all the wholsome

[1] 1 *New Haven Colonial Records*, 19.   [2] *Ibid.*, 137.

lawes and orders thatt for present are or hereafter shall be there made and established by lawful authority and thatt I will neither plott nor practise any evill agst the same, nor consent to any thatt should so doe, butt will timely discover the same to lawfull authority here established, and thatt I will as I am in duety bounde, maintaine the· hono^r of the same and off the lawfull magistrates thereoff, promoting the publique good of the same whilest I shall eontinue an inhabitant there.   And whensoever I shall be duely called as a freeburgesse according to the fundamentall order and agreem^t for governm^t in this jurisdictiō to give my vote or suffrage touching any matter which concerneth this Comowealth, I will give itt as in my conscience I shall judge may conduce to the best good of the same w^{t}hout respect of persons, so help me God &c.[1]

CONNECTICUT.

The oath of a Hartford freeman was almost precisely like that required in New Haven.[2]

After 1703 the following oath was prescribed:[3]

You, A B, being by the providence of God an inhabitant within this her majesties Colony of Connecticut, and now to be made free of the same, DO swear by the Ever living God, that you will be true and faithful to her Majesty Queen Anne, (and to her lawful Successors,) and to the Government of Her Majesties said Colony as Established by Charter. And whensoever you shall give your Vote or Suffrage touching any matter which concerns this colony, being called thereunto, you will give it, as in your conscience

---

[1] The London Edition of the laws (1656) contains an oath made up of sentences taken from each of the preceding oaths (2 *New Haven Coloniai Records*, 616).

[2] See 1 *Connecticut Colonial Records*, 63.   *Laws*, ed. 1653, Title *Oaths*, 53.

[3] *Session Laws*, ed. 1754, 45.

you shall judge may conduce to the best good of the same without respect of persons, or Favor of any Man. SO HELP YOU GOD.

NEW YORK.

General Oath to be taken by every voter, if required.[1]

YOU shall swear that you are a freeholder of the County of   and have improved Land or Tenement to the Value of forty pounds, lying at   within the said county of   Freehold: And that you have not been before Polled at this Election, nor have you procured this freehold to give your Voice in this election. SO HELP YOU GOD.[2]

In New York city elections one of the following oaths must be taken by every voter, according to his status, if required by a candidate or an officer:[3]

Freeholder's Oath.

You shall swear, or affirm, that you are a Freeholder in the Ward in which you now offer to vote, and have Lands or Tenements to the Value of Forty Pounds lying in the said Ward; that you do not hold the same in Trust for any Body Politic or Corporate, or for any pious or religious Use whatsoever, and that you have possessed the same for one Month next before the day of this Election (except he has his Freehold by Descent or devise), and that you have not been before polled at this Election nor have you procured this Freehold under any obligation or Promise to reconvey the same to the Seller after this Election. SO HELP YOU GOD.

---

[1] 11 Will. III, chap. 74, § 14, Van Schaack's *Laws*, 28.

[2] Part of this oath is taken from the English statute of 7 and 8 Will. III, chap. 25.

[3] 11 Geo. III, chap. 1492, Van Schaack's *Laws*, 620.

Freeman's Oath.

YOU do swear or affirm that you are a Freeman of the City of New York, and have been so for three months now last past, and have actually resided in the Ward in which you now offer to vote, one Month next before the Day of this election, and that you have not been before polled at this Election. SO HELP YOU GOD.

NEW JERSEY.

Oath to be taken by electors.[1]

I A B do in the presence of God, Declare and Swear, That I am and have been a freeholder and Resident in this County, City or Town, One whole Year, and that the Estate for which I claim to give my Votes in this Election, is my proper estate and that it is not conveyed to me in Trust, or on Condition that I shall give my vote in this Election for any person.

PENNSYLVANIA.

If required by any inspector, an elector was bound to declare upon his solemn affirmation,[2] " That he is Twenty-one Years of age and a Freeholder for the County of   and has fifty acres of land or more, well seated and twelve Acres thereof or more cleared; OR, that he is otherways worth Fifty Pounds, Money of this Province, clear Estate, and hath been resident·therein for the Space of two years and that he has not before been polled at that Election."

When the system of regularly elected inspectors came into effect, an oath or affirmation was necessary unless the qualification of a voter was generally known, " or some one or more of the inspectors shall or will openly declare as to the

[1] 12 Geo. I, chap. 40, Nevill's *Laws*, 142.
[2] 4 Anne, chap. 129, Franklin ed., 1742, 67.

rest that they know such elector to be qualified as afore-said."[1]

MARYLAND.

All Papists or persons suspected of being such must take the following oaths before being permitted to vote.[2]

Allegiance.   I A B do sincerely promise and swear that I will be faithful and bear true allegiance to his Majesty King George. SO HELP ME GOD.

Abhorrence.   I A B do swear, That I from my Heart ab-hor, detest and abjure as impious and heretical, that Damn-able Doctrine and Position That Princes excommunicated or deprived by the Pope or any Authority of the See of Rome may be deposed and murthered by their subjects or any other whatsoever.   And I declare That no foreign Prince Person Prelate State or Potentate hath or ought to have Jurisdiction, Power, Superiority, Preeminence, or authority, Ecclesiastical or Spiritual within the Kingdom of Great Britain or any of the Dominions thereunto belonging.   SO HELP ME GOD.

Abjuration.   I A B do truly and sincerely acknowledge, profess, testify and declare in my conscience before God and the world, That our Sovereign Lord King George is law-fully and rightfully King of the Realm of Great Britain and all other the Dominions and countries thereunto belonging. And I do solemnly and sincerely declare that I do believe in my conscience that the person pretended to be the Prince of Wales, during the life time of the late King James, and since his decease pretending to be and taking upon himself the Stile and Title of King of England by the name of James the Third, or of Scotland by the Name of James the Eighth, or the Stile and Title of King of Great Britain hath not any

---

[1] 13 Geo. I, chap. 284, Franklin ed., 1742, 346.

[2] 3 Charles Lord B., chap. 1; 1 Chas. Lord B., chap. 5, Bacon's *Laws.*

Right or Title whatsoever to the Crown of the Realm of
Great Britain or any other the Dominions thereto belonging.   And I do renounce refuse and abjure any Allegiance
or Obedience to him.   And I do swear that I will bear Faith
and True allegiance to his Majesty King George and him
will defend to the utmost of my power against all traitrous
Conspiracies and Attempts whatsoever which shall be made
against his Person Crown or Dignity, and I will do my
utmost Endeavor to disclose and make known to his Majesty
and his successors all Treasons and traitrous Conspiracies
which I shall know to be against him or any of them.   And
I do faithfully promise to the utmost of my Power to support maintain and defend the Succession of the Crown against
him the said James, and all other Persons whatsoever,
which Succession by an act entitled " An act for the further
Limitation of the Crown, and better securing the Rights and
Liberties of the Subject" is and stands limited to the Prin-
cess Sophia, Electress and Dutchess Dowager of Hanover
and the Heirs of her body being Protestants.   And these
things I do plainly and sincerely acknowledge and swear,
according to these express words by me spoken and according to the plain and common Sense and understanding of the
same Words, without any Equivocation, mental Evasion or
secret Reservation whatsoever.   And I do make this Recognition, Acknowledgment, Abjuration, Renunciation and
Promise, heartily willingly and truly upon the true Faith of
a Christian.   So HELP ME GOD.

Test.   I A B do declare, That I do believe there is
not any Trans-substantiation in the Sacrament of the Lord's
Supper or in the Elements of Bread and Wine at or after
the Consecration thereof by any person whatsoever.

VIRGINIA.

Oath to be taken by voters upon request of any freeholder.[1]

YOU shall swear that you are bona fide a freeholder in this county of   or towne   of to the best of your knowledge.

In case the elector were a Quaker, the following declaration must be first made :

I, A B, do declare in the presence of Almighty God, the witness of the truth of what I say.

After 1705, this oath was required of all voters :[2]

YOU shall swear that you are a freeholder of the county of   and that you have not been before polled at this election.

Thirty-one years later the following oath must be taken if required :[3]

YOU shall swear, That you are a freeholder in the county of   and have at least one hundred acres of freehold lands unseated, lying and being in the parish of   in the county of   in your sole possession or in the possession of your tenant or tenants for years ; and that the greatest part of the said land doth lie in the county of OR, that you are a freeholder and sole owner of twenty five acres of land with a house and plantation upon it, lying and being in the county of   in your sole possession, or in the possession of your tenant or tenants for years ; OR, that you are a freeholder and sole owner of a house and lot, or a house and part of a lot, in your possession, or in the possession of your tenant or tenants lying and being in the city and town of   , and that such freehold estate hath not been made or granted to you fraudulently on purpose to

[1] 11 Will. III, chap. 2, 3 Hening 172.
[2] 4 Anne, chap. 2, 3 Hening 336.
[3] 10 Geo. II, chap. 2, § vii, 4 Hening 475.

qualify you to give your vote; and that you have not been polled before at this election.[1]

NORTH CAROLINA.

Locke's Constitution required all persons seventeen years of age or over to take the following oath before they could have any rights in the province. In this respect it falls under the head of a voter's oath, though of course the elector must be a freeman of the proper age.[2]

I A B do promise to bear faith and true allegiance to our sovereign Lord King Charles the Second, his heirs and successors, and will be true and faithful to the Palatine and Lords Proprietors of Carolina, their heirs and successors, and with my utmost power will defend them and maintain the government,according to this establishment in these fundamental constitutions.

Oath to be taken upon challenge by any person present.[3]

YOU shall swear, That you have been possessed of a Freehold, of Fifty acres of Land for Three Months past in your own Right, in the County of   and have been Six Months an inhabitant of this Province; and that you have not given in your vote before in this Election. SO HELP YOU GOD.

In 1760 the following oath was substituted for the above:[4]

YOU shall swear that you have been Six Months an Inhabitant of this Province, and that you have been possessed of a freehold of Fifty acres of Land for three months past, in

---

[1] A portion of this oath is taken from the English statute of 10 Anne, chap. 23. For additional oaths see 15 Geo. II, chap. 26, § iii, 5 Hening 204; 3 Geo. III, chap. 1, § xiii, 7 Hening 519.

[2] Art. 117, 2 *North Carolina Colonial Records*, 205.

[3] 17 Geo. II., chap. 1, Davis ed., 1752, 177.

[4] 33 Geo. II., chap. 1, Davis ed., 1773, 247.

your own Right in the County of   , and that such land hath not been granted you fraudulently, on Purpose to qualify you to give your Vote; and that the place of your abode is in the County of   and that you have not voted in this election. SO HELP YOU GOD.[1]

In Vestry elections the following oath was prescribed:[2]

You shall swear (or affirm) that you are in actual Possession of a Freehold of Fifty Acres of Land in your own Right (or the Right of some other Person); or a Lot in the Town of   saved according to Law, in the Parish of   and that you have not given your Vote before in this Election. SO HELP YOU GOD.

SOUTH CAROLINA.

Oaths covering the qualifications were administered to every voter.[3]

GEORGIA.

Oath to be administered at the request of one of the candidates or of any two persons qualified to vote.[4]

I AB, do swear that I am legally possessed in my own Right of a freehold Estate of fifty acres of Land in the Township or District of   and that such Estate is legally or bona fide in my own right and not made over or granted to me purposely or fraudulently to intitle me to vote at this Election.

---

[1] The latter part of this oath is similar to that prescribed in England by statute of 10 Anne, chap. 23.

[2] 5 Geo. III, chap. 2, Davis, ed., 1773, 305.

[3] Act 1704, no. 227, 2 Cooper, 249; Act 1716, no. 365, 2 Cooper, 683.

[4] Act 1761.

§ 2.   *Election Officers.*

MASSACHUSETTS.

"Oath to be administered to those that sort and number the votes."[1]

Whereas yow A B C are appointed and betrusted ffor the opening the Proxies sent in by the Freemen, and receiving sorting and numbering the Votes for the choice of Gou'no[r] Deputy Gou'no[r] , Assistants and other public Officers of this Jurisdiction to be Chosen on the ellection Day yow doe now sweare by the Name of Almighty God that yow will deale truely and uprightly therein as also that you will not either directly or indirectly discouer either persons or number of Votes until the Election is ended.   So help you God.

CONNECTICUT.

At the election to fill the vacancy caused by the death of Governor Winthrop, in 1707, the tellers chosen to count the votes of the legislature took the following oath:[2]

You, AB, CD &c being appointed to sort the votes now to be given in for the choice of a Governour doe swear that you will faithfully do the same and declare who is chosen by the major part of this assembly.   So help you God.

[1] Orders at Court of Feb'y 4th, 1679-80; 5 *Massachusetts Colonial Records*, 262.
[2] 5 *Connecticut Colonial Records*, 38.

APPENDIX B.

PENNSYLVANIA.

LAWS 1700, CHAPTER 28.[1]

An Act to Ascertain the Number of Members of Assembly And to Regulate the Elections.

For the prevention of all dispute and uncertainty for the future, what persons shall be accounted freemen of this Province and Territories and have right of electing or being elected members of Assembly. Be it Enacted by the Proprietary and Governor and by and with the advice and consent of the freemen of this Province and Territories in General Assembly met and by the authority of the same, That there shall be four persons elected yearly in said respective county of this Province and Territories to serve as members of Assembly. And that no inhabitant of this Province and Territories shall have the right of electing or being elected as aforesaid unless he or they be natural or native born subject or subjects of England or be naturalized in England or in this Province and Territories and unless said person or persons as aforesaid be of the age of twenty-one years or upward and be a free-holder or free-holders of this Province

---

[1] This statute was incorporated by reference in Penn's Charter of Privileges, and confirmed by that instrument as establishing the qualifications of electors. (See 1 Proud, *History of Pennsylvania*, 444, for a copy of the charter.) The present act is referred to by title in most of the editions of the Pennsylvania colonial statutes. The copy now published was obtained from the office of the Secretary of the Commonwealth of Pennsylvania, where the original is of record.

or Territories and have fifty acres of land or more well
seated and twelve acres thereof or more cleared and improved or be otherwise worth fifty pounds lawful money of
this Government, clear estate and have been resident therein
for the space of two years before said election. And to the
end that elections on which the good of the Government so
much depends may not be corruptly managed or obtained.
It is Enacted by the authority aforesaid that all elections
of the said Representatives shall be free and voluntary and
that the elector that shall receive any reward or gift for his
vote shall forfeit his right of electing for that year and be
fined in the sum of five pounds to the use of the Proprietary
and Governor. And that all and every person and persons
that shall give, offer or promise any reward to be elected or
that shall offer to serve for nothing or less allowance than
the law prescribes shall be fined in the like sum of five
pounds for the use aforesaid and be incapable of serving for
that year and the Representatives so chosen as above
directed shall yield their attendance accordingly and being
in Assembly shall be the sole judges of the regularity or
irregularity of the elections of the respective members
according to this Act. And if any person or persons so
chosen to serve as aforesaid shall be wilfully absent from the
service he or they are elected unto, every such person or
persons shall be fined in the sum of twenty pounds to the
use aforesaid unless his or their excuse shall be allowed by
the Assembly. And in case any person or persons so
chosen as aforesaid shall die in the meantime or be rendered
incapable, then and in such cases it shall be lawful for the
Proprietary and Governor and his successors and his or their
Lieutenant and Governor for the time being after knowledge
thereof to issue his or their writ or writs to the Sheriffs of the
respective counties for which the said person or persons
were chosen immediately to summon the freemen of the same

to elect another member or members in the room and stead of such absent or deceased or incapable person or persons and to return the same duly executed. And for the prevention of all such exceptions or complaints for want of due notice of elections, Be it Enacted by the authority aforesaid that publication of all and every writ or writs for elections as aforesaid shall be made by the several Sheriffs of this Province and Territories in their respective counties or by some others by them severally appointed to read the same in the capital town or most public place within their respective Bailiwicks between the hours of ten in the morning and two in the afternoon with an advertisement posted upon some tree or house in the way of leading from every hundred or precinct to the said capital towns or places respectively and also upon the Courthouses and public fixed meeting houses for Religious worship in the said respective counties with all convenient speed after he receives the writ and also give notice thereof to every Constable of the several hundreds and townships which Constables are required to promulgate the same under penalty of five pounds each for each offence. And in case any sheriff shall be deficient therein he shall be fined in the sum of fifty pounds for each offence and in case any Sheriff shall misbehave himself in the management of the aforesaid elections he shall be punished accordingly at the discretion of the Governor and Council for the time being. And be it further Enacted by the authority aforesaid that every member chosen or to be chosen by the freemen as aforesaid to serve in the Assembly shall be allowed the sum of six shillings by the day and the Speaker ten shillings per day during his or their attendance on the service thereof and that every member of Assembly shall be allowed toward his travelling charges after the rate of three pence for each mile both going to and coming from the place where the Assembly is or shall be held. And be it further Enacted by the authority aforesaid that all Laws hereafter to be made in this Province and Territories shall be fairly engrossed in rolls of paper or parchment before the final passing thereof.

* * * * * * *

Passed November 27, 1700.

Recorded A. Vol. I. page 15.

Repealed by the Queen in Counsel, February 7, 1705.

MARYLAND.

4 ANNE, CHAPTER 35.[1]

An Act directing the Manner of Electing and summoning Delegates and Representatives to serve in succeeding Assemblys.

FORASMUCH as the chiefest and only foundation and support of any Kingdom State or Commonwealth is the providing establishing and enacting good and wholesome laws for the good rule and government thereof and also upon any necessary and emergent occasion to raise and levy money for the defraying the charges of the said Government and defence thereof neither of which according to the Constitution of this province can be made ordained established or raised but by and with the consent of the freemen of this province by their severall delegates and representatives by them freely nominated chosen and elected to serve for their severall citys and countys in a Generall Assembly. And forasmuch as the safest and best rule for this province to

---

[1] Bacon refers to this act by title and declares it to be obsolete. We have thought it unnecessary to publish the act of 4 Will. and Mary, chap. 76, because on comparison we find that it is similar to the law passed in the third year of Charles Lord Baltimore (1678), *mutatis mutandis.* The latter statute was reprinted a few years ago in the *Maryland State Archives* (3 *Proceedings and Acts of Assembly*, 60–63), and is therefore easy of access.

follow in electing such Delegates and Representatives is the presidents of the proceeding in parliament in England as near as the Constitution of this province will admit. The Governour Council and Delegates of this present Generall Assembly do humbly pray that it may be enacted and BE IT ENACTED by the Queens most excellent Majesty by and with the advice and consent of her Majestys Governour councill and Assembly of this province and the authority of the same that for the future when and as often as his excellency the Governour of this province for the time being shall be upon any accident and urgent affair of this province think fitt to call and convene an Assembly and to send writts for election of Burgesses and Delegates to serve in such Assembly the form of the said writt shall be as followeth.

(*Here follows the form of writ as given in Appendix A of the present work.*)

And be it further enacted by the Authority aforesaid that two citizens to serve in the said Assembly for the city of St. Marys shall be nominated elected chosen and appointed by the major Recorder Aldemen and comon councill as heretofore hath been usual.

And be it further enacted by the authority aforesaid that the aforesaid four Delegates to be elected in the respective countys within this province and the two citizens of the city of St. Marys be and are hereby bound and obliged to attend the time and place of the meeting of such Assembly without any further writt or sumons to bee to them sent under the penalty of such fines as shall be by the house of Assembly imposed upon them unless upon sufficient excuse to be admitted by the said house of Assembly their absence be excused withall any law statute usage or custom to the contrary notwithstanding.

And be it also further enacted by the authority aforesaid that any sheriff that shall refuse and neglect to make return of the Delegates so elected by Indenture as aforesaid before the day of sitting of such Assembly or that shall make any undue or illegall returns of such elections shall for every fault be fined two hundred pounds ster'l the one half to her Majesty her heirs and successors for the support of Government and the other half to the Informer or him or them that shall sue for the same to be recovered in any Court of record in this province wherein no essoyn protection or wager of Law to bee allowed.

PROVIDED nevertheless that this act or anything herein contained shall not extend to be construed to exclude any County or Countys city or citys Burrough or Burroughs hereafter by her Majesty her heirs or successors to be erected and made within this province from the liberty of such elections of Delegates and Representatives as is before expressed But that such writt as aforesaid shall upon calling every Generall Assembly for this province for the future issue to the sheriff of every such county when the same shall be erected and made into a county as aforesaid and to the major Recorder and Aldermen of every such city or Burrough comanding such sheriff or major recorder and aldermen to cause four freemen of the said County and two freemen of the said city or Burrough qualifyed as in the said writt is expressed to serve as Delegates and Representatives of the said county city or Burrough in the Generall Assembly then next ensuing which said four Delegates for every such county and two for the city and Burrough shall from henceforth be reputed and esteemed to be members of the house of the Generall Assembly of this province anything in this Act to the contrary in anywise notwithstanding.

Provided also that no ordinary Keeper within this province during the time of his keeping ordinary shall be elected chosen or serve as a Deputy or Representative in the said

Generall Assembly so to be hereafter called convened and appointed as aforesaid.

Sept. 23rd, 1704	Sept. 26th 1704
Read and assented to by	Read and assented to by
the house of Delegates	her Majestys Honble Councill
W SAYLARD Clk H. D.	W BLADEN Clk Councill

Maryland October 3d 1704

On the behalf of her Maty I will this be a Law

Jo: SEYMOUR.

{ Seal of Maryland }

I, J Frank Ford, Clerk of the Court of Appeals of Maryland do hereby certify that the foregoing is a full and true Copy of an Act of the Provinciall Assembly of Maryland as taken from Liber L. L. No 3 Folios 90 &c. one of the Record Books of this Office.

{ Seal of the Court of Appeals of Maryland. } In testimony whereof I have hereunto set my hand as Clerk and affixed the seal of the said Court of Appeals this 10th day of June 1892.

[Signed] J. FRANK FORD

Clerk Court of Appeals of Maryland.

NORTH CAROLINA.

10 GEORGE I, CHAPTER 2.[1]

An Act intituled an additional Act relating to biennial and other Assemblies and regulating Elections and divers other things relating to Towns.

Whereas by the Act intituled an Act relating to Biennial

---

[1] The act of 1723 is referred to by title in the several editions of the North Carolina laws as chapter 2 of the statutes passed in that year. Davis and Swann (ed. 1752, 67; ed. 1773, 37,) give the title of another law, "an act for Regulating towns and Elections of Burgesses," passed Nov. 6th, 1727. On account of the sup-

and other Assemblies and regulating Elections and Members. And by a late Act intituled an Act for enlarging and Encouragement of the town called Edenton in Chowan precincts the inhabitants of Several Towns in this Government have Liberty to elect a Representative to Sit in all succeeding Assemblies but there being no particular directions how such Representative or the votes shall be qualified for the better regulating thereof.

Be it Enacted by his Excellency the Palatin, &c.

And it is hereby enacted by the authority of the same that no person or persons shall be admitted Representative or Burgess for any town in this government unless he be a Freeholder or owner of a saved lott in the said town and hath been so for eighteen months preceeding the said election and doth constantly maintain and keep an habitable house thereon.

And be it further enacted by the authority aforesaid that no person or persons whatsoever shall be admitted to elect or vote for a representative or burgess for any town in this Government, unless he be an owner of a saved lott in the said town and doth constantly keep an house or houses in repair thereon not lett or tenanted to and by a person capable of voting in the said town, though not residing therein. Provided nevertheless that where any person who hath paid the preceeding years levy or pole tax doth rent and live in and on any such house or lott in the said town not tenanted shall have a right of voting for a Representative or Burgess, but if the tenant by law have not a right to

posed destruction of the original manuscript laws passed between the years 1723 and 1743 (see footnote p. 89, *ante*), it has not been possible to procure a copy of this statute. A search among the papers of the Public Record Office in London has failed to bring to light a copy of the act of 1727, or of either of the South Carolina election laws of October 15th, 1692 (No. 78, 2 Cooper) or of March 10th, 1696–7 (No. 152, 2 Cooper, 130) respectively, to which reference has several times been made in this work.

vote, then the owner thereof and not the tenant shall have the vote and no other person or persons than what are above expressed, shall have any vote for any member or representative in such towns, any Law Usage or Custom to the contrary notwithstanding.

And be it further enacted by the authority aforesaid that no person or persons whatsoever, not having resided within this Government eighteen months next preceeding any succeeding elections shall be capable of being elected or chosen as a representative or member of assembly for any town or precinct within the Government.

(The remainder of this statute relates to subjects wholly foreign to the topic treated in the present work. It is therefore omitted.)

I, J. C. Birdsong, State Librarian, do hereby certify that the foregoing is a true copy of "An Act intituled an additional Act relating to biennial and other Assemblies and regulating elections and divers other things relating to towns," passed "At a General Biennial Assembly begun and held at Edenton, the 4th day of November, 1723, and continued by several adjournments to the 23rd day of the same," the same being now on file in the State Library of this State.[1]

[Signed]   J. C. BIRDSONG,
State Librarian.

December 23rd, 1892.

8 GEORGE II, CHAPTER 2.[2]

An Act for repealing a Clause in an Act Intituled an Act relating to Bienial and other Assemblies, which empowers Freemen of the several precincts to vote for Members of Assembly ; And declaring what persons shall be qualified to

---

[1] There is also a copy of this act in the Public Record Office in London.

[2] This act is quoted by title in Davis and Swann (ed. 1752, 79; ed. 1773, 45). The copy now published was found in the British Public Record Office in London.

vote for members to sit in General Assembly; And also qualification of Members for the future.

Whereas it hath been found inconvenient for the Freemen of each precinct to vote for members of Assembly; And His Majesty by his Royal Instruction having been pleased to direct that only only the Freeholders of this Province should be Intituled to vote for Members of Assembly. Therefore be it Enacted by His Excellency Gabriel Johnston Esqr Governour, the Council and General Assembly, That no person hereafter shall be admitted to give his vote in any Election for members of Assembly for the precincts in this Province, unless such person has been an Inhabitant in the precinct where he votes at least six months, and has bona fide a Freehold in his own Right of at least fifty Acres of Land in the said precinct, which he shall have been possest of Three Months before he offers to give his vote.

And be it Enacted by the Authority aforesaid, That hereafter no person shall be deemed qualified or admitted to sit in the Assembly, unless he has been one full year an Inhabitant of this Province, and is possessed in his own Right of at least one hundred acres of Freehold Land in the precinct where he is Elected or Chosen.

And it is hereby Enacted that those parts of the two clauses in an Act Intituled "an Act relating to the Biennial and other Assemblys; wherein the Freemen of the respective precincts of the County of Albemarle, and the Freemen in each precinct, in Every other County, are Impowered to vote for Members to Sit in the General Assembly; as also that part of the clause in an Act Intituled "an Act for regulating Towns and Elections of Burgesses;" that permit persons to vote who have been resident six Months in the precinct where they vote, are hereby declared repealed. And be it further Enacted by the Authority aforesaid, that if any dispute or Challange shall arise touching the qualification of any person or persons offering his or their vote according to the true Intent and meaning of this Act, that then and in such Case, it shall and may be Lawful for the person who is authorized to take the Poll, to administer an Oath to such person or persons so off'ring his or their vote, that he or they are quallified pursuant to this Act; and that the same Oath be administred to every candidate upon any Challenge made of his being quallified, as is in this Act Provided, any Law heretofore made to the Cóntrary in any wise notwithstanding. And be it further Enacted by the Authority aforesaid, that from and after the ratification of this Act, That all Elections of Members to sit in General Assembly, shall be held and taken at the Court House in Every precinct & in Case there should be no Court house in any of the said precincts, that then and in such case, it shall and may be lawful for the Inhabitants of such precinct, to meet and Convene at the place appointed for such Court house to be built; and if no place for that purpose appointed, then at the usual place in the said precinct to Elect as aforesaid; any Law Custom or Usage to the Contrary, in any wise notwithstanding.

GEORGIA.
ACT OF JUNE 9, 1761.[1]
AN ACT

To assertain the manner and form of Electing Members to represent the Inhabitants of this Province in the Commons House of Assembly—

[1] This statute is quoted by title in Watkins, *Digest of the Laws of Georgia,* as act number 73. It is said that the session laws passed under the provincial government were printed annually at Charleston and Savannah, commencing in 1756. Copies of these are extremely rare, and we have not been able to find a trace of one. The celebrated Charlemagne Tower collection is wanting in this particular, and as a reprint of some of the Georgia colonial statutes made in 1881 does not contain the election law of 1761, it has been thought advisable to insert it in this connection.

Preamble to—

Whereas the manner and form of chusing Members of the Commons House of Assembly to represent the Inhabitants of this Province and the Qualification of the Electors and those elected Members of the Commons House of Assembly has never yet been appointed, fixed and determined by any Laws of this Province, We therefore pray your most Sacred Majesty that it may be Enacted—

Enacted.

AND BE IT ENACTED by his Honor James Wright Esquire Lieutenant Governor and Commander in-Chief of this his Majesty's Province of Georgia by and with the advice and Consent of the Honerable Council and the Commons House of Assembly of the said Province in General Assembly met and by the authority of the Same That. from and after the passing of this Act all Writs for the Election of Members of the Commons House of Assembly shall be issued out by the Governor or Commander in Chief for the time being with the Consent of the Council and shall bear teste forty days before the day appointed for the Meeting of the said Members and shall be directed by the Provost Marshal in the said Writs to Cause such Elections to be made and to return the Names of the Persons eleclected to be Members of the Commons House of Assembly and the Provost Marshal is hereby empowered and required to execute such Writ to him directed and for the faithful and due performance of which according to the true intent and meaning of this Act the Provost Marshal shall cause publick Notice in writing to be affixed at one or more noted

Writs for electing Members of Assembly to be issued by the Governor with Consent of the Council to bear teste 40 days before the day appointed for meeting, and to be directed to the Provost Marshall who is to cause such Election to be made and return the names of the Persons elected.

Provost Marshall to cause publick Notice to be made in writing of the Time and Place of Election, at least 10 days before the day of Election.

place or places in such Parish, District or Town or Village for which the election of a Member or Members by him is to be taken at least ten days before the day of Election of the time and place where such election is by him to be taken. AND BE IT FURTHER ENACTED by the authority aforesaid that every free white man and no other who has attained to the age of Twenty One years and hath been Resident in the Province Six Months and is legally possessed in his own Right of fifty Acres of Land in the said Parish District or village for which the Member or Members is or are to be elected to represent in the General Assembly shall be deemed a person qualified for Electing a Representative or Representatives to serve as Member or Members of the Commons House of Assembly for the Parish District Town or village wherein he is possessed of the above Qualification. And for preventing frauds as much as may be in all Elections, It is hereby Enacted by the Authority aforesaid that the Returning Officer shall come to the place at the time appointed by the publick notice given and shall enter the Names of every person presented or presenting himself as a Candidate in a Book or Roll leaving a fair Column under each Candidates Name for the names of the Voters and when a Voter comes and Votes the Returning Officer shall repeat distinctly the person or persons Names for whom the vote is given before he writes the Voters Name in the fair Column under the name of such Candidate or Candidates as shall be voted for by that person and

Marginal notes:

Every free white man of the age of 21 years and hath been Resident in the Province 6 months and possessed in his own Right of 50 Acres of Land in the Parish &c where a Member is to be Elected, deemed qualified to vote for such representative.

Returning officer to enter the Names of the Candidate or Candidates in a Book or roll, and the Name of the Voter under the Name of the Person voted for, and no Voter to alter his vote after entered, or vote twice at the same Election.

that no Voter shall alter his vote after it be entered or vote twice at one and the same Election and that the Candidate or Candidates who after the Poll is closed and the votes summed up shall be found (upon Scrutiny made if demanded) to have the Majority of votes shall be deemed and declared to be a Member or Members of the succeeding Commons House of Assembly. AND BE IT ENACTED by the Authority aforesaid that the time for taking votes at any election shall be between the hours of Nine of the Clock in the forenoon and Six in the afternoon and that at adjourning the Poll at Convenient hours during the time of an Election the Returning Officer shall first sum up the votes given for each Candidate and declare the same to the Candidates present and also declare the same when he has opened the Poll at the ensuing Meeting and that the said Election shall not continue longer than two days unless Scrutiny is demanded. PROVIDED NEVERTHELESS that the Returning Officer is hereby empowered and required to close the Poll when he or they have waited two hours after the last vote has been given or at any time by and with the consent and desire of all the Candidates then present. AND BE IT ENACTED by the Authority aforesaid that every person who shall be elected and returned as is before directed by this Act to serve as a Member in the Commons House of Assembly in this Province shall be qualified in the following manner (viz) That he shall be a free born Subject of Great Britain or of the dominions thereunto belonging or

The Candidate or Candidates having the Majority of votes (upon Scrutiny made if demanded declared a Member of Members of the Assembly.

Vote to be taken between the hours of 9 in the forenoon and 6 of the Clock in the afternoon and no election to Continue longer than 2 days, unless a Scrutiny is demanded.

Proviso Returning Officer to close the Poll two hours after the last vote given or at any time with Consent of the Candidates present.

Every person returned to be a Member of the Assembly to be a free born subject or a foreign person naturalized professing the Christian Religeon of the age of twenty-one years and a Resident of this Province for a year, and possessed of 500 Acres of Land therein.

a foreign person naturalized possessing the Christian Religeon and no other and that hath arrived at the age of Twenty One years and hath been a Resident in this Province for twelve months before the date of the said Writ and being legally possessed in his own Right in this Province of a Tract of Land Containing at least five hundred Acres. AND BE IT EN-ACTED by the Authority aforesaid that if any Member or Members chosen or hereafter to be chosen to serve in this or any other Commons House of Assembly shall refuse to serve or any Member or Members should die or depart this Province or shall be expelled the House so that his or their Seat or Seats become vacant then and in such case the House shall by address to the Governor or Commander in Chief for the time being Signify the Same and desire that a new Writ or Writs may issue to elect a Member or Members to fill up the vacancy or vacancies in the House and in Con-sequence of such Address a new Writ or Writs shall be issued to chuse in that Parish District Town or Village such other Member or Mem-bers to serve in the place or places of such Member or Members whose seat or seats are become vacant and every person so chosen and returned as aforesaid shall attend the Com-mons House of Assembly and shall be reputed, deemed and judged a Member thereof. AND BE IT ENACTED by the Authority aforesaid that if any returning officer as aforesaid shall admit of or take the vote of any person refusing at the request of one of the Candidates or any two

Any Member or Members chosen to serve in the Com-mons House of As-sembly refusing to serve or shall die or depart the Province or be expelled the House. The House to address the Gov-ernor to issue new Writ or Writs to elect a Member or Members to fill up such vacancy.

Returning Offi-cer not to take the vote of any Person refusing to take the oath herein pre-scribed.

persons qualified to vote to take the following oath: "I, A B do swear that I am legally

"possessed in my own Right of a freehold Estate of fifty acres of Land in the Township "or District of ———— and that such Estate "is legally or bona fide in my own right and "not made over or Granted to me purposely or "fraudulently to intitle me to vote at this "Election"—or at the request of any Candidate or any two freeholders shall refuse to administer the following oath to any Candidate who is hereby obliged to take this Oath if so required: "I, A B do swear that I am

"in my own Right truly and legally—possessed "of five hundred Acres of Land within this "Province and that the said Right is truly and "Bona fide within myself and not fraudulently "made over or granted to me for the purpose "of qualifying me to be a Representative in "General Assembly" or if the Provost Marshal

shall make any fraudulent return or shall influence or endeavor to influence or persuade any Voter not to vote as he first designed shall forfeit for each and every such offence the sum of fifty pounds Sterling to be to his Majesty for defraying the expence of the sitting of the General Assembly and to be sued for and recovered in the General Court of this Province by Bill Plaint or Informa-

tion. AND BE IT ENACTED by the Authority aforesaid that the Provost Marshal or any person properly authorized by him to manage an Election as aforesaid shall not return himself as a Member to serve in General Assembly and if the Provost Marshal refuses or neglects on a Summons from the Commons House of Assembly to attend that House to inform them to the best of his knowledge of any matter or dispute that did arise or may have arisen about the election of the Member or Members by him returned to serve in Assembly or refusing to shew the Poll taken shall forfeit for every such offence fifty Pounds Sterling to be applied and recovered as herein before directed. AND BE IT FURTHER ENACTED by the Authority aforesaid that if any person or persons whatsoever shall on the day appointed for the Election of a Member or Members to serve in the Commons House of Assembly as aforesaid presume to violate the freedom of the said Election by any Arrest Menaces or Threats or attempt to over awe Affright or force any person qualified to vote against his Inclination or Conscience or otherwise by Bribery obtain any vote or who shall after the said Election is over menance despightfully use or abuse any person because he has not voted as he or they would have had him every such person so offending upon due and sufficient proof made of such his violence or abuse menacing or threating before any two Justices of the Peace shall be bound over to the next General Sessions of the Peace himself in Twenty Pounds Sterling money and two Sureties each in Ten Pounds like money and to be of good behavior and abide the Sentence of the Said Court where if the offender or offenders are Convicted and found Guilty of such offence

[margin notes:]

ter about the Election of Members returned by him, or refusing to show the Poll taken to forfeit £50 to be applyed as before directed.

Any Person on the day of Election attempting by any arrest or threat to overawe any Person to vote against his Inclination or by Bribery obtain any vote or after the Election menace or abuse any person for not voting as he would have had him, on sufficient proof before two Justices to be bound over to the next General Session of the Council and if convicted to forfeit a sum not exceeding £20.

or offences as aforesaid then he or they shall each of them forfeit a sum not exceeding Twenty Pounds Sterling money and be Committed to Goal without bail or Mainprize till the same be paid which fine so imposed shall be paid as before directed. AND BE IT FURTHER ENACTED by the Authority aforesaid that no Civil Officer whatsoever shall execute any Writ or other Civil Process whatsoever upon the Body of any person qualified to vote for Members of the Commons House of Assembly as before in this Act directed either in his Journey to or in his return from the place of such election providing he shall not be more than forty eight hours upon his Journey either going to, returning from or during his stay there upon that account or within forty eight hours after the Scrutiny for such election is finished under the Penalty of a sum not exceeding Twenty Pounds Sterling Money to be recovered of and from the Officer that shall arrest or serve, any Process as aforesaid after such manner and form and to be disposed of as herein before is directed and all such Writs or Warrants executed on the Body of any person either going to or being at within the time limited by this Clause or returning from the place where such election is appointed to be managed he being qualified to give in his vote thereat are hereby declared void and null. AND BE IT ENACTED by the Authority aforesaid that this Act or any part thereof shall not extend to debar the Commons House of Assembly of the Right to Judge and determine

No Civil Officer to execute any Writ on the Body of any Person qualified to vote in his Journey to or on his return from the Place of Election provided he be not more than 48 hours in his Journey to, returning from or during his stay there on that account, or within 48 hours after the Scrutiny for such Election is finished under the penalty of a sum not exceeding £20 and Writs executed on the Body of such Persons within the time limited declared void.

This Act not to extend to debar the Commons House of the right to Judge agreeable to the direction of this Act the Qualification of their Mem-

agreeable to the direction of this Act the Qualification of any Member or Members of that House or to take away from the General Assembly or any part thereof any Power or Priviledge whatever that any General Assembly or any part thereof heretofore of Right had might could or ought to have had in the said Province anything herein Contained to the Contrary in anywise notwithstanding. PROVIDED ALWAYS that this Act or any part thereof shall not be construed to take away the power and prerogative given the Governor or Commander in Chief for the time being from the Crown to adjourn prorogue or dissolve any General Assembly of this Province when and as often as he shall think fit and expedient so to do or to take any other power or Prerogative whatever had from the Crown.

bers, or to take away any Priviledge any General Assembly heretofore had in the Province.

Proviso.

By order of the
Upper House.
JAMES HABERSHAM.

By order of the
Commons House of Assembly.
GREY ELLIOTT, Speaker.

In the Council Chamber
the Ninth day of June, 1761.
Assented to,
G. A. WRIGHT.

An Act.

To ascertain the manner and form of Electing Members to represent the Inhabitants of this Province in the Commons House of Assembly.

Read
{
first Time 27th March.
Second Time 30th ——
third Time 9th April
and passed the Commons
House of Assembly.
} 1761.

THOS. BARRINGTON, Clerk.

Upper House.

Read
{
first Time 10th April.
Second Time 13th ——
third Time 10th May
and passed.
} 1761.

CHAS. WATSON, C. G. A.

9 June 1761.

OFFICE OF THE SECRETARY OF STATE.

ATLANTA, GA., April 21st, 1892.

I hereby certify that the foregoing Seven (7) pages contain a true and correct copy of An Act now of file in this office, "to assertain the manner and form of electing members to represent the inhabitants of this Province in the Commons House of Assembly." Assented to June 9th, 1761.

Given under my hand and official seal.

{ Seal of the State of Georgia. }   [Signed]   PHILIP COOK,
Secretary of State.

APPENDIX C.

AUTHORITIES QUOTED.

ALBANY. *Collections on the History of Albany.* 4 vols. Albany, 1865-70.

ALLINSON'S LAWS. See NEW JERSEY.

AMES AND GOODELL. See MASSACHUSETTS.

ARNOLD, SAMUEL G. *History of the State of Rhode Island and Providence Plantations. 1636-1790.* 2 vols. New York, 1859-60.

BACON'S LAWS. See MARYLAND.

BALDWIN, SIMEON E. *Early History of the Ballot in Connecticut.* Publications of the American Historical Association, pt. iv, 90, Series of 1890.

BANCROFT, GEORGE. *History of the United States.* 9 vols. 23rd ed. Boston, 1870.

BELKNAP, JEREMY. *History of New Hampshire.* 3 vols. Philadelphia, Boston, 1784-92.

BOZMAN, JOHN LEEDS. *History of Maryland.* 2 vols. Baltimore, 1837.

BRIGHAM. See PLYMOUTH.

BRODHEAD, JOHN ROMEYN. *History of the State of New York.* 2 vols. New York, 1859-71.

BRYCE, JAMES. *The American Commonwealth.* 2 vols. 2d ed. London, 1889.

CENTURY DICTIONARY. 6 vols. New York, 1889-91.

CAMPBELL, DOUGLAS. *The Puritan in Holland, England and America.* 2 vols. New York, 1892.

CHALMERS, GEORGE. *Political Annals of the Present United Colonies.* London, 1780.

COFFIN, JOSHUA. *Sketch of the History of Newbury, Newburyport and West Newbury.* Boston, 1845.

COLDEN, CADWALLADER. *History of the Five Indian Nations of Canada.* London, 1747.

COLONIAL CHARTERS. *A list of copies of Charters from the Commissioners for Trade and Plantations.* London, 1741.

CONNECTICUT. *Laws.* Cambridge, 1673.

CONNECTICUT. *Acts and Laws of His Majesties Colony of Connecticut in New England.* New London, 1715.

This is the edition generally referred to in the course of this work as *Session Laws.* In Connecticut as well as in one or two of the other Colonies the laws passed at each successive session of the general court were printed and paged in continuation until a new revision was made.

—— *Acts and Laws.* New London, 1750.
The second revision.

—— *Acts and Laws.* New London, 1769.

—— *Public Acts.* 1819.

—— *Public Records of the Colony of Connccticut, 1636–1777.* 15 vols. Hartford, 1850–90.

COOPER. See SOUTH CAROLINA.

COX, EVERSHAM. *Antient Parliamentary Elections.* London, 1868.

DE FRANQUEVILLE, ALFRED, C. E. F. *Le Gouvernment et le Parlement Brittaniques.* 3 vols. Paris, 1887.

DELAWARE. *Laws.* Printed by B. FRANKLIN and D. HALL. Philadelphia, 1752.

—— *Laws, Vol. II.* Printed by JAMES ADAMS. Wilmington, 1763.

—— *Laws, 1700–1792.* 2 vols. Printed by JAMES ADAMS, New Castle, 1797.

DOUGLAS, WILLIAM. *A Summary Historical and Political, &c., of the British Settlements in North America.* Boston, 1747.

DUKE'S LAWS. See PENNSYLVANIA.

ENGLAND. *The Statutes at Large.* Magna Charta to 25 Geo. III.

There are a number of editions of the Statutes, that of Ruffhead (18 vols. London, 1763-1800), probably being the best.

FARMER, JOHN and MOORE, JACOB. *New Hampshire Historical Collections.* 3 vols. Concord, 1822–24.

GEORGIA. *Digest of the Laws of the State of Georgia.* Compiled by WATKINS. Philadelphia, 1800.

—— *A Codification of the Statute Law of Georgia.* By WILLIAM A. HOTCHKISS. New York, 1845.

—— *Acts passed by the General Assembly, 1755–1774. Now first printed.* Philadelphia, 1881.

GNEIST, RUDOLF VON. *History of the English Constitution.* 2 vols. Translated. New York, 1886.

GORDON, THOMAS F. *The History of Pennsylvania.* Philadelphia, 1829.

HARRINGTON, JAMES. Works, edited by TOLAND. London, 1771.

HAWKS, FRANCIS L. *History of North Carolina.* 2 vols. Fayetteville, 1857–8.

HENING. See VIRGINIA.

HOUSE OF COMMONS. *Resolutions and Orders of the House of Commons.* This is the Journal of the House of Commons. From 1547 to 1860, 115 volumes were published, the first seventeen volumes covering the period from 1547 to 1714.

HOWARD, GEORGE E. *An Introduction to the Local Constitutional History of the United States.* Vol. I. Baltimore, 1889.

LEAMING AND SPICER. See NEW JERSEY.

LECHFORD, THOMAS. *Plaine Dealing; or Newes from New England.* London, 1642.

MCMAHON, JOHN V. L. *An Historical View of the Government of Maryland.* Baltimore, 1831.

MARTIN, FRANCIS XAVIER. *The History of North Carolina.* 2 vols. New Orleans, 1829,

MARYLAND. *Acts of Assembly.* Printed by JOHN BASKETT. London, 1723.

—— *Laws of Maryland at Large.* Edited by THOMAS BACON. Baltimore, 1765.

This is the edition referred to as Bacon's *Laws.* The pages are not numbered, but are headed with the regnal or proprietary years.

—— *Archives. Proceedings and Acts of the Assembly, 1637–83.* 3 vols. Baltimore, 1883–9.

MASSACHUSETTS. *The Book of the General Laws and Libertyes.* Cambridge, 1660.

—— *The General Laws and Liberties.* Cambridge, 1672.

There were numerous supplements to the editions of 1660 and 1672.

—— *Laws.* Edited by Wait. Boston, 1814.

This reprint contains nearly all the laws issued under the charter of 1628.

—— *Records of the Governor and Company of the Massachusetts Bay in New England.* 5 vols. in 6. Boston, 1853–4.

—— *Acts and Resolves of the Province of Massachusetts Bay.* Edited by AMES and GOODELL. 4 vols. Boston, 1869.

This reprint contains nearly all the session laws made under the charter of 1691.

MASSACHUSETTS HISTORICAL SOCIETY. *Collections.* Vol. 23. Boston, 1833.

MOORE, JOHN W. *History of North Carolina,* 2 Vols. Raleigh, 1880.

NEVILL'S LAWS. See NEW JERSEY.

NEW HAMPSHIRE. *Acts and Laws.* Printed by DANIEL FOWLE, Portsmouth. 1761.

—— *Acts and Laws.* Printed by DANIEL and ROBERT FOWLE, Portsmouth, 1771.

—— *Provincial Papers.* 16 vols. Concord, 1867–87.

NEW HAVEN. *Laws.* London, 1656.

—— *Records of the Colony and Jurisdiction. 1638–1665.* 2 vols. Hartford, 1857–8.

NEW JERSEY. *Laws.* Printed by WILLIAM BRADFORD. New York, 1704.

—— *The Acts of the General Assembly.* Edited by SAMUEL NEVILL, Esq. Philadelphia, 1752.
A second volume published in 1761 contains the laws enacted after 1752.

—— *The Grants, Concessions and Original Constitutions of the Province of New Jersey. The Acts passed during the Proprietary Governments.* Edited by AARON LEAMING and JACOB SPICER. Philadelphia, 1758.

—— *Acts of the General Assembly.* Edited by SAMUEL ALLINSON. Burlington, 1776.

—— *Archives of the State.* 10 vols. Newark, 1880–8.

NEW YORK. *The Laws.* Printed by WILLIAM BRADFORD, New York, 1710.

—— *Journal of the Votes and Proceedings of the General Assembly of the Colony. 1691–1765.* 2 vols. New York, 1764–66.

—— *Laws of New York from 1691 to 1773 inclusive.* Edited by PETER VAN SCHAACK. 2 vols. paged consecutively. New York, 1774.

—— *Documents relative to the Colonial History of the State of New York.* 14 vols. Albany, 1856–1883.

—— *Manual of the Common Council of New York.* New York, 1868.

NEW YORK HISTORICAL SOCIETY. *Collections.* 3d series. Vol. III, pt. i. New York, 1857.

—— *Collections for the year 1885. The Burghers of New Amsterdam and the Freemen of New York, 1675–1866.* New York, 1886.

NORTH CAROLINA. *A Collection of all the Public Acts of Assembly.* Edited by SWANN. Printed by JAMES DAVIS, Newbern, 1752.

—— *A Collection of all the Acts of Assembly.* Newbern, 1764.

—— *A complete Revisal of all the Acts of Assembly.* Printed by DAVIS, Newbern, 1773.

—— —— *Colonial Records, 1662–1776.* 10 vols. Raleigh, 1886–90.

O'CALLAGHAN, E. B. *History of the New Netherland.* 2 vols. New York, 1846–8.

—— *Introduction to the Journal of the New York Legislative Council.* Latter in 2 vols. Albany, 1861.

—— *Laws and Ordinances of New Netherland, 1638–74.* Albany, 1868.

PALFREY, JOHN G. *History of New England.* 4 vols. Boston, 1859–75.

PENNSYLVANIA. *A Collection of all the Laws of the Province of Pennsylvania Now in Force.* Printed by B. FRANKLIN, Philadelphia, 1742. This as well as most of the other editions of the Pennsylvania laws, contains the charters.

——— *Votes and Proceedings of the House of Representatives of the Province of Pennsylvania, 1682–1776.* 6 vols. Philadelphia, 1752–76.

——— *The Charters and Acts of Assembly.* 2 vols. Printed by PETER MILLER and Comp. Philadelphia, 1762.

——— *The Acts of Assembly.* Printed by HALL AND SELLERS. Philadelphia, 1775.

——— *Archives.* 12 vols. Philadelphia, 1852–6.

——— *Colonial Records.* 17 vols. Philadelphia, 1852–60.

——— *Charter and Laws, 1676–1700.* Printed by Authority of the State. Harrisburg, 1879. This edition contains not only the laws and charters of Penn's government down to 1700, but also the Duke of York's Book of Laws. The latter is the code promulgated at the East Hampton convention of 1664, together with the additions and amendments made subsequently by the court of assizes. See p. 19, *ante*.

PLOWDEN, EDMOND. *Commentaries.* English Law Reports, 1550–80. 2 vols.

PLYMOUTH. *Laws.* Edited by BRIGHAM. Boston, 1836. Most of the laws contained in this volume were also reprinted in the eleventh volume of the Plymouth Colony ·Records.

——— *New Plymouth Colony Records.* 12 vols, in 10. Boston, 1855–61.

POORE, B. PERLEY, editor. *Federal and State Constitutions.* 2 vols. Washington, 1877.

PROUD, ROBERT. *History of Pennsylvania.* 2 vols. Philadelphia, 1797.

PRYNNE, WILLIAM. *Brevia Pariamentaria Rediviva.* London, 1662.

RAMSAY, DAVID. *History of South Carolina.* 2 vols. Charleston, 1809.

RHODE ISLAND. *Acts and Laws.* Boston, 1719.

——— *Acts and Laws.* Printed by JAMES FRANKLIN, Newport, 1730.

——— *Acts and Laws.* Printed by the WIDOW FRANKLIN. Newport, 1744.

——— *Acts and Laws.* Printed by J. FRANKLIN. Newport, 1752.

——— *Acts and Laws.* Printed by SAMUEL HALL. Newport, 1767. This is Hall's *Code.*

——— *Acts and Laws.* Printed by SOLOMON SOUTHWICK. Newport, 1772.

——— *Records of the Colony of Rhode Island and Providence Plantations.* 10 vols. Providence, 1856–65.

RHODE ISLAND HISTORICAL SOCIETY, *Proceedings of.* Providence, 1872–3.

RIDER, S. S. *An Inquiry concerning the Origin of the Clause in the Laws of*

Rhode Island (1719–1783) disfranchising Roman Catholics. Providence, 1889.

RIVERS, WILLIAM JAMES. *Sketch of the History of South Carolina.* Charleston, 1856.

SALKELD, WILLIAM. English Law Reports. 1689–1712. 3 vols.

SHARPE, GOVERNOR HORATIO. *Correspondence*, 1753–61. 2 vols. in *Maryland Archives.* Baltimore, 1889–90.

SMITH, SAMUEL. *History of New Jersey.* Burlington, 1765.

SOUTH CAROLINA. *The Laws.* Edited by NICHOLAS TROTT. Charleston, 1736.

—— *Statutes at large of South Carolina.* Edited by T. COOPER. 4 vols. Columbia, 1836–8.

STEVENS, WILLIAM B. *History of Georgia to 1798.* 2 vols. New York, Philadelphia, 1847–59.

STITH, WILLIAM. *The History of the First Discovery and Settlement of Virginia.* Williamsburg, 1747.

STUBBS, WILLIAM. *Constitutional History of England.* 3 vols. 4th ed. Oxford, 1883.

SWIFT, ZEPHANIAH. *A System of the Laws of Connecticut.* 2 vols. Windham, 1795–6.

TROWARD, RICHARD. *A Collection of the Statutes in force relating to Elections.* London, 1790.
Most of the English *Statutes at Large* which have been quoted in this work are to be found in Troward's collection.

WALSH, ROBERT. *An Appeal from the Judgments of Great Britain.* Philadelphia, 1819.

WEISE, ARTHUR J. *History of Albany.* Albany, 1884.

WHITEHEAD, WILLIAM A. *East Jersey under the Proprietary Governments.* 2d ed. Newark, 1875.

WINSOR, JUSTIN, editor. *Memorial History of Boston.* 4 vols. Boston, 1880–1.

—— *Narrative and Critical History of America.* 8 vols. Boston, 1889.

WINTHROP, GOVERNOR JOHN. *Journal.* Edited by JAMES SAVAGE, under the title of: *The History of New England, 1630–1649.* Hartford, 1790.

VAN SCHAACK'S LAWS. See NEW YORK.

VINER, CHARLES. *A general Abridgment of Law and Equity.* 30 vols. 2d ed. London, 1791–4.

VIRGINIA. *The Statutes at Large; being a Collection of all the Laws of Virginia from the first session of the Legislature in the year 1619.* Edited by WILLIAM WALLER HENING. 13 vols. New York, Richmond, Philadelphia, 1819–23.

NOTE: Besides the editions of the statutes mentioned in the foregoing list, the writer has made a personal examination of the Charlemagne Tower collection of American colonial laws, in the Library of the Pennsylvania Historical Association. In addition he has consulted the collections of the New York Bar Association and of the New York Historical Society, which are excelled in completeness only by the Philadelphia collection, and which contains some volumes not included in the latter. A few statutes which it is believed were not published in any of the known editions of the colonial laws, were transcribed from the originals now on file in the capitals of the various States or from copies in the British Public Record Office in London, and are published in Appendix B of this work.

APPENDIX D.

TABLE OF BRITISH REGNAL YEARS,

FROM THE FIRST PARLIAMENT UP TO THE CLOSE OF THE COLONIAL PERIOD.

FOR CONVENIENCE OF REFERENCE TO THE STATUTES AT LARGE.

Sovereign.	Commencement of Reign.	Number of Regnal Years.
Edward I	November 20th, 1272	35
Edward II	July 8th, 1307	20
Edward III	January 25th, 1326	51
Richard II	June 22nd, 1377	23
Henry IV	September 30th, 1399	14
Henry V	March 21st, 1413	10
Henry VI	September 1st, 1422	39
Edward IV	March 4th, 1461	23
Edward V	April 9th, 1483	..
Richard III	June 26th, 1483	3
Henry VII	August 22nd, 1485	24
Henry VIII	April 22nd, 1509	38
Edward VI	January 28th, 1547	7
Mary	July 6th, 1553	6
Elizabeth	November 17th, 1558	45
James I	March 24th, 1603	23
Charles I	March 27th, 1625	24
The Commonwealth	January 30th, 1649	11
Charles II.[1]	May 29th, 1660	37
James II	February 6th, 1685	4
William and Mary[2]	February 13th, 1689	14
Anne	March 8th, 1702	13
George I	August 1st, 1714	13
George II	June 11th, 1727	34
George III	October 25th, 1760	60

[1] Although Charles II did not ascend the throne until May 29th, 1660, his regnal years were computed from the death of Charles I, January 30th, 1649. The year of the restoration of Charles II is therefore styled the twelfth year of his reign.

[2] After the death of Mary on December 28th, 1694, William reigned alone under the style of William III.

TABLE OF PROPRIETARY YEARS OF THE LORDS BALTIMORE.

FOR CONVENIENCE OF REFERENCE TO THE MARYLAND STATUTES.

Proprietor.	Commencement of Proprietorship.	Number of Proprietary Years.
Cæcilius	June 20th, 1632............	44
Charles [1]	November 30th, 1675........	40
Benedict	February 20th, 1714........	..
Charles	April 16th, 1714............	37
Frederick	April 23rd, 1751............	20

[1] From August, 1691, to May, 1715, the government of Maryland was administered by the Crown.

George Calvert, the first Lord Baltimore, died before the Charter passed the Great Seal. He was therefore never proprietor. The title ceased with Frederick, sixth Lord Baltimore, who died in 1771, leaving no legitimate issue.

The compound dates (e. g. 1635–6) used in the course of this work refer to that part of the calendar year which preceded the commencement of the new year. Until after the adoption of the New Style by act of Parliament in 1751, the new year began in the month of March. January, February and part of March were therefore reckoned in both years.